KU-313-905

THE
SECRET
LIFE OF
DOROTHY
SOAMES

JUSTINE
COWAN

———

THE
SECRET
LIFE OF
DOROTHY
SOAMES

A FOUNDLING'S
STORY

virago

VIRAGO

First published in the United States in 2021 by HarperCollins Publishers
First published in Great Britain in 2021 by Virago Press

1 3 5 7 9 10 8 6 4 2

Copyright © 2021 by Justine Cowan

The moral right of the author has been asserted.

All rights reserved.
No part of this publication may be reproduced, stored in a
retrieval system, or transmitted in any form or by any means, without
the prior permission in writing of the publisher, nor be otherwise circulated
in any form of binding or cover other than that in which it is published
and without a similar condition including this condition being
imposed on the subsequent purchaser.

A CIP catalogue record for this book
is available from the British Library.

Hardback ISBN 978-0-349-01318-3
Trade paperback ISBN 978-0-349-01317-6

Printed and bound in Great Britain by
Clays Ltd, Elcograf S.p.A.

Papers used by Virago are from well-managed forests
and other responsible sources.

Virago Press
An imprint of
Little, Brown Book Group
Carmelite House
50 Victoria Embankment
London EC4Y 0DZ

An Hachette UK Company
www.hachette.co.uk

www.virago.co.uk

FOR PATRICK

To do a great right, you may do a little wrong.

—Charles Dickens, *Oliver Twist*

CONTENTS

THE
SECRET
LIFE OF
DOROTHY
SOAMES

1

DOROTHY SOAMES

I always knew my mother had a secret. She guarded it fiercely, keeping it under lock and key. That was how I envisioned it—a hidden chamber tucked away in the recesses of my mother's twisted mind. But her secret was too big to be contained, and it would ooze out like a thick slurry, poisoning her thoughts and covering our family in darkness.

When I was nineteen, my mother accidentally gave me a clue to her past, yet it would take me years to gather the courage to learn more. Eventually I followed a trail of bread crumbs that led me across an ocean into an institution's macabre and baroque history. Only then did I discover the agony of generations of women scorned by society, and of thousands of innocent children imprisoned although they had committed no crime. And I would dredge up family secrets that forced me to reassess everything I had ever known.

Of course, I didn't know any of that when the phone rang that morning. I only knew it was an odd time for my father to call.

"I need your help. It's your mother."

His voice was strained and loud.

I had trouble concentrating as he described the events that had unfolded earlier that morning—my mother tightly clutching the steering wheel as she careened through a labyrinth of twisting hillside roads, my father racing close behind in his matching black Jaguar, desperate to stop her. Luckily, he'd caught up with her before she could run herself off the road.

"She said she had to go to the hospital."

"The *hospital*? Why? Was she hurt?"

"No." My father offered no further information, but he wasn't really calling to explain. And I wouldn't find out where my mother had been trying to go that day until years after her death.

"I have to be in court today."

I don't care, I wanted to say, but the words stuck in my throat. One thing I'd picked up in my nineteen years was the intuition to dread what I knew was coming next.

"It's not safe to leave her alone."

Images flashed before me. Jagged shards of glass on an Oriental rug, a papier-mâché piñata swinging from a tree, broken dolls strewn across sleek hardwood floors. I pulled my textbooks out of my backpack and returned them to the desk as my arms began to tingle, my fingers going numb. I usually had more time to prepare myself.

I tried not to think about what I would find as I drove across the Bay Bridge, watching the city's skyline come into view before heading south, toward Hillsborough.

We'd left San Francisco when I was six, my father eager to escape the damp city fog that triggered his claustrophobia, my mother more than happy to relocate to one of California's most prestigious zip codes. On the face of things, the wealthy enclave where we landed was a magical place for a child, and the neighborhood kids had the run of its wide, quiet streets. We'd duck into gaps in the hedges that concealed manicured gardens, using the holes in the thick vegetation as secret tunnels to evade capture during our games of hide-and-seek. On our corner stood an empty manor house we'd crawl into through an unlocked window, running through its grand rooms with our arms spread wide as if we were flying, or taking turns riding from floor to floor in the dumbwaiter. One at a time we would climb into the small wooden box to be hoisted and lowered by the rest of the group, the ropes creaking as they threaded their way through the rusting pulleys.

But Hillsborough lost its brilliance as I got older, and soon I could see only its blemishes, reflected in my mother's eyes—her blind idolatry of wealth and status, how she name-dropped the famous people who lived around the corner in the English accent she hadn't lost despite her decades in the States, her triumphant grin when we scored the best table at an exclusive restaurant.

My eventual escape to Berkeley had given me the perfect antidote to an upbringing I'd grown to despise, the clamor of urban life providing a comfort our home never could. I basked in the grittiness of noisy streets, the beatnik cafés and bookstores, the street vendors and shirtless hippies whooping through games of hacky sack on Sproul Plaza. Even though I was only forty minutes away, my life felt like my own.

By the time I pulled into the driveway, my father was gone. I parked a few feet behind my mother's shiny black Jaguar, in its usual spot. Nothing seemed out of place. The lawn was freshly mown, the roses untrammeled. I climbed a set of brick stairs to the front door, surveying the row of arched windows that lined my childhood home for any hint of what awaited me.

The front door was unlocked. I took a deep breath as I pushed it open and peeked into the living room, where the gold-upholstered furniture perfectly complemented the giant hand-woven rug, and the various objets d'art gathered by my mother on her frequent trips to Butterfield & Butterfield were strategically placed on antique tables and in glass display cases. It was the sort of room designed to impress or intimidate. But I was only looking for signs of disarray—a couch cushion off-kilter, a toppled figurine.

None of the ornate furnishings appeared to have been disturbed, so I inched down the hallway, gently dragging my fingertips along the bright white walls. Each week a young woman who spoke little English spent hours mopping the floors, scrubbing the bathrooms and the kitchen, dusting every room and nook and cranny, though rarely to my mother's satisfaction. After the house cleaner had finished her tasks, I often found my mother wiping the walls with a vinegar-soaked rag. Scratches and red patches on her knuckles were telltale signs that she'd been on her hands and knees, rescrubbing the bathroom floor.

My shoes made no sound as I approached my mother's room and knocked lightly, hoping she was asleep.

"Justine, is that you?" she called out.

I tiptoed inside, feeling a familiar wave of guilt over the fact that I didn't actually want to see or speak with her. The room was dim, but I could make out my mother's silhouette as she sat up in bed. Her nightgown reflected the light streaming through the gaps in the heavy white curtains.

She was holding a notepad. I immediately recognized her old-fashioned calligraphic script, with its precise bends and curves. I couldn't make out the words in the shadowy light, but I saw deep indentations in the thinly lined paper, along with dark smudges and small tears where it looked like a pencil might have broken.

She turned the notepad toward me, and a splash of morning light illuminated the page. Each line contained a name, written over and over, with the same unwavering precision. It was a name I had never heard before, and would not hear again for many years.

Dorothy Soames Dorothy Soames Dorothy Soames

2

GHOSTS

I didn't love my mother, but I cried when she died.

Twenty-five years had passed since I left California and moved into an adult life that kept my mother at arm's length, and I'd made it to her bedside with hours to spare. Her battle with Alzheimer's had been lengthy, but at the end her decline was swift. In a matter of months the disease had transformed my mother into a soon-to-be corpse that bore little resemblance to the woman who had raised me. Gone was the imposing figure who radiated nervous energy and was rarely at rest. Any idle moment would be spent flitting around the house, tidying up invisible clutter. Even while sitting still, shoulders square, her spine barely touching the back of her chair, she would fiddle with her fingers or pick nervously at the skin on her arms until she bled. Now, no longer able to speak or move as she slipped in and out of consciousness, her arms sank into the thin hospital blanket like leaden stumps, her contorted fingers curved under her bent wrists.

I sat solemnly beside her, watching her die. My father and sister were in the room, too, but we rarely spoke. The stillness was broken only by the quiet wheezing that emerged from the back of my mother's throat as she struggled for air. Once she'd heaved her last, gasping breath, I rushed from the room and huddled on a small bench in the hallway, sobbing wildly, struggling to breathe, my head between my knees. The wails erupted from deep inside, one after the other, as if they had a life of their own.

During the days that followed, I would be bewildered by the strength of my feelings for a woman who had caused me so much pain. Eventually I transitioned into a heavy fatigue, palpably weighed down by the emotions that had overtaken my body. I found it difficult to perform even the most mundane tasks, and sought escape in sleep whenever I could find it. When I did leave the house, I was prone to weeping at inopportune moments. Strangers would approach to ask if I needed help. The woman who took my dry cleaning came from behind the counter just to hug me.

"My mother died," I told her as she wrapped her arms around me.

But she was comforting a fraud, a cheat. Would she have held me with such compassion had she known how I truly felt about my mother?

We buried her in the town of Rogersville, where my father was born, in a small cemetery near the Great Smoky Mountains of Tennessee. She was laid to rest beside long-deceased family members of his, people she had never met, in a town where she had never lived. My father had picked out their plots long ago, and my mother didn't object, having no family of her own.

A year later he joined her, in a grave not far from where his own parents had been buried.

I never spoke to my mother about Dorothy Soames, or the day she'd taken off through the winding streets in her shiny black car. Not even as I watched Alzheimer's whittle away at her brain, stealing a few words here, a memory there.

I didn't want to know her secrets. Perhaps I suspected that her story would be too painful for me to carry. More likely, I feared that knowing the truth would give her a power over me that I couldn't bear.

She had tried to tell me, but only years after I had left home. Once I'd graduated from Berkeley, I moved as far away as possible. I traveled to Asia on a whim, living for a year on the wages I earned teaching English to schoolchildren, then on to Washington, DC, North Carolina, Tennessee, and Georgia, always ensuring that there were thousands of miles between us.

I was living in Nashville when I got the letter. It was brief, with few details. She wanted me to call her. It should have been an easy thing to do—pick up the phone, ask her what she meant by the cryptic phrase she'd dropped near the end of the letter.

She wanted to tell me about her life as a foundling.

It was an old-fashioned word, not one I'd ever heard uttered in our household. But it soon slipped my mind as I tucked my mother's letter under a stack of unopened mail. I had long since stopped caring about her secrets or her motivations, a mode of self-preservation I'd refined into a precise form of science.

She called me later that week, asking if I had received the letter. "We can go to London if you like, together," she said. "I can show you where I was raised, and where it all happened."

Instead of piquing my curiosity, her call aroused my suspicions. It had always been understood that my mother's past was off-limits. To bring up the subject was to risk a swift rebuke—or, worse, a retreat, my mother disappearing into her bedroom and emerging hours later, eyes red and swollen. Now she was proposing a visit to her homeland? Lunch would have been a stretch. A girls' trip to London seemed as distant a possibility as a quick trip to the moon.

"I want to tell you everything," she added, her voice filled with an unfamiliar buoyancy. Her willingness to talk seemed sudden, to say the least, and I was dogged by the fear that whatever she had to say would somehow be used against me.

"It's too late," I told her.

She didn't need me to expand to understand what I meant, and her disappointment was unmistakable. But I was unmoved, resolute in the stance that my mother's past meant nothing to me.

And that was true. Until twenty years later, when I went to London with the man who'd recently become my husband.

The trip was a belated honeymoon of sorts, a monthlong tour of Europe. Our actual honeymoon to Costa Rica had been cut short—a car accident on a curvy mountain road, followed by a tropical illness that sent Patrick to the hospital. It was just as well. In the months surrounding our wedding, we'd buried Patrick's mother, his sister-in-law, and both of my parents.

Our trip to Europe was supposed to be our fresh start, the beginning of a promising life unburdened by the past or our mutual grief. Our ambitious itinerary reflected our hopes, with stops planned in London, then Paris, Bruges, Amsterdam, Florence, and Rome.

A visit to London would be no different than traveling to any other city, I tried to convince myself. We would visit the sights, sample the local food, and come home with full bellies and a spring in our step, ready to begin our new life together.

My husband didn't understand why I'd avoided England so stubbornly. He'd heard stories from my traveling days—how I'd pedaled a bicycle from Salzburg to Vienna with my belongings strapped on a rack, stopped alongside the Danube to eat cheese and bread, crisscrossed Europe on high-speed trains. Once I'd seen enough of Europe, I traveled to Southeast Asia, flouting government warnings to venture into conflict-ridden jungles, and through western Africa, braving military checkpoints to discover villages untouched by modern technology.

But the thought of London tied my stomach up in knots.

It's going to be different, I remember Patrick saying. *She's dead now. She can't hurt you anymore.*

We'd met late in life, as adults, and married in our mid-forties. We were an unlikely pair, at least on paper. Patrick was a laid-back jazz musician and animation artist, while I was a driven public interest environmental attorney hell-bent on taking down polluters. Yet our connection was instant.

He was quick-witted and handsome, with curly hair, an infectious smile, and kind brown eyes. I could hardly believe my luck. He could have his pick of women, I thought. Why had he chosen me? He showered me with compliments, told me I was perfect, beautiful, and brilliant. I chided him, accusing him of flattery, but he continued, undeterred. And so I learned to keep my doubts to myself, silently answering his praise with a ready-made list of my imperfections.

We were matched by one of those online services that promises to find your soul mate based on answers to a series of questions. *If your friends could describe you in four words, what would they be? What are you thankful for? What's your favorite book?* I'd answered dutifully and earnestly, hopeful that my responses would bring me the love I yearned for. Instead I spent my evenings reviewing seemingly endless profiles of men who didn't appeal to me, or vice versa. An early match who'd seemed promising asked me outright about my relationship with my family, his line in the sand. If you didn't have a good relationship with your family, then how could you have a good relationship with your partner? His reasoning filled me with anxiety, my troubled relationship with my mother casting a pall over a process that was already difficult.

The issue continued to gnaw away at me as things with Patrick got more serious. The last thing I wanted was to scare off a prospective partner by introducing him to my mother. So I tested the waters slowly, gradually revealing eccentricities like her belief in ghosts, or her inside scoop on government plots to poison our water supplies. I carefully watched his reactions, fearful that if he had any inkling of the sickness that afflicted our family, he would run for the hills.

None of that mattered to Patrick, who never batted an eye as I slowly unraveled the complexities of my family dynamics.

As we descended into London, he reached over and took my hand, squeezing it as the plane touched down on the tarmac.

We stayed in Westminster, in a boutique hotel overlooking the Royal Mews of Buckingham Palace. Brimming with old English charm and replete with cozy rooms and the requisite afternoon tea, it was staffed by an attentive doorman clad in traditional livery, complete with a top hat. His accent delighted me, a thick cockney brogue that sounded like it belonged in a Dickens novel.

My mother would have disapproved.

I could easily see her curling her lip, raising an eyebrow ever so slightly to register her displeasure as the doorman gave us directions to Victoria Station. I'd been taught at an early age that a person's status in society could be discerned by his or her diction, and my mother took particular objection to those who spoke with a cockney accent. Riffraff, she called them. She had little tolerance for the working class, in any context.

I heard her voice as we wandered through London's narrow

alleys or popped into a pub to escape the wintry rain. The fish and chips we feasted on brought back the tastes and smells of my early childhood. Our cupboards were always stocked with the malt vinegar we used to generously anoint the lightly battered cod she regularly served for dinner. The vinegar's pungent odor would linger on my fingers for hours.

Like a ghost, she appeared in Harrods in a small hallway at the bottom of an escalator, where a memorial statue of Princess Diana and her lover, Dodi Fayed, had been erected several years after their deaths. Just for a moment, I saw my mother's large brown eyes, pools of tears spilling down her face when she heard the news.

And so my mother had gotten her way, traveling with us through London. Hers was a constant and familiar voice in my head, fading only when our plane landed back in the States. We had gone together, after all.

As the wheels touched the ground, I reflexively reached for my phone.

My mother would always call after my adventures, sometimes several times, ostensibly to make sure I had arrived home safely. I resented those calls, knowing they would inevitably lead to arguments, harsh words, tears, and phones slammed down onto the receiver, followed by the inevitable follow-up call from my father. *Why couldn't you just keep the peace?* As soon as technology gave me the gift of caller ID, I would send her straight to voice mail, only calling her back when guilt overcame my misgivings.

This time there would be no call from my mother. No one checking to see if I'd made it home in one piece. My older sister and I had been estranged since my father's funeral, eleven months after my mother's. In the space of a single year, my birth family had vanished.

I'd have expected to feel relief in my mother's absence. Instead warm tears streamed down my face as the plane taxied toward the gate.

I had spent a lifetime loathing my mother, moving thousands of miles away to be rid of her, only to be haunted by her after she was gone.

When I returned home, instead of organizing photos or turning my focus back to work, I began my search for Dorothy Soames.

IT STARTED SLOWLY, as small chunks of time surfing the web. I don't know what I expected to find, or even exactly what I was looking for. My efforts amounted to aimless googling of a few words in various combinations—"Dorothy Soames" and "England," for example—each of which yielded disappointing results. I found a reference to Lady Mary Spencer-Churchill Soames, best known as a member of London society and the daughter of Winston Churchill. A connection to Winston Churchill wouldn't have been unwelcome, but even if his daughter *had* married into a Soames clan with some relationship to my mother, it was difficult to imagine how they could have been connected. My search uncovered various other people named Dorothy or Soames, but none of them wound up giving me any clues into my mother's past.

I could have stopped there. At that point, my level of curiosity hadn't progressed beyond a vague interest. But ever since I returned from London, I had felt a growing sense of unease. My mother's letter, the one she sent all those years ago, kept on tickling the back of my brain—along with the specific word she had used to describe herself.

I stared at the computer screen, the cursor blinking as if

awaiting instructions. I placed my fingers gently on the keyboard and typed:

Foundling London

And there they were, right there at the top of the page, the words that would take me back across the Atlantic to find the answers to questions I didn't yet know I had: the Foundling Hospital.

"I THINK SHE may have been my mother."

I had no idea if anyone at Coram would be able to help me when I sent an email through the general contact channels, asking for any information about a girl named Dorothy Soames.

The Hospital for the Maintenance and Education of Exposed and Deserted Young Children, or the Foundling Hospital, as it was commonly called, was founded by a shipbuilder named Thomas Coram and granted a royal charter in 1739. Its stated mission was to care for "helpless Infants daily exposed to Destruction."[1] More than two hundred and fifty years later, the institution still exists, though now it's known simply as Coram, in honor of its founder.

I waited for a reply, checking my in-box multiple times a day.

A few days later, it came. Yes, someone would look into the files to see if the institution had records on Dorothy Soames. But the promise of assistance came with a caution—don't expect much. Even if they could find her records, it would be unusual for a search to unearth many details. The most I could hope for would be a confirmation of whether and when a child had been at the Foundling Hospital. Only in exceptional circumstances would there be anything more.

At the time, Patrick and I were living in Florida. He had landed a job on a team creating high-end video games, and we'd packed everything up and headed south from Atlanta. Leaving behind my position as the director of a nonprofit environmental law firm had been a difficult decision to make. Holding polluters accountable had once been my dream job, the reason I'd gone to law school. I filed lawsuits against unscrupulous paper mills, coal plants, and waste management companies for spewing dangerous toxins like mercury, arsenic, and lead into the air and water. Each case was grueling, the stakes always high, and my never-ending responsibilities ran the gamut from supervising staff to drafting briefs, managing the budget, and raising money for the cause. I was filled with an intoxicating sense of purpose. But after thirteen years, I was exhausted.

Overnight, my life morphed from a continuous flurry of court hearings, meetings, and phone calls to days with seemingly endless hours to fill. We'd moved to Orlando's historic district, a tree-lined neighborhood with an eclectic mix of 1920s Craftsman bungalows and Mediterranean-style homes. I took on a few clients, but spent most days roaming the brick streets shaded by ancient oaks laden with Spanish moss, their sturdy branches fanning out above me as the humid air weighed me down like a blanket. I sat for long hours on a bench at a nearby lake, monitoring the progress of a pair of swans giving flying lessons to their cygnets. I wandered through the old cemetery, where I discovered an eagle's nest in the fork of a lone pine tree and a pair of nesting owls perched on the branch of a cypress. The days spread out with a slow pulsing rhythm, my mind freed from the specter of endless meetings and impending court deadlines.

With little to occupy my time, I ordered one of the books I had come across during my brief inquiry into the Foundling Hospital. Written by a former chief executive of the institution, it was a quick read, and soon I purchased another, this one by an academic and historian. Each page was dense with facts and statistics chronicling the early years of the hospital, and I would sit on my back porch, turning the pages slowly as I listened to the chorus of frogs that lived among the ferns and bromeliads, occasionally glancing up to see a lizard scamper across the burnt-orange Saltillo tiles.

Eventually I heard back from Coram. A woman named Val confirmed what I had already suspected: my mother had been raised in the Foundling Hospital under the name of Dorothy Soames. Val provided me with some general information—a timeline, a confirmation of my mother's stay at the institution. If I wanted to know more, I would need to come back to London to look at the files in person.

Months passed as I stalled on making any kind of decision, the contents of the books I'd read fading away in my mind. I was beginning to imagine that my dive into the Foundling Hospital's history had been a momentary diversion, a fleeting detour into some mildewing family archives, when Patrick nominated Barcelona as his destination of choice for our annual getaway.

"We could stop off in London first," I responded, the words spilling from my mouth without forethought. "There's a direct flight," I added, as if I were indifferent to the outcome, my suggestion only a matter of logistics.

Looking back, I don't believe that I consciously decided to return to London to research my mother's past. Why would I? The five years since my mother had died had been calm, even peaceful.

Nothing would be served by stirring up the past.

During the summer days of my youth, I'd taken riding lessons at an equestrian center nestled below the ridge that ran from Santa Cruz to San Francisco. After hours of demanding instruction, I would sneak away and ride through the labyrinth of trails that crisscrossed the adjacent hills and mountains. The sun would soon disappear as I followed the well-worn bridle path through a gap in a stand of giant redwoods. I would ride aimlessly for hours, no map or plan to guide me, turning onto one path or another, enticed by the way a root curved along the ruts and grooves worn down by rain, the bend of a tree limb, or how a ray of dwindling sunshine snuck through the canopy to cast a shadow on a flowering bush, all of it demanding further investigation. The air was cool and damp, and in the dappled light, I would let the reins go lax. Allowing my steed to choose the path, I would stroke her wide neck as if to encourage her to make her own choice, content to see where she would take me next. When I lifted my chin toward the sky, I could see only ancient trees towering over me. And without any conscious aim or desire on my part, there I would be.

Deep in the forest.

That is how my journey began—without a blueprint or master plan, or any carefully weighed options. Yet once our plane landed in London that second time, there would be no turning back.

After a fitful night of rest at our hotel, I found myself in the lobby of Coram, in the heart of Bloomsbury, a fashionable area of central London. I anxiously tapped my feet, glancing nervously over at Patrick as a woman approached us with a purposeful gait, a file folder tucked under one arm. Her gray hair was thick and wavy, with white tresses that cascaded around her face. Her attire was understated and professional, an unassuming button-down blouse and a simple wool skirt. She introduced herself as Val, and while up until that time we had exchanged only emails, I felt instantly at ease in her presence. She smiled sympathetically as she greeted me, as if she knew that my journey of discovery would not be easy.

She led me to a small room, then placed the file folder carefully on a table. I recalled her earlier words of caution about managing my expectations, not to hope for much. Still, my heart beat a little faster when I noticed that the folder was several inches thick. I tried not to look at it as we exchanged pleasantries about my flight.

"We can make copies to take with you, if you'd like. And after you have looked at the files, we can head over to the museum."

Once Val had stepped out of the room, Patrick put his arm around my shoulders and squeezed. I took a breath and turned my attention to the file, which seemed to pulse with anticipatory energy. As I began gently spreading out the thick stack of documents yellowed with age, my eyes fell on a bundle of letters dating back to the 1930s. Some were delicately handwritten in thick black ink, faded with time and difficult to decipher. Other letters were more formal, usually a sentence or two, with no name, just the word *Secretary* typewritten where a signature would be. There were a few photos interspersed among the letters, and what appeared to be reports, some several pages in length.

On some of the letters, I could make out a signature: *Lena Weston*. The first name didn't ring any bells. But the last name did. It was my mother's maiden name, and my stomach churned at the sight of those six familiar letters.

I'd never heard my mother mention anyone named Lena. Then again, I'd rarely heard my mother mention anyone beyond the immediate sphere of our neighborhood, my school, and my father's office. From time to time she mentioned a friend who lived in Europe, but I knew little about her—only that her name was Pat.

There were too many files to review, and the feeling in the pit of my stomach gave me the sense that I'd be better off examining the contents on my own, somewhere private. After flagging a stack of promising documents for Val to copy, we walked over to the Foundling Museum, located just a few steps away at 40 Brunswick Square. The Georgian-style brick building, once the site of the Foundling Hospital's administrative offices, had been turned into another kind of public institution: a place for the curious to learn about the history of the hospital and the "foundlings" who were raised there.

A foundling, I'd learned over the course of my initial research, was not an orphan. And the Foundling Hospital was neither a hospital nor an orphanage.

An orphan was a child whose parents were dead, whereas a foundling likely still had parents, somewhere. Perhaps due to poverty, or more likely because of illegitimacy, those parents had given their child over to the care of the Foundling Hospital. Which meant that, despite its name and the fact that it did provide medical care, the "hospital" was more akin to an orphanage. The term *foundling* was technically a misnomer in the case of the children who'd ended up at the institution, for only a child who had been abandoned could be properly described as a foundling. For most of the hospital's history, admissions were limited to children who were personally handed over by a parent, following a rigorous process of review.

The files I'd begun to thumb through contained some early clues, in the form of a document on parchment, from an era before ballpoint pens and mechanical typewriters. "The Foundling Hospital" was written across the top in elegant calligraphy; just underneath was a simple title in block print—"Rules for the Admission of Children." As I scanned the document, my eyes lingered on a few choice phrases: *previous good character, in the course of virtue, the way of an honest livelihood*. I would learn more later.

At the museum I wandered through exhibits on the daily life of the foundlings, photos of identically dressed children filling row after row of a chapel. There was a small black iron bed, along with a display of the uniforms that the children were required to wear. They hung neatly in a row, on rounded pegs. The serge cloth was thick and coarse, a homely russet brown, chosen as a symbol of poverty, humility, and, as I would later learn, disgrace.

The garments were strangely familiar to me.

I had grown up in a wealthy family, but while other children at my school wore clothes purchased at upscale department stores, my mother frequently sewed my clothes by hand. I remember watching her work, hunched over her sewing table, lips pursed as she skillfully guided the fabric under the rapidly dancing needle. The clothes were flawless, with tight stitches and straight hems, but always brown and loose-fitting. I would plead with her to let me wear something else. The drab and shapeless clothes would make me the target of ridicule, I told her. She told me that I was too fat to wear anything else, and that children wouldn't tease me. Both statements were equally false.

I remember standing in the center of the playground, wearing one of the brown skirts that my mother had carefully sewn for me. The hem fell below the knees, too long to be fashionable. The outfit was completed by an oversized shirt, plain white socks, and sturdy brown shoes, which did nothing to help the cause.

My eyes were fixated on the rectangles forming a hopscotch pattern in the asphalt beneath me. I counted the numbers drawn in brightly colored chalk as I tried to drown out the taunts of my classmates.

When my mother picked me up, she had a different take on the playground dynamics. I wasn't the freak, the weirdo in ill-fitting clothes—and the children's taunts were just a cover. "It's because you play the violin," she whispered as if she were sharing a secret. "They're just jealous." I turned my head and watched her as she spoke, but the expression on her face revealed nothing other than a pure, fiery certainty in her convictions. I remember it vividly, her breathless voice and wide eyes. It was a small, insignificant moment, but it may have been my first realization that I wasn't the only member of my family who was out of step with the outside world.

As I gently ran my fingers over the uniforms the foundlings had worn, I wondered whether they were the reason my mother had dressed me as she did. Perhaps, for her, coarse brown sacks that might as well have been used to transport potatoes were simply what children wore.

I headed upstairs to the Court Room, the place where the "governors" of the Foundling Hospital had conducted their business. This room, where the men responsible for the administration of the hospital had spent countless hours debating the fates of their charges, had a familiarity about it as well—the formal furniture and lush Persian rugs reminded me of pieces my mother had chosen to decorate our home.

As I wandered into the picture gallery, adorned with large-scale portraits and a marble fireplace, my breath caught in my chest at the sight of two tall, ornate chairs. Featured prominently in the center of the expansive room, with intricate carvings that crept up their upright backs, they looked stately, like wooden thrones. They'd been used in the chapel, I was told. The resemblance was more than uncanny. The chairs were indistinguishable from a pair that were prominently displayed in the living room of my childhood home.

Wandering through the museum, I was overcome with a certainty that *this* was the place where it had begun—the darkness that consumed my mother, smothering any chance for tenderness or affection in our household.

Everyone I encountered treated me with kindness—the docent who showed me around the museum, the curator I met with later that afternoon. They must have known my interest wasn't purely academic. Maybe my reddened eyes gave me away. Some appeared to know to exactly what had brought me to the museum. One woman approached me and explained that she herself had been a ward of the hospital in the early 1950s. We chatted for a while.

"We were fortunate," she volunteered. "Where else would we have gone?"

I shouldn't have been surprised by the woman's gratitude to the institution. I'd passed right by Coram's motto that very morning: "Better chances for children since 1739." And as I roamed through the halls of the museum, I was surrounded by portraits of the dukes, earls, and other noble men extolled for their roles in creating and managing the Foundling Hospital throughout the centuries. The men in their elegant clothing, perched atop richly brocaded furniture, seemed to radiate pride in their philanthropic achievement.

I stood for a long time under the portrait of Thomas Coram, depicted in his later years, with white hair and a ruddy face, wearing a sturdy coat spun of worsted wool, and surrounded by evidence of his travels and station in life. The oil painting was mounted in a burnished golden frame. As I contemplated the face of the man whose vision had carved out a place for children like my mother, I felt a familiar bitterness rise up in my chest.

3

Secrets

I began my life two miles from the epicenter of the sexual revolution, in 1966. As I was taking my first steps, tens of thousands of the movement's foot soldiers had converged on San Francisco for the Summer of Love. The drug-fueled Haight-Ashbury district had become ground zero for a cultural revolution in which activists, artists, and half-lucid dreamers challenged deep-seated norms of behavior. Almost overnight, stigmas that had haunted women for centuries began to lose their power, and several years later one of the revolution's cornerstone tenets would be ratified into law. An unmarried woman who found herself pregnant and alone would no longer be forced to bear a child in the shadows, only to leave it at the doorstep of a parish church or, worse, seek out a back-alley abortion that could leave her disfigured or dead.

But in Forest Hill, an affluent neighborhood of gracefully curved streets atop one of San Francisco's famous peaks where I spent the first six years of my childhood, life went on as it always had. Lawyers and bankers left their imposing homes, many with ocean views, to make their daily trek to the financial district, while mothers took their children to feed the swans at the Palace of Fine Arts, untouched by the turmoil brewing a short drive away.

The sexual revolution had come too late for my mother, anyway. Her fate had been sealed centuries before, by the stroke of a king's quill pen and the accident of her birth.

No one told me that my mother was illegitimate. It wasn't a topic to be brought up at the dinner table or in casual conversation. Yet from my earliest memory, the fact of her illegitimacy was an integral part of my family's narrative. Somehow we just knew, perhaps because the clues simply spilled out into our daily lives.

Unlike other kids, in my world there were no grandparents bearing gifts or sending cards on birthdays or at Christmas. My paternal grandmother had died giving birth to my father, and my paternal grandfather had succumbed to a heart attack years later. I'd heard stories about them and would ask my father about his dad from time to time, questions any child might ask. *What was he like? Do you look like him? How old was he when he died?* But to bring up my mother's parentage was taboo. *What were their names? Where did they live? Were they alive or dead?* I didn't know the answers to even the most basic questions.

From time to time, I'd overhear tidbits about my mother's heritage. She was a descendant of Welsh nobility, but her rightful place in society had been taken from her—*stolen,* she would say. We had blue blood pulsing through our veins, she declared, and *that* no one could change.

I didn't know what she meant, and imagined that my blood was somehow different from that of other children. I had no reason to doubt her, not back then, given the precision of her speech and the high-toned nature of her extracurricular pursuits. She was as skilled at sketching with a pencil as she was at oil painting, and she played the piano with an effortless grace. Her tales of her studies at London's Royal Academy of Music, England's oldest conservatory, founded by the 11th Earl of Westmorland in 1822, only served to fuel my fantasies. So did her obsession with her Welsh ancestry and a long-running effort to help restore a crumbling Welsh castle. She would occasionally show me photographs of the imposing turreted stone structure, set on a vast empty moor, and over the years she spent thousands of dollars organizing posh dinner parties to raise funds for rebuilding the castle to its former glory.

When I was about eleven, I found a letter that hinted at the unknowns percolating in the background of my family life. The composition of the blood that surged through my veins was in question, it turned out. My parents had gone on an errand, and I'd taken the opportunity to snoop around my father's office. It was a bold move on my part, uncharacteristic of my rule-abiding nature. I glanced nervously out the window to make sure the coast was clear and then opened and closed a few desk drawers before turning to my father's file cabinet. This imposing piece of furniture was made of shiny lacquered oak, with antique brass handles on each of its four drawers. The cabinet had always seemed mysterious to me, so different from the gray industrial cabinets that lined the halls of my father's law office in San Francisco's financial district. Unsure of what I was looking for, I reached over and pulled on the top drawer.

"Bills," "House," "Insurance." The contents were mundane, but a file all the way in the back, at the very end of the alphabet, caught my eye. Its label sported a single name: "Weston."

Carefully sliding the file out of the cabinet, I sat on the hardwood floor and thumbed through its contents—a few articles about England that didn't seem particularly important, then a copy of a letter on my father's stationery. The letter was addressed to someone in England, and it began with a formal salutation: "Dear Sir."

"We are confident . . ." "The evidence shows . . ." The topic was a property in a place called Shropshire, and I managed to piece together that my father was trying to prove that my mother was somehow entitled to this land. Near the end of the letter was the string of words I found most surprising of all: "even her daughter looks like a Weston."

I'd always been told that I looked like my mother, a comparison I resented and one that my sister used as a taunt. "You're just like Mom" was the ultimate insult in our home. My sister and I had never been close; we were separated by four years, and then by geography when she was sent off to boarding school in Arizona as a young teen. We would never live in the same house again, or even in the same city. By the time she returned, I was off at boarding school myself. But my sister's words were seared into my memory, and I secretly clung to the hope that despite her assertions I was, in fact, nothing like my mother. The physical resemblance, however, was irrefutable. I had the same smooth brown hair, the same pale skin splattered with freckles. We both had large eyes and thick black eyebrows, although her eyes were brown and mine blue-green, like my father's. And now I looked "like a Weston," whatever that meant. Despite the sting of confirmation, my wish for individuation faded slightly as I realized my possible role in proving my mother's noble birthright.

Her claims had never seemed strange or unusual, and I had never questioned her status as a member of the aristocracy. After all, she made her disdain for the poor crystal clear (while reserving her greatest derision for the nouveau riche, calling them the "tackiest of the lot"). Her concern with the social strata was all-consuming, infiltrating every aspect of our home life. In fact a great deal of the misery in our household, at least as it applied to me, centered around my mother's enduring attempts to turn me into a proper upper-crust British girl—presumably the kind of girl she'd been raised to be.

OUR MORNING ROUTINE began before dawn. My mother would wake me, shaking me gently, breakfast already on the table.

There was no conversation as the car moved silently through the empty streets. My nose pressed up against the window, I'd watch as the moon followed us closely behind, dodging in and out from between passing trees and houses whose windows were still dark.

I was six when we started our early-morning treks to the home of Dr. Haderer, a respected professor of music who had studied in Japan with the renowned Dr. Shinichi Suzuki. At the time, few teachers had been trained in Suzuki's innovative "mother-tongue" approach, a theory of instruction that uses principles of language acquisition such as listening and repetition in teaching children violin. Dr. Haderer was in high demand, but my mother would settle for nothing but the best, even if that meant taking a six-in-the-morning slot.

After the lessons we would rush to the series of prestigious schools I attended. Always punctual, my mother would be back on the curb when classes let out, silently handing me a thermos full of warm split-pea soup as we headed to the next lesson— ballet, tap, tennis, horseback riding. Weekends or evenings, tutors were ushered into the dining room, where we'd work at the long oak table under the soft light of the vintage gold sconces and large chandelier. My skin pressed uncomfortably against the carvings that wound up the stiff back of my wooden chair as we went over my French, creative writing, and drawing assignments to ensure that no area be neglected.

Among the revolving cast was a private handwriting tutor who taught me how to hold a pen, how much pressure to exert on the paper, and the exact stroke needed to create a perfectly shaped letter. My lessons took place at her home, a cream-colored mansion with a red-tiled roof. Once through the spacious foyer, I would follow her long white hair and free-flowing gray tunic up a spiral staircase to a cozy room in a tower overlooking the forest behind her house. We would sit side by side at an antique desk as she gently pressed her hand on top of mine to guide my writing instrument. The lessons were painless, but they still caused me worry. Handwriting had never been my forte, and my mother was highly critical of my deficiencies, down to the last pen stroke.

She was relentless in her quest to mold me into an accomplished and refined young lady, going so far as to teach me to spell using the Queen's English. When my teachers at school would correct me—"It's t-h-e-a-t-e-r, *not* t-h-e-a-t-r-e"—I'd insist that my version was "real" English. "This is America," they would sensibly respond, and so I learned to spell one way for my mother, another for my teachers.

Once the tutors had gone and we'd cleared my notebooks off the dinner table, our in-house curriculum began. How to butter bread (break off a bite-sized piece first), which fork to use, and how to get that last drop of soup in the bowl (never tip the bowl toward you).

After dinner, the lessons would turn to diction. "Repeat after me," she would begin:

Betty had a bit of butter
But the butter was too bitter
So, Betty bought some better butter to make the bitter butter better.

30

Our routine was repeated night after night. Where my tutors were patient, encouraging, my mother would ridicule. "It's not bud-d-d-d-der," she would mock, drawing out the "d," her face rumpled in disdain. "Say it again, but *properly* this time." Yet I could never quite get it right, my tone of voice or accent unrefined, too American.

As early as first grade, teachers started sending me home with notes expressing concern over my habit of worrying, the way an inconsequential error would send me into a chasm of self-doubt and anxiety. The smallest mistake would cause acute physical pain that left me weakened and anguished for days after the inciting event. This was a pattern that would be repeated throughout my life, the slightest criticism sending me into a spiral of defensiveness and shame. Work supervisors admonished me for being "too sensitive" to feedback. Friends and coworkers told me not to worry so much or take it so hard. Their well-intentioned suggestions did little to quiet the critical voices in my head. Sometimes I could prevent myself from spiraling by digging a thumbnail into the palm of my hand to create a dull throbbing, or counting cracks in the sidewalk as I walked to and from meetings—anything to distract myself from my inner thoughts. These efforts weren't always successful, and occasionally my fears and anxieties would seep out as harsh words directed at colleagues or inopportune tears when I discovered a missed typo. A few times my panic landed me in the emergency room when my symptoms too closely resembled those of a heart attack. I would spend decades on a therapist's couch, working to overcome the intractable belief that I was a failure, unworthy of love and respect. But no matter how hard I tried to silence the voices in my head, I carried around my list of personal defects like a thousand-pound weight.

I saw my anxieties as a byproduct of my mother's relentless

criticism, her unending desire to mold me into a person I never wanted to be, fashioned in her own image. I placed all of my miseries squarely upon her shoulders. But I would come to discover that any real mistakes she made paled in comparison to the injustices she had endured in the past.

4

SCRUTINY

A burst of adrenaline would rush through my tiny body when I heard the front door latch each day around six o'clock. Promptly putting a stop to whatever I was doing, I would sprint to the front of the house on my stubby legs and hurl myself into my father's arms, breathlessly offering to carry his briefcase. With both of my hands gripping the well-worn leather handle, we would walk slowly down the long hallway as he listened intently to the highlights of my day—what I'd learned in school or a picture I had drawn in art class.

An old-fashioned lawyer, a true gentleman, and a statesman built on a bygone template, my father was brilliant and honorable. He never had a bad word to say about anyone, and he was honest to a fault. He would return a nickel if it were given to him in error, or leave a note if he barely nicked the paint on another car.

He held me to the same exacting ethical standards. Even an inconsequential lapse in judgment would become a teaching moment, a reminder of the importance of living a life of integrity.

I spent most of my weekend days at an equestrian center in nearby Woodside, a small town known for its horse culture, with trails in place of sidewalks and hitching posts for parking meters. When I was ready to be picked up, I would call my father from a pay phone located near the barn's tack room. A friend gave me an idea on how to save money—call collect, and when the operator connects the call, just hang up. The aborted call would send the signal that I was ready. A clever way to save a quarter, it seemed.

"We can't do that," my father explained patiently when I proposed the idea. "That would be cheating the phone company, which is wrong."

His corrections were always gentle, delivered without anger or judgment.

My favorite time of day was just before I drifted off to sleep, when my father would knock softly on my bedroom door, kiss me gently on the forehead, then prop himself up on the second twin bed. Curling onto my side, I could just make out his silhouette in the moonlight streaming in through the sheer white curtains. Resting my head on my clasped hands, I would let the slow and deliberate droning of his voice soothe me like a lullaby.

"Do you know what asbestos is?"

Instead of listening to fairy tales, each night I learned about what happened when a worker was injured on the job. My father was the managing partner of one of the leading workers' compensation defense firms in California. Some of his stories were mundane—details on the burgeoning field of litigation due to the common use of asbestos, a mineral considered an excellent fire retardant that was commonly mixed with cement and used in construction. The "magic mineral" likely prevented thousands of untimely deaths by fire, but it was later discovered that the material's tiny fibers could be inhaled, damaging workers' and residents' lungs and making them sick. When I discovered that the pipes leading to our own furnace were wrapped with asbestos, I worried that our entire family would fall sick, maybe even die. My father assured me that they had been properly covered, the hazard long since contained, but I still was fearful each time I ventured down into the basement. Some of his cases seemed like scenes out of a TV show, like the time he hired a private investigator and caught a man doing aerobics when he had claimed he was too injured to work. I imagined the investigator slinking between the bushes outside a gym, snapping photos of the con artist as he did knee raises and grapevines, oblivious to the fact that he had been caught red-handed. Another time, my father exposed a fraudulent claim by a member of the Mafia and was advised to hire a bodyguard. (He didn't.)

Some of the bedtime stories came from the time before my father moved to California, when he served in the Tennessee legislature. There was corruption everywhere, he said. It was like the Wild West. Men would walk into the capitol building with canvas bags filled with cash ready to be delivered to legislators whose votes could be bought. Not long after my father took office, a former Tennessee Supreme Court justice approached him with promises of campaign contributions if my father could just "find a way" to support an upcoming bill. My father refused in no uncertain terms, establishing his reputation as a man whose vote wasn't for sale.

I dreamed of becoming a workers' compensation attorney, commuting each day to an office building in the San Francisco financial district, working alongside my father at his firm. That's when I learned a new word: *nepotism*. "I don't believe in it," he explained when I asked him if he would hire me. "If you work hard, and you are the best candidate for the job, then you can work for me."

I was disappointed, crestfallen actually, but my father told me that his work was boring, that if he could do it all over again, he would have joined the Peace Corps. Or, he went on, perhaps he would have taken a parallel path, but become a public interest lawyer.

"Do something good with your life," he urged me. "Use what you have to help people."

Following in the footsteps of my father's dream career twenty years later, I knew that he had been right. Sorting through government files and reviewing inspection reports and toxicology records was exhilarating. I treated each case like a treasure hunt as I searched for data I would use to right a wrong. I would spend hours navigating bureaucratic mazes, making phone calls, camping out in government offices, and chatting up file clerks to uncover evidence of environmental improprieties.

Digging for gold amid dusty files and combing through volumes in search of empirical evidence was second nature to me—so much so that applying those same skills to the documentation I brought home from that second trip to London felt like finding an old friend. Many of the accounts of the Foundling Hospital's history were out of print, written decades or generations ago. I looked forward to hearing the doorbell ring, and finding brown-papered packages from used-book sellers on the doorstep. Soon my desk was covered with books by historians, academic researchers, and learned governors who'd led the institution centuries ago—men whose names I didn't recognize, like Jonas Hanway and John Brownlow. No book was too obscure for my notice.

The Foundling Hospital had been established in the middle of the eighteenth century to fill a dire need, I quickly learned. An unwed mother of limited means would have had few options in providing for her infant at the time. She would likely have been shunned by her family, perhaps forced out of her home. Existing poorhouses were frequently filthy and dangerous—temporary shelters filled with vagrants and lunatics, the aged and the ill. In contrast, the Foundling Hospital offered a clean and orderly environment, and women desperate to find a home for an unwanted infant flocked to its doors in great numbers. Administrators couldn't keep up with the quickly escalating demand, and it wasn't unheard of for fights to break out among waiting mothers desperate to give their children a safe home. On the sideline of the melee would be fashionably attired spectators who paid a fee to watch the admission process unfold.

To mitigate the chaos of the hordes of women gathered outside its doors, the hospital instituted a lottery system in 1742. The system amounted to little more than a mother drawing colored balls from a leather bag. If she drew a white ball, her child would be accepted, pending the results of a medical examination. A red ball meant that the child would be wait-listed, in case a child whose mother had drawn a white ball failed the medical test. A black ball doomed a child to rejection.

The lottery system didn't last long. Criticized for relegating life-or-death decisions to a game of chance, it was followed by a second system termed the "General Reception." A woman could drop off a child with no questions asked, or simply leave her infant in a basket hung on the hospital gate, ringing a bell to alert the porter before disappearing into the night. The General Reception had disastrous results. There was massive influx of children, 117 on the first day alone, and the numbers only increased. Soon the hospital was overwhelmed. Nearly 15,000 children were admitted during the four-year-long General Reception period; more than 10,000 of them died.

After much trial and error, the Foundling Hospital created a set of admission procedures that were honed for efficiency and left little to chance. Adopted in the 1800s and implemented well into the following century, the Foundling Hospital's "Rules for the Admission of Children" included precautions ensuring that children of legitimate birth would not be inadvertently accepted: "The children of Married Women and Widows cannot be received into the Hospital."[2] Couples too poor to care for their children or women who had been widowed or abandoned by their husbands would have to look elsewhere for assistance. Unlike those born out of wedlock, their children had a chance in life—a chance to receive an education, take on a trade, and become productive members of society.

But even the women who met the basic criteria set forth in these rules would not find immediate relief. The admission process was lengthy. It could last weeks, even months, not for any reason related to the child but because it took time to determine whether the mother was worthy of the generosity of the Foundling Hospital.

For Lena Weston, my grandmother, the process lasted eight weeks.

IN 1931 LENA was unmarried, in her thirties, pregnant, and alone.

As a young woman living in the interwar period following World War I, one of the deadliest conflicts in human history, she was part of a lost generation of women consigned to a solitary existence. The war had claimed the lives of hundreds of thousands of British soldiers, leaving behind a grim cohort whose chance to marry would never come. Their husbands-to-be lost to the battlefield, unmarried women frequently wound up living with relatives. If the relatives were male, most typically brothers, the women would serve as housekeepers while their brothers ran the farms or worked outside the home. Entirely dependent upon their living male relatives for support, they developed few skills other than tending house. Those women who lived with their female relatives fared a bit better, such arrangements generally being more egalitarian, with the housework shared and no objections raised to the pursuit of a vocation outside of the home. In either case, however, the women were unlikely to end up with a proposal of marriage.

Lena's parents were deceased, and her sister, Lily, had immigrated to the United States, where she was living in the renowned Waldorf Astoria while working for the jazz composer Cole Porter. Perhaps following in Lily's footsteps would have been feasible at some point, but by the time Lena entered her thirties, her only option was to join her brother on a farm in the county of Shropshire, a largely unpeopled land near the Welsh border, with a smattering of farms and the occasional castle. It was a landscape of vast meadows carpeted with dark purple wildflowers, of rolling hills whose wild escarpments were thick with untamed roses and rhododendrons. Most of the local inhabitants were farmers or laborers at a nearby ironworks, although there were a surprising number of landed families with knightly aristocratic roots. There were no cities to speak of, only quiet villages and hamlets. The closest escape from the Weston farm was the market town of Wellington, whose quaint shops lined a narrow lane bordered by brick-terraced houses and an old stone church.

With only the steady rhythm of daily chores and Sunday sermons to fill the solitude of her days, Lena's chances at finding intimacy, tenderness, and love would have been few to nonexistent. Unlike single men, who were simply "sowing wild oats" when they engaged in sex outside marriage, a woman who dared to seek companionship in the arms of a lover would be labeled promiscuous and shunned from proper society. Then there were the practical considerations—limited access to birth control, at least for women like Lena, and no legal path to abortion. The first birth control clinic in England was established in 1921 by the British women's rights advocate Marie Stopes. Stopes was a prominent eugenicist, and her repugnant views on race left an irredeemable mark on her legacy. But her advocacy for reproductive rights was considered revolutionary, and she openly defied the church's disapproval of birth control. Lena would not benefit from these advances, however; the clinic's contraceptive services were available to married women only.

Lena could have resigned herself to her fate: a life of solitude, endless days on a farm tucked away in the countryside, with only her brother to keep her company.

But that is not what happened.

The files that I brought home from London chronicled the sequence of events that had brought Lena to the Foundling Hospital's doorstep. Where there were gaps, it was easy enough to imagine the subtext that went unspoken as Lena recounted her circumstances to the strangers who would determine the fate of her child. It was February 1931, and after selling eggs at the market, Lena had settled herself in for her customary cup of tea at a café near the center of Wellington. It was there that she met him. Perhaps she noticed him smiling at her from across the room, or tipping the brim of his hat to her. With only her brother to keep her company, Lena may have been unusually susceptible to the charms of a man. Or maybe that's a bit of conjecture on my end. Maybe she knew full well what she was doing. Maybe it had happened before.

Either way, that day in February would change the course of Lena's life, and the lives of generations to come.

The affair was brief, and the repercussions swift. After a bitter quarrel, Lena's brother kicked her out, forcing her to make her way to London in search of institutional support. Single and with a child on the way, Lena had few options. A woman in her circumstances could petition for child support, but she would have to establish the father's identity through legal proceedings. The process would take place in open court, exposing her to shame and ridicule. Society was not kind to women like Lena, considering them "fallen" and deserving of punishment, a view held even by those who advocated for women's rights. Marie Stopes, who had campaigned for a married woman's right to access birth control, herself condemned illegitimacy, asserting that the illegitimate child is "inherently inferior to the legitimate, through the fact that his mother has failed to maintain her self-respect and the respect of the father."[3] Maude Royden, a well-known feminist and Christian preacher, argued against providing benefits to unmarried women, which might encourage single parenting and promiscuity. Even John Bowlby, a pioneer in child psychology whose theories exalted the role of the mother in child-rearing, considered an unmarried mother to be "emotionally disturbed," and her "socially unacceptable illegitimate baby" to be a "symptom of her neurosis."[4]

These deep-seated prejudices were memorialized in the laws of the time. The Mental Deficiency Act of 1913 went so far as to categorize unmarried mothers "in receipt of poor relief" as defective, grouping them in with "idiots," "imbeciles," and the "feeble-minded," thus empowering government officials to institutionalize them and separate them from their children. So-called bastardy bills, designed to improve conditions for illegitimate children or allow for a path to legitimization, were frequently introduced in the House of Lords but consistently rejected. The Legitimacy Act finally passed in 1926 allowing unmarried parents to marry and retroactively claim their child as legitimate, but it did not apply to children who were the result of adultery. Similarly, post-1906 liberal welfare reforms ushered in a wave of progressive policies that provided a range of support services for seemingly everyone else—factory workers, the unemployed, children, the elderly and the infirm—but denied unmarried mothers maternity and unemployment benefits.

Not until World War II, when illegitimacy rates soared, would the government adopt a more compassionate view of unmarried mothers. Those changes would come too late for Lena, who would be forced to wait out her pregnancy at the Constance Road Institution, a workhouse established in the nineteenth century to house "imbeciles and lunatics" and the "aged and infirm." Closer to her due date, she was transferred to Dulwich Hospital, built by the Guardians of the Poor of the Parish of St. Saviour, where, on January 1, 1932, she gave birth to a healthy girl.

Keeping the child had never been an option, not without her brother's support.

Within a day or two of her daughter's birth, Lena wrote a letter that would be the first of several. The handwritten note was dispatched to an address on Brunswick Square that was already familiar to me by the time it came into my hands, some eighty-five years after she'd written it. The contents of the letter were difficult to decipher, the ink faded with time, the penmanship sometimes illegible. I brought the photocopied replica closer to my face, squinting to make out the words.

Dear Madam,

I am writing to ask you if you would kindly help me if you are able. Through my misfortune, I have given birth to a daughter here, and I cannot find the father, and worst I have no parents. If I was able to have someone to look after the child, I should be able to go back to work. I should be very glad if you could come and see me, if you please can find it convenient [illegible] explain to you and tell you.

> Yours faithfully,
> Lena Weston

In reply, the secretary of the Foundling Hospital provided Lena with an application form and a copy of the Foundling Hospital's "Rules for the Admission of Children"—the same rules that had been adopted more than a century before.

The form contained some perfunctory questions about the child, its sex, and the date of its birth, but the remainder of the questions focused on the circumstances that had led to Lena's pregnancy. *Who is the father? What is his full name? Did you become engaged to marry him? Who introduced you to him? Does the father know of your trouble? Has he promised to provide for the child?*

In my research, I learned that the hospital's primary purpose was to provide a home for illegitimate children who would otherwise fall through the cracks of the social order. It was understood, however, that the institution would serve a second and arguably more important purpose: that of restoring a fallen woman to her former standing. That she be prevented from becoming a prostitute, according to John Brownlow, secretary of the Foundling Hospital during the mid-1800s and a former foundling himself, was imperative. He was particularly concerned about the woman who had become the "unsuspecting victim of treachery," and who, without the assistance of the Foundling Hospital, would become "delirious in her despair."[5] Brownlow felt compelled to help such a woman. "Preserving the mere vital functions of an infant," he reasoned, cannot be put in competition with saving from vice, misery, and infamy, a young woman, in the bloom of life, whose crime may have been a single and solitary act of indiscretion. Many extraordinary cases of repentance, followed by restoration to peace, comfort, and reputation, have come within the knowledge of the writer of this note. Some cases have occurred, within his own observation, of wives happily placed, the mothers of thriving families, who, but for the saving aid of this Institution, might have become the most noxious and abandoned prostitutes. Very rare are the instances, none has come within notice, of a woman relieved by the Foundling Hospital, and not thereby preserved from a course of prostitution.[6]

Helping a woman regain her dignity and virtue was a noble and essential purpose, and the rules of the institution reflected the gravity of the task. To have her child admitted to the Foundling Hospital, a mother had to prove to the satisfaction of the governors who administered the process that all requirements had been met.

Each rule had been designed to determine whether a woman was of sufficient moral character that her reputation *could* be repaired, and that, if granted the great favor of being allowed to relinquish her child, she would return to her station in society. The rules on this score were unforgiving:

No child can be admitted unless the Committee is satisfied, after due enquiry, of the *previous good character* and present necessity of the Mother, and that the Father of the child has *deserted* it and the Mother; and also, that the reception of the child, will, in all probability, be the means of replacing the Mother in the course of virtue, and the way of an honest livelihood.[7]

Nor were ladies of great wealth spared the rigors of the process. Infants delivered to the hospital in fine lace bonnets or intricately embroidered gowns, with expensive toys clutched between their tiny fingers, would still have been vetted to the full extent of the rules.

Once a child had been admitted, its mother could rest easy, knowing that the very existence of the child would be a closely guarded secret. The hospital's clerk entered the name of the mother and the sex and age of the child in a central register, the only record of the mother's true identity. The register, along with any other identifying tokens or documents, was placed in a billet that was to be "kept with great Secrecy and Care," and "never to be opened but by Order of the [Hospital's] General Committee."[8] The child would go by a new name, and in correspondence or in response to inquiries, he or she would be identified only by a letter and the date of admission. At first children were given the names of distinguished public figures to honor them, a practice that began in 1741, when the hospital's first two charges were named after its founder, Thomas Coram, and his wife, Eunice. The naming system was abandoned when grown children began laying claims upon their namesakes, and the earls and dukes who had lent their names were forced to defend themselves against spurious claims of descent.

On my first sort through the documents back in that small room across from the Foundling Museum, I'd noticed that Lena hadn't named the father on her application form, instead listing him anonymously as a "commercial traveller." When Val came back to check on us, I'd asked her curiously if he might have been a traveling salesman. My own frame of reference called up a particularly American notion of the trade—a humdrum man in a cheap suit knocking on doors, selling encyclopedias or vacuum cleaners. Maybe I could track down the identity of my grandfather by researching companies that had employed salesmen in the area. But Val gently disabused me of these notions, along with my hopes of finding out more. It was common for applicants to the Foundling Hospital to claim that the men who'd impregnated them were travelers passing through town, to hide their true identities.

There was another clue in Lena's statement of her case:

> My brother is my nearest relation. . . . I have written to him to ask if he could take the child and myself, but writes to say that he could not do with the child but would give me some assistance. . . . I am making this application to you asking for your help, if you would kindly take the child off my hands now that I can get work, and trust that some day I shall be in circumstances to have the child again. The tragic part—I do not know the father or much about him as I met him casually as a ~~stranger~~ stranger he never told me either his name or address, unfortunately only now realize my foolishness! Trusting that you can understand and help me through, this most awful fate.

Lena's handwritten strike through the word *stranger* was telling. Maybe she'd had a moment of indecision on that score because her "commercial traveller" was in fact someone she knew—not a stranger but an acquaintance, or perhaps a married lover. But her letters revealed nothing about the man's identity.

The file was a jumble of loose papers in no particular order when I received it, and on my return from London I spent the better part of two weeks combing through its contents and carefully cataloging the documents. Years of work as a public interest attorney preparing for trial without the help of teams of paralegals had honed my organizational skills. Approaching the task as I would any legal case, I had painstakingly organized the documents using color-coded tabs. Chronologically, the next letter was a typed response from the Foundling Hospital back to Lena, dated January 7, 1932:

Dear Madam,

I am in receipt of your application form, but regret to inform you that your case cannot be entertained unless you are able to furnish me with the name of the man you allege to be the father of your child, the address where he lived or worked when you knew him and some corroboration to your story.

Yours faithfully,
Secretary

As I read the typewritten letter, with its detached tone and seeming indifference to the plight of a distressed mother, I imagined Lena in her bed at Dulwich Hospital, possibly alone and almost definitely fearful. Perhaps she was clutching the child who would one day be my mother as she read this discouraging response. But the following letter in my chronologically organized folder gave me a hint of Lena's character. Just three days later, she tried again:

Dear Sir,

Thanking you for your letter of Thursdays date. I note that you cannot accept my application under the circumstances.

Would you kindly give permission for an interview, I should then be able to give a better and further description of details of my case. I feel sure would not be rejected, awaiting your reply.

I am,
Yours respectfully,
Lena Weston

Her persistence paid off, and on January 25 she received the following reply:

Dear Madam,

Referring to your application, will you please attend at these Offices tomorrow (Tuesday) afternoon at 3.30 o'clock to be interviewed by the Committee.

Please do not bring the child with you.

Yours faithfully,
Secretary

"Please do not bring the child with you." The last line of the letter spoke volumes about the type of interview Lena could expect at the hands of the "Committee" of governors who would ultimately make the decision to admit or deny her child. The governors who'd been given the power to manage the Foundling Hospital and shape the future of the mothers and children who came before them would not be swayed by an apple-cheeked infant. As they decided which children would be admitted, they would cast judgment solely upon the mothers.

By design, the committee of governors was comprised of men of wealth and influence, many of them of noble birth. Notably missing from their ranks were any women, though, as I would later learn, women had been key to the hospital's founding. A plan to allow them to formally participate in the governance of the institution was proposed, but ultimately rejected, since women were "excluded by Custom from the Management of publick Business."[9] Instead, only men would decide the fate of thousands of mothers and their children—determining not only who would be admitted but also how they would be raised and educated, and even the methods used to punish them. Almost two centuries would pass before a woman would sit among their ranks.

I was no stranger to inequality, having spent much of my career as an attorney in the South, litigating high-profile cases, often in small rural towns. To succeed, I'd had to navigate a world dominated by men—the federal judge who addressed only the male lawyers during an in-chambers hearing, the former attorney general who would speak to me only through his female secretary, opposing counsel who described me as a bit "too strong" in advocating on behalf of my client (a trait generally admired in male litigators). But these men and their underestimation of my skills had inspired me to advocate with a deepened sense of purpose, to be more outspoken, and to take any opportunity to challenge norms I viewed as antiquated and unfair.

It was a trait that often got me in trouble.

I was seven when I first challenged a man—and he was at least six times my age. Mr. Nakamoto was a parent who shared carpool duty with my mother, ferrying me and his daughter back and forth from the violin recitals that were a regular part of the Suzuki music curriculum.

"What do you want to be when you grow up?" he asked us one afternoon.

"The president!" I boldly proclaimed as I climbed through a window into the jump seat in the back of his tan station wagon.

"Why, you can't be the president, Justine! You're a girl!"

"You're wrong," I countered. "I can!"

He continued to school me on my gender's limited prospects, and I continued to argue back without hesitation until he gave up, no match for my willfulness. I folded my arms in defiance and glared at him as he closed the back gate of the wagon. He never asked me any questions again.

It was that same brazenness that fueled me to challenge a

group of male attorneys two decades later, between my second and third years of law school, during a friendly game of softball. I was serving as a summer clerk for a prestigious law firm in Nashville. If all went well, they would offer me a job upon my graduation.

It was my turn at bat, and I approached home plate.

"Take first," instructed the umpire as he pointed his glove toward first base. Puzzled, I was informed of a long-standing league rule: if the pitcher walks a male batter who precedes a female in the lineup, the female batter automatically "gets a walk" to first base. The rule was designed to prevent savvy pitchers from walking a strong and skilled male batter in order to strike out the next batter—the weak and inept female.

My male teammates, the lawyers who would determine whether I was worthy of employment with their firm, urged me to take the base. I hesitated, but not for long.

"You've got to be kidding me," I retorted as I took my place at bat, ignoring their groans. I can still hear that *crack* as the bat made contact, hurtling the ball into the outfield. I did little to hide my smirk as I breezed past first base and took my place on second.

While I eventually made it to home plate, I didn't get the job offer.

I had been so proud of my performance that day, viewing myself as a trailblazer of sorts—a regular Susan B. Anthony! But reading about Lena's struggles, I felt foolish, the feather in my cap won so easily and with so little risk. While the law firm's rejection stung, I had other options. Lena did not. Nor did she have the bulwark of higher education, as I did, or the help of an advocate. On the afternoon of January 26, 1932, she pleaded her case alone before a panel of the wealthiest and most highly educated men she had ever encountered. The meeting took place in a wood-paneled room on the second floor of the administrative offices of the Foundling Hospital at 40 Brunswick Square, an oblong space that no longer exists in its original form. The walls were adorned with fine art, the molded ceilings decorated with elaborate plasterwork. A crystal chandelier hung in the center of the room. A large fireplace provided warmth for the governors who sat along one side of a long table, perhaps in high-backed chairs like the one I'd seen in the Foundling Museum and recognized from my childhood home.

There are no detailed records of what transpired that day. The London Metropolitan Archives contained only perfunctory minutes reflecting who was in attendance and the committee's final decision. The meeting was chaired by Sir Roger Gregory, a hospital governor who served from 1892 until his death in 1938. I didn't uncover much about Gregory, only that he was a solicitor who served as a senior partner at the prominent London firm Gregory, Rowcliffe, & Co. A portrait of Sir Gregory hangs in the Foundling Museum gallery today. In it, his rumpled black suit seemed modest compared to the attire of other governors I'd seen portraits of, and he had the look of a charitable man, with tufts of gray hair, a trimmed mustache, and kind eyes. Eight other men, listed in the archives' minutes only by their surnames, joined Sir Gregory that day. The notes reveal nothing of how they treated Lena, whether they expressed sympathy or judgment. Lena would have sat alone on the other side of the table, allowed no assistance from counsel or even a trusted friend, as the governors deposed her about the details of her misfortune. The proceedings typically included an inquiry into the nature of the liaison that had led to the unwanted pregnancy.

How long have you known the father?
Did he use force?
Was there alcohol involved?

I don't know whether Lena stuck to her story—a stranger passing through town, no promises made, no information exchanged. According to a scholarly article detailing the process of admissions, an applicant who claimed a promise of marriage prior to sexual intercourse was more likely to receive admission for her child. Lena might have understood that answers reflecting a woman's naïveté and a man's duplicity were much more likely to lead to her desired outcome. In her written application, she had included few details of her illicit liaison, only that in February 1931 a man had taken "liberties" with her during a walk to the Wrekin, an iconic rock formation on the outskirts of Wellington, and that this had been "repeated the two subsequent weeks." The timing of Lena's story would have resulted in an improbably long pregnancy, and I had no way of knowing whether the governors conducting the interviews were astute enough to question Lena's chronology of events. With no record of the details of the meeting, I knew only that her pleas were successful as she received a letter the following day.

27th January, 1932

Dear Madam,

   With reference to your application for the admission of your child to this Hospital—the Governors decided yesterday to have enquiries made into your case.

   Yours faithfully,
   Secretary

Despite its dry tone, the letter was an indication of success. I silently cheered when Lena passed through the first threshold of the arduous process, but there was more to come. Next, the governors would investigate whether Lena was who she claimed to be—a respectable woman. She had already assured them in her application that she was virtuous, and that "this is the only occasion on which I have ever been interfered with, and if the Governors relieve me of my child I propose to return home to look after my brother." But Lena's word would not be enough. Instead, the governors sought corroboration from the men who knew her—her brother, her doctor, and her pastor. Her family's physician, Dr. Mackie, supplied a reference vouching for Lena's respectability, while censuring the "lapse" that had occasioned her current situation:

> I have been Medical Attendant to the Weston Family for years and have always had a great respect for them all. . . . I have never heard the slightest hint or suggestion of any moral turpitude in her character, in fact the recent lapse came as a great surprise to me, and from what I know of her I am pretty certain it will never happen again.

Her pastor, Reverend Nock, added his voice to the chorus: "This is to certify that I have known Miss Lena Weston for a number of years and she is of a most respectable family and attends my Church as one of my Church followers." The underlining, presumably added by a governor reviewing Lena's case, was telling—respectability was essential for an applicant to succeed.

The governors were exceedingly thorough in the execution of their task, going so far as to dispatch an investigator to interview each of the letter writers personally. More notes and documentation would follow. During his interview, Reverend Nock reiterated his earlier assessment, that Lena came from "respectable people," adding that they were "highly thought of in the district." He described Lena as "truthful, reliable and dependable," and he "had never seen her about with any men." Dr. Mackie affirmed Reverend Nock's assessment that Lena came from a "very respectable family," adding that "the girl was quite straight-forward, but easily led." The not-so-subtle implication behind the assurances from these male guarantors was that Lena wouldn't stain the Foundling Hospital's reputation by repeating her mistake—nor were they at risk of housing the offspring of the worst kind of repeat offender, a common prostitute. For his part, Lena's brother, Harry, attested that "his sister had always been a very nicely conducted girl" and that "if the Governors helped her, he was quite willing to have her back." (Quite a turnaround, given that he'd thrown her out just a few months earlier.)

Shuffling through the reports and letters, I could feel the blood rushing to my head. How freely these men rendered their opinions! Scrutinizing my grandmother, adjudicating her virtue, deciding whether she measured up to their exacting standards; it all seemed to come so easily to them. I felt oddly protective of a woman I had never known, whose name had held no meaning for me until so recently.

In the end, Lena succeeded. Vouched for by her doctor, her pastor, and her brother, she received the following letter a month after her interview:

24th February, 1932

Dear Madam,

Referring to your application—the same was considered by the Governors at their Meeting yesterday and I am pleased to inform you they decided to receive your child. You must bring her to these Offices yourself on Wednesday morning next, the 2nd proximo, punctually at 10.30 o'clock.

Please acknowledge this letter and be punctual as there are

other children for admission the same day and if you are late it will upset the whole arrangements.

It will not be necessary for you to provide any additional clothing for the child.

Yours faithfully,
Secretary

As instructed, at the appointed time, Lena Weston brought her baby girl to 40 Brunswick Square. Just blocks from the fashionable Russell Square, where gray-and-white buildings with brightly colored doors and large brass door knockers housed wealthier inhabitants of London, the Foundling Hospital was modest, constructed of common red brick, its windows adorned with crisp white trim that gave the facade a well-ordered and tidy appearance. There was only one entrance, a set of plain concrete steps that led to an unassuming wooden door.

How Lena must have trembled as she walked up those stairs, the hope of sparing her family from disgrace fueling her with the strength to lift her each step. In truth, I don't know much about Lena's character or her thoughts on that day, since the only trace left of her is the trail of administrative bread crumbs in the Foundling Hospital's files. But by the measure of the times, Lena had been given a rare gift, one that would allow her to regain her respectability and no small degree of security.

In return, she was asked to do only one thing—forget that her daughter had ever existed.

5

BASTARDS

To understand Lena's choice, I'd have to go back to the eighteenth century, to images that seem barbaric to us now—dead or dying babies tossed into open sewers or thrown atop piles of refuse on London's streets. Medieval as it sounds, the disgrace of an unwanted pregnancy was still so ruinous at the time that a woman from any walk of life might find herself turning to infanticide. Where better to hide the evidence of her crime than among butchers' bones strewn along narrow alleys, where a child's discarded corpse would be buried under the excrement dumped from chamber pots emptied from the windows above?

Not all children died at the hands of their desperate mothers, of course. Many were simply left to fend for themselves. A thousand children or more might be abandoned on the streets of London in a given year, and those fortunate enough to survive past infancy were often relegated to lives of begging, theft, and prostitution. The wickedness of London's streets was so commonplace that it was reflected in the art of the time, memorialized most famously by William Hogarth. A leading eighteenth-century art-ist who would eventually find a sideline saving children cast off by society, Hogarth captivated London in the early 1730s with his *Rake's Progress* series of paintings. The story of a man who forsakes his pregnant fiancée and squanders his fortune on wild parties and orgies would have resonated at the time. Of course, punishment awaited: the final painting depicts the rake's demise at Bedlam, London's infamous mental asylum.

London's ruling class had a long history of providing for children whose fathers had died honorably or were too long at sea, serving their country. But the growing number of illegit-imate children abandoned along the city's streets was another matter altogether. Members of high society didn't see fit to help children born outside of marriage, an act that would have been considered immoral, against the teachings of Christ. Eighteenth-century philanthropist and author Jonas Hanway summed up the prevailing view in describing the failure of earlier attempts to save forsaken children during the reign of Queen Anne: to help a child born out of wedlock "might seem to encourage per-sons in vice, by making too easy provision for their illegitimate children."[10]

Not all members of society shared this view. Thomas Co-ram, whose own tragic childhood would inform his life's work, viewed these discarded children not as the wages of sin but as a worthy cause. Born in 1668, Coram started life unluckily, losing his mother when he was four, a few days after she gave birth to a younger brother who also perished. At the age of eleven, the poor, motherless Coram was sent to sea by his father, later be-coming an apprentice for a shipwright. Somehow, with no ped-igree or resources, the competent and tenacious boy managed to turn that apprenticeship into a successful career as a shipbuilder. From there he made his way in society, sailing for Boston in

1694 to stand up a shipbuilding business. He traveled the world, became a trustee of the brand-new colony of Georgia, and developed a plan (implemented by the Earl of Halifax, among others) for the settlement of Nova Scotia. Yet no matter how changed his own circumstances, he could never turn a blind eye to the tiny corpses or starving children with outstretched hands on London's streets, as so many Londoners did. Instead he made a pact with himself—he would find a way to care for these forgotten children.

Coram's quest would not be an easy one. The practical difficulties of carrying out any philanthropic efforts in this area were compounded by his countrymen's moral objections.

It is difficult to imagine an entire nation turning its back on defenseless infants. But as historian Ruth McClure noted in her meticulously detailed account of the Foundling Hospital, eighteenth-century foundlings had been effectively dehumanized: "The most difficult obstacle to overcome, as Coram soon found out, was prejudice because, for the most part, the attitude of the average Englishman towards foundlings was not recognized as a prejudice. Everyone took for granted the equation: foundling equals bastard; . . . everyone also took for granted the corollary: bastard equals disgrace. That was the accepted order of things in God's universe and all decent English society; few questioned it."[11]

There was an exception; the very highest members of society did not always share in loathing the illegitimate child. Among their ranks, bastard births were remarkably common. Perhaps that is why women of great status and wealth were among the first constituency to rally by Coram's side—"Ladies of Quality and Distinction," as he called them.

The first woman to support Coram's efforts was Charlotte, the Duchess of Somerset, whose husband, Charles Seymour, the

6th Duke of Somerset, was one of the richest men in England. Her rank allowed her to support the cause without running the risk of censure, paving the way for the others that soon joined her—daughters and wives of barons, marquesses, earls, and dukes. Twenty-one of them would sign the "Ladies Petition" calling for the establishment of an institution to care for deserted children. The document was presented to King George II in 1735, and although the plea did not immediately persuade the king, it was thought to be the key to Coram's ultimate success, as it provided respectability to an otherwise taboo subject. The ladies also had the ear of the king's bride; many of them served as ladies of the bedchamber to Queen Caroline.

Even so, the pleas of women would not be enough to persuade the king. Coram would need to recruit men to his cause— powerful men who owned property, controlled the nation's assets, held seats in Parliament, and they would not be easily won over. Their influence and prosperity were dependent on primogeniture, the system whereby the eldest male heir inherits his father's estate. An illegitimate child could alter the future, change fortunes, transfer wealth and power. A system that allowed such a child to be cared for, and perhaps one day to challenge the established lines of succession, was not in their best interest. Leaving that child to die on the streets of London was, for these men, the price of assuring the social order's smooth functioning.

Their intransigence would stall Coram's scheme for seventeen years. But Coram was playing a long game. And when a game-changing opportunity finally arose, he seized it.

When Coram first took on the cause of London's abandoned children, the city was mired in financial uncertainty brought on by the failure of a venerable financial institution. After promising vast riches, the celebrated South Sea Company had collapsed, ruining its stockholders and sending economic shock waves throughout Great Britain. The time was not ripe for charity. But in the ensuing years the economy recovered, and a growing confidence in the future allowed the elite to live a little more lavishly. Construction boomed, requiring stonemasons, brickmakers, carpenters, and roofers.

This rise in prosperity was set against the backdrop of Britain's desire to build its empire by expanding its influence on the European continent and abroad. Conflict was brewing in North America, and England was already engaged in a series of ongoing territorial wars—the Nine Years' War against France, then the wars of the Spanish Succession and the Austrian Succession. With war and economic growth came a serious and pressing need for a resource that had become all too scarce: able-bodied men and women—men to fight, and women to wait on a growing elite in need of servants. Thomas Coram was a clever man, and he saw an opportunity within these developments to advance his cause, boldly cloaking his pet project in a brand-new argument. Caring for foundlings, he now maintained, was no mere charitable act but a public good that could address the government's need by creating "useful members of the commonwealth . . . in order to supply the government plentifully with useful hands on many occasions, and for the better producing good and faithful servants from amongst the poor and miserable cast-off children or foundlings."[12]

The foundlings had been rebranded as servants and soldiers—the essential building blocks for England's burgeoning empire.

Coram's new approach was a success. On July 21, 1739, he submitted three petitions to King George II: one with his own signature; a second with the signatures of dozens of dukes, earls, and knights, the entire Privy Council, the Speaker of the House of Commons, and the prime minister; and the last with signatures from justices of the peace. Less than a month later, on August 14, 1739, the king granted a royal charter officially opening the Hospital for the Maintenance and Education of Exposed and Deserted Young Children.

On November 20, 1739, Coram proudly presented the charter to the Duke of Bedford, who served as the hospital's first president, thereby opening what became England's first secular charity. Over the next two centuries the Foundling Hospital, as it quickly came to be known, went on to care for thousands of children who likely would have otherwise perished or been consigned to London's rough streets.

Coram's achievement would secure him a place as one of the greatest philanthropists in England's history, but his success came with a price, one that would be paid for generations to come. While he'd saved these children, he had made a devil's bargain, committing them to a hard life of scrubbing floors and changing chamber pots, or being sent to war to defend a nation that viewed foundlings as disposable.

And so a foundling was to begin life disgraced by the illicit union between his mother and father. His parents would be spared the shame of their actions, the child safely tucked away out of society's notice. But there would be little hope for the foundling, no chance of a better life, only the one already laid out before him in which he would serve the needs of England's ruling class.

Two centuries later, a woman with dark brown hair and a pale complexion would abandon her child at the Foundling Hospital to protect the honor of her family. That child would be scorned and belittled for the shame of her birth, her fate as a servant to society's elite forever sealed, it seemed. She would not even be allowed to keep her own name.

Instead, she was known as Dorothy Soames.

6

RUNNING

I had no mental image of my grandmother, the color of her hair, whether she was plump or wiry, how her eyes creased when she smiled—or if she smiled at all. As a child, my mind was a sponge, porous, ready to be filled with even the smallest bit of information about her. A passing comment would have been enough to fill my imagination. But the subject was off-limits. My mother never spoke of her. There were no photos on the mantel or stories around the dinner table. I didn't even know her name.

Combing through the Foundling Hospital files, holding Lena's letters in my hand, I felt a growing sense of our kinship. The files contained no photographs of her, but Lena's spirit, tenacious and determined, had acquired a shape and heft of its own.

Would I have had the strength to do what Lena did? I wasn't sure. She had committed one of society's greatest taboos—bearing a child out of wedlock. But she had also gone against another equally powerful societal norm in abandoning her own flesh and

bone, leaving her daughter in the hands of strangers. Our librar-
ies are filled with books that revere women who make sacrifices
for their children, and revile those who do not. The artwork
on the walls of the world's most venerated museums deifies the
mother as an ethereal, saintly figure, her love able to transform
and redeem. The lesson of history is unequivocal—nothing is
more sacred than the bond between a mother and her child.

Lena had abdicated her role as a mother, yet I felt no judgment toward her. She had been shunned by her family and would
have been unable to access government resources reserved for
mothers whose husbands had died or abandoned them. Had she
kept her child, her only certainty would have been a lifetime of
hardship and scorn.

My own decision to break the sacred bond between mother
and child, to repeatedly ignore and reject my mother in the name
of self-preservation, seemed almost petulant in comparison. While
my family wasn't particularly religious, a biblical verse had been
a constant refrain in my head in the years since I sought distance
from my mother:

HONOUR THY FATHER AND THY MOTHER: THAT THY DAYS MAY BE
LONG UPON THE LAND WHICH THE LORD THY GOD GIVETH THEE.

It wasn't just any Bible verse. It was one of the Ten Com-
mandments, given the same weight as prohibitions against lying,
cheating on your spouse, and murder.

As a daughter, I had only one job—to honor the woman
who'd brought me into this world. She'd kept up her end of the
bargain, after all, performing all of her motherly duties. She bore
me, she disciplined me without ever raising a hand to me, she
clothed me and fed me and tucked me in each night.

In return, I shunned her.

I never cut off all contact, and we were never estranged in the typical sense of the word. But we may as well have been—when I finally left, I'd logged five thousand miles by my first stop.

I was working as a temp for a financial firm in San Francisco shortly after college graduation when I ran into a friend who mentioned his plans to move to Japan. He gave me the name of a company that was hiring Americans to teach English to business professionals and schoolchildren. Less than a month later, I arrived at Tokyo's Narita International Airport.

My new employer set me up in a small apartment in the city of Kasukabe, just north of Tokyo. I was instantly spellbound by Japan's distinctive culture, its sights, smells, and tastes so different from anything I had ever before encountered. A trip to the supermarket was an adventure. I would wander up and down the aisles, examining row after row of canned goods adorned with kanji characters and unfamiliar images. The fruits and vegetables in the produce section were strange and wonderful, and the massive bags of rice weighing fifty pounds or more posed an insurmountable engineering challenge for my bicycle ride home (solved when I learned that the mini-mart sold "small" five-pound bags). I boldly sampled street food that I had never heard of before—*donburi*, *zaru soba*, sesame snacks with tiny whole dried fish in every handful, or *natto*, gooey fermented soybeans that even the Japanese considered an acquired taste. When I wasn't teaching, I spent my days exploring nearby Tokyo. At night I would drift off to sleep to the wails of the *yakisoba* man as he drove through the streets, selling his traditional stir-fried buckwheat noodles to drunken "salarymen."

I ate rice and dried fish for breakfast, learned to read and speak Japanese (at least enough to get by), and after a few weeks could navigate the complicated public transportation system like a native. Home was thousands of miles away, and I gave it little thought. It was the late 1980s, and there was no email to keep me connected to family. The phone in my tiny apartment couldn't receive international calls. My connection to my parents was limited to the occasional letter, and that suited me just fine.

When I returned to the United States a year later, I brought back a valuable lesson. My happiness increased exponentially with the number of miles between me and my mother. I experienced no guilt at my discovery. That would come later. All I knew was that being away just felt . . . *better.*

Then, to make sure the universe got the message, I kept on moving.

My next plane ticket took me to Washington, DC, for a fellowship with the National Wildlife Federation. Each day I wandered the halls of the Capitol Building, dropping off letters for congressional staffers or taking notes at hearings on environmental legislation. My experience working to protect the environment at the centers of power lit a fire in my belly, and I took the next logical step, applying to law school. Though I was accepted at universities in California, I chose Duke in North Carolina, conveniently located across the country from my family. My mother's relentless training paid off through the grueling three-year experience. Hard work came naturally to me. I was selected for law review and, after graduating with honors, landed a prestigious clerkship with a federal judge in Nashville, Tennessee.

With a clerkship under my belt, I was offered a job at one of the South's oldest and most prominent law firms. I turned it down for a low-paying job in Atlanta that would launch my career as an environmental attorney. I drove through small towns in rural Georgia, took water samples from wells and streams near wastewater treatment plants and factories, paddled canoes through blackwater swamps looking for illegal discharges. I immersed myself in my work, basking in the identity it created for me and rising each morning with an invigorating sense of purpose.

My preferred line of work had the benefit of introducing me to a world of like-minded people—a core group of friends who would become my new chosen family. There was Ed, my best friend—a quirky and irreverent gay man who'd escaped his fundamentalist upbringing in rural Tennessee to become a respected attorney in Atlanta; Carolyn, whose friendship with me dated back to college, our conversations filled with fits of laughter over an unlimited supply of private jokes; Julie, a respected civic leader who would drive for hours through the Tennessee mountains to be by my side each time I buried a parent; Angie, whose back deck hosted innumerable sessions of late night "drunken Scrabble" with seemingly endless pitchers of margaritas; and "Porch," the fiercely loyal crew of friends named for our weekly porch parties where we shared food, mirth, and drinks. My family of choice enveloped me with an unconditional love that I freely returned. For the first time, I felt secure enough to let my guard down and be myself.

My adult life seemed idyllic. I had achieved everything I had ever wanted. I was a successful attorney doing meaningful work, my free time spent with a tight-knit group of friends who were loyal and kind.

But then it would come in like a wave, with a force that could knock me off my feet. Other times, I feared it would swallow me up like quicksand, pulling me down into the darkness.

I remember sitting on the back steps of my house, staring down at the stairs, my eyes focused intently on the gray paint whose peeling revealed a dingy layer of cement, trying to hold myself up against the weight of a depression that sat like lead on my shoulders. Shame took a seat on top. I had no right to feel the way that I did, and I mentally ticked off all the good things in my life—particularly the privileged upbringing that would make most people envious. I rarely shared details about my upbringing, unintentionally hiding my upper-crust background behind the cheap haircuts and well-worn clothes that were the hallmarks of a public interest salary and milieu. While I was never dishonest, I would have felt awkward discussing the bevy of private tutors who had filled my childhood days, and I was so successful at hiding my parents' wealth that sometimes my closest friends were taken by surprise. When I was living in Nashville, a law school classmate came to visit and was wandering around my modest one-bedroom apartment. Before long he emerged from the bedroom with an odd look on his face.

"There's a painting of a horse on your wall. It says you're the owner?"

My mother had commissioned the portrait of my horse, Chelsea's Folly, when I was a teenager. I had never liked the painting, but after I left home she shipped it to me, insisting that I hang it on the wall.

"So your parents are rich?"

Nothing in our relationship changed, but I felt like a liar.

Even more than the judgment of others, my own conscience was a constant drumbeat in my head. Keenly aware of the advantages I'd had as a child, I was ashamed of my unhappiness. You should be grateful, I reasoned. Again and again, I presented my brain with a logical argument for the case against depression.

The dynamic only worsened when I visited my parents in Pebble Beach, where they had retired. Within a day or two the arguments would begin. They were usually set off by my mother's criticisms on subjects ranging from my clothes to the length of my hair, my weight, or the condition of my skin. There was hardly an area of my body that wasn't subjected to her scrutiny.

Fights would erupt when she would return from a shopping excursion with unasked-for bags full of clothing for her twenty-five-year-old daughter, every item several sizes too big. The point behind her "generous" gesture was hard to miss. I would tell her that the clothes were too large, that I hadn't asked for them in the first place and didn't need them. "You're bigger than me," she would counter, by way of explaining her innocent mistake. I remember standing half naked in front of her, humiliated, as she forced me to try them on, the items slipping off my body one after the other because they were so wildly oversized. There was no compassion in her eyes as tears streamed down my face. I was ungrateful, she told me, and didn't appreciate her thoughtfulness.

The hardest visits would be at the end of the year, when my mother was on edge. Our holiday fights were always more intense, and my depression would accelerate as the leaves turned from green to bright red and orange. To me, fall meant that soon I would be going home.

And then one Christmas we had a terrible argument, a fight to end all fights. My recollection of the events leading up to the argument has been wiped from my memory bank. But what happened next appears in my mind like a slow-motion playback, as if I'm watching a stranger instead of myself.

Throwing furniture around the house was usually my mother's domain. This time it's not her I see but me, picking up a stool and throwing it across the kitchen with a force that shouldn't have come from my five-foot-tall self. The room became eerily silent, neither of us saying a word. I retreated to my bedroom, and the event was never mentioned again.

That was the last time I went home for Christmas.

The next year I spent the holidays with friends. Making the decision was a relief, and that Christmas was filled with laughter and warmth. The spell was soon broken by a flurry of phone calls from my mother, and then my father, telling me that I was cruel, thoughtless, inconsiderate, selfish. *What kind of daughter won't come home for Christmas?*

Their words were potent, and shame seeped into every crevice of my body. But for the first time in my life, the waves of once-intractable depression began to recede. Each time I put additional distance between myself and my mother, it felt like a chink had been chipped away from a stone monolith that had loomed over me for most of my life. I saw glimmers of light inversely related to the amount of time I spent with my family.

My rules and regulations multiplied as I realized that no amount of physical distance between myself and my mother could ever be enough. She would burst into my workday with a phone call whenever an idea popped into her head, each conversation dragging me back into the depressed state I had fought so hard to keep at bay.

My parents continued to call me cruel, and sometimes I was. "I will only talk to you on Sundays," I told them. "If you call on any other day, I will hang up the phone."

My parents were devastated by each new addendum, but I stuck to my plan, and another chink in the monolith crumbled. I felt empowered by every limit I enforced. I was clinical in my approach, heartless, severing our connection one piece at a time.

Next I tackled my mother's visits, not long after I bought my first house in Atlanta. It was a blue-gray Cape Cod fixer-upper with white trim and a Craftsman door. I was instantly drawn to the small cottage, with its dormer windows and curved walkway shaded by a large oak tree. I rehabilitated a swing that the previous owners had hung on a branch, slathering it with thick white paint to mask the weather-worn wood. I lined the walkway, buckled by a particularly large tree root, with purple and pink impatiens. It was my first real adult home, but it needed work. When my parents announced their intention to visit, I asked them to stay in a hotel. I didn't even have a bed for them, I explained. A few days later a check arrived in the mail, along with a handwritten message from my father:

Go buy a bed. We will be staying with you.

When they arrived, my mother surveyed the house, remarking that it was "quaint" and had some "nice features" for those who might prefer "small houses." She quickly drew a sketch of how I could renovate it, by which she meant make it more grand, a plan that included moving a staircase and knocking down a few walls, a gargantuan and costly task for a house that boasted only about fourteen hundred square feet. My mother dismissed my objection that I couldn't afford the renovations on my salary.

A few days into their visit, I came home from work to find that she had rearranged my furniture and gone through my closet. On the kitchen table she had carefully laid out a pile of clothes she deemed in need of repair, a note affixed with a safety pin to each with instructions in her meticulous handwriting: "iron," "mend the collar," "replace the third button." On my winter coat, she indicated a small tear on the inside of the right front pocket. Somehow that was the final straw.

Now you're going through my pockets?

The fight unfolded in the usual manner.

You ungrateful brat! I was only trying to help!

As the weekend approached, my parents offered to take me shopping for furniture, to buy me something as a housewarming gift. I found an old oak wardrobe, modest but full of character. It had a dark brown finish, with lighter spots where the stain couldn't penetrate the wood's thick knots. The doors were inlaid with simple hand carvings. On one side there was an old-fashioned keyhole with an oil-rubbed bronze key.

"It's too rustic," my mother complained. She had another one in mind. "Elegant and refined," she said. The armoire argument lasted for days, and my father begged me to give in. *Please, it's not worth it! My life will be hell if you don't get it!* So I gave in. The oversized shiny lacquered armoire sat like a behemoth in my small cottage home until shortly after my mother's death, fifteen years later, when I gave it away to a friend.

The armoire remained in my house, but my mother would not. I firmly informed her that she would need to find another place to stay the next time she visited.

There were repercussions, of course. I was subjected to a relentless stream of commentary on my selfishness, my lack of feeling, how I didn't care about family. My father wrote me letters begging me to let them stay with me during the next visit. "Please just keep the peace," he pleaded.

I never gave in, resolute in keeping my mother at bay, but my father's words planted deep seeds of self-doubt. When I confided in friends about my troubled relationship with my mother, I came to expect the familiar refrain: *But she's so charming!* Or from those who had never even met her: *Every mother and daughter fight sometimes. But I know you still love her. After all, she's your mother!*

I would find few allies; only my closest friends understood my struggles. It shouldn't have surprised me. My mother had mastered her public persona, delighting those around her, masking what lurked beneath. She was always gracious, and she carried herself with a captivating air of sophistication, her chin slightly raised when she spoke. Her voice was never too loud. Even her laugh seemed refined. Her clothing was simple—linen suits or wool blazers in muted colors, never anything too bright, her outfit accented with a stylish necklace she had picked up at Neiman Marcus or Gump's.

My parents' home was littered with photos of my sister and me at play, holding wildflowers as we leaned casually up against a tree, photos that told the same misleading story. My mother had painstakingly memorialized a curated version of our lives, hiring professional photographers to take pictures of our happy family. At Christmas she sewed dresses made of green-and-red-plaid taffeta for us to wear, creating elaborate sets on our front porch. One year she hired actual live reindeers. I remember being entranced by the animals I had seen only in fairy-tale picture books, but equally terrified of being impaled by their antlers.

On one occasion prior to our Christmas fight, I attended a lavish party my mother had organized to benefit the Welsh Society, or some other similar cause. The living room had been cleared of its usual furniture, filled instead with round rental tables adorned with white linen tablecloths, silver place settings, and tasteful floral arrangements. I watched as my mother flitted around the room, checking in with guests, my father by her side. I was placed at a table with several older couples I had never met before. When they learned that I was my mother's daughter, the conversation focused on how "lovely" she was, and how "lucky" her daughter must be.

I had heard it all before. Everyone thought my mother was lovely, that our house was lovely, that our life was *lovely*.

Everyone except me.

And so, when I was living in Atlanta in my thirties and opened my mailbox to find a large mustard-yellow envelope addressed in my mother's meticulous handwriting, I already had a sense of what I was going to do.

Inside was a sheath of papers bundled together with a thick rubber band, with a note addressed to me. I skimmed the contents of the note impatiently, somehow knowing already what the enclosed pages contained. Several years had gone by since she last brought up the subject of her past, when I was living in Nashville and she sent me the letter telling me that she had been a foundling. Unlike that brief note, what I held in my hands was a tome fifty pages long, bound in a spiral fastener with a sheer plastic cover.

"I'm also enclosing some material that backs up my story," my mother wrote. "I thought that you, as an attorney, would appreciate that, since it is out of the ordinary."

My mother had written a memoir. The first page was a table of contents, complete with a title: *Coram Girl*. After years of secrecy, of hiding her past from me and my sister, refusing to answer basic questions about her family and upbringing, she wanted me not only to tell about her past but, presumably, to share it with the world.

I could only assume that my father had read the manuscript and helped her prepare it. It was carefully typed, and I had never seen my mother use a computer or a typewriter. My sister had also received a copy, and she called a few weeks later, asking what I thought. She had skimmed through it, she said; it was "interesting." But that was the extent of our conversation.

To my mind it was simply too late. I had no interest in learning about my mother's past, and I rejected this incursion into my carefully calibrated, semi-motherless existence. And with the last line of her note, my mother unintentionally affirmed the decision I had already made: "I'm grateful and proud that despite my bad parenting you managed to become a remarkable person."

I should have welcomed her admission of guilt, since she usually blamed me for our familial strife. It was the only time she had explicitly acknowledged her role in our troubled relationship. Rereading the note decades later, I see it as an apology, a recognition of her failures. But that was not how I saw it then. My mother wasn't apologizing; she wanted absolution. She wanted to share her tale of woe, in the hopes that I would forgive her, maybe even love her.

That was something I simply was not prepared to do.

I wonder now if anything would have been different between us if I hadn't put the pages back in the envelope and stuffed them into a file. Tucked away in the back of a filing cabinet, the manuscript remained unread; five years passed, then ten, then twenty. From time to time I thought about it, but it wasn't until after that second trip to London that I reached back into that file cabinet to extract my mother's secrets from the past.

The manuscript was still in the same envelope, and I slowly opened the flap. I held the manuscript at arm's length at first, as if the words on the pages could reach out and cut me. Slowly my eyes focused on the black print, and I began to read about my mother's life as a foundling.

I was accepted by the Foundling Hospital and my mother handed me over at the institution's London headquarters at 40 Brunswick Square, on March 2, 1932. I was 2 months and one day old. How thankful she must have felt that I was accepted into the renowned and prestigious Foundling Hospital. I think she imagined that I would be exceptionally well cared for. At least now she could go back to Shropshire without the burden of shame the knowledge of an illegitimate child would have brought her. . . . Thus my mother was liberated from her "disgrace" and saved from scandal and scorn, her secret secure—and I am glad of that. For me, the stigma of illegitimacy would remain.

The voice my mother adopted, that of a calm, reliable narrator in possession of a factual story to impart, wasn't one I recognized.

The words in the typewritten pages I'd set aside so long ago might as well have come from a stranger. The disturbed woman who'd scrawled a name I didn't recognize on a crumpled piece of paper, over and over again, was nowhere to be found. Also missing from the pages were the aristocratic airs and closely guarded secrets that were my mother's defining characteristics. In setting down the memories she'd hoped to share with me before she died, my mother gave me the first of many jolts to come.

7

ADMISSION DAY

My mother had no recollection of the day she was left with strangers. She didn't know whether Lena cried or held her two-month-old baby one last time. Instead, her earliest memories were of a woman with an angry face and a stern voice who found fault in her every action.

Within a short period of time Dorothy Soames, as she would now be known, was sent to the country to be raised by a foster mother paid from the hospital's coffers. At the age of five, she would be returned to the custody of the Foundling Hospital, to a facility in Berkhamsted on the periphery of London—a place my mother referred to as "a Dickensian institution, without the squalor."

Sending young children out to foster families was a practice that had been adopted nearly two centuries before. Like many outmoded customs at the Foundling Hospital, it was initially born of necessity.

Contrary to its founder's aims, the hospital's earliest iteration had failed to stem the tide of infant deaths; in fact, it was common for more than half of those admitted to perish, and mortality rates sometimes exceeded 80 percent. While admission to the Foundling Hospital yielded better odds than the workhouses where infant deaths were almost certain, to increase the chances of survival, the hospital implemented a work-around—babies would be sent to the countryside to be wet-nursed. Only at the age of five would they return to London, once they were safely past the toddler stage and sturdy enough to survive institutional life. While the new approach yielded dismal statistics by modern standards, in the context of the times, the approach was a success—by some estimates, only 39 percent of the foundlings raised in the country died.

Medical advances over the next two centuries would improve prenatal care and reduce infant mortality rates all over Europe, but sending young children to live in the country—only to cruelly remove them later—remained part of the Foundling Hospital's protocol, a tradition ingrained in its fabric. Even if improved health outcomes were no longer the point, for many foundlings these first few years with a foster family yielded some psychological benefits. They would begin their lives in bucolic country settings, nurtured by women who raised them as their sons and daughters, allowing them to play in the fields alongside their own children, as brothers and sisters. For these lucky foundlings, memories of their time in the country were filled with happiness, acceptance, and love.

That wasn't my mother's experience.

I'm not sure that any of the many foster mothers on the Foundling Hospital payroll took in the children for love over money, but I know of many Foundling girls who had loving, nurturing foster homes. I was not so fortunate.

The Foundling Hospital's files didn't contain any clues as to why Louise and Thomas Vanns decided to take in my mother and two other foundlings, both boys. But the family was poor, and money was hard to come by. The Vanns, their son, and the three foundlings lived in a plain, mock-Tudor council house—the British version of public housing—in Hadlow, a small town south of London. Thomas worked as a laborer at a local brewery and later as an estate gardener; Louise, as a seasonal crop picker.

My mother's account of Louise Vanns is remarkably sharp. Louise's black hair was cut just below the chin and pulled back with a pin to one side. When she wasn't working in the fields, she wore flowered dresses, sometimes with a pinafore. The floral print and bright colors might have looked cheerful on some women, but on Louise the bright clothing only provided contrast to a weary face wrinkled by age and hard work.

Louise had no kind words for Dorothy. Maybe the hours spent toiling in the fields, raising children, and tending to her husband left her with little energy for love. Thomas Vanns, Dorothy's foster father, typically had no words at all for his young charge. He was slight of build and quiet, and often wore a traditional flat cap. He spent most of his time at a pub or going to football games. At home he retired to a small front parlor, where he read the newspaper or listened to the radio behind a closed door. The chapter on my mother's years in foster care is short, and only once does she remember Mr. Vanns showing her any attention:

> I have one special memory of my foster father when he was
> attentive to me. I had made a miniature rag floor mat, having
> sewn a few strips of fabric onto another piece of fabric about
> a foot square. I must have tried to copy a rag rug already in
> the house. When he came home from work, I asked him to

go back out the door and come back in again and step on my mat, which he did with a big smile and exclamation of approval, stepping on it with one foot, which was all it had room for.

Dorothy had never forgotten that small moment, and the pages that followed told me everything I needed to know about why. It was no wonder the nonevent had been seared into her memory—it was the only act of kindness she would receive until almost a decade later, when the world was at war.

Though those early years were bereft of love or tenderness, my mother did manage to find some happiness. During crop-picking season, when Louise Vanns worked in the cherry orchards and hop fields, she would bring her foster children along. Dorothy would play with the other children in piles of vines that had been stripped of their hops. Or they would peek into the pungent and dark interior of the oast house—the kiln where hops were dried for brewing—frightening one another with stories of what lurked within. Other times, the children went "scrumping" for apples, mischievously climbing trees and pinching a few before scampering off to a nearby hiding place to eat their loot. One of those children was Isabel Hockley, another foundling who lived a few doors down from the Vanns on Carpenter Lane, and who would be Dorothy's closest friend during their years at the Foundling Hospital.

But the bitter transition that awaited them could not be postponed forever. At age five, nurtured or neglected, loved or unloved, every foundling boy or girl would be removed from the care of his or her foster mother and placed under the charge of the joyless administrators of the Foundling Hospital. As with all the rules of the institution, there were to be no exceptions, even when the child had a chance for love.

It should have surprised no one that the women hired to raise infants, suckle them, nurture them, and watch over them for five years might grow attached to their charges. But during most of the Foundling Hospital's history, a woman who wanted to raise a foundling as her own would face considerable legal obstacles. Britain didn't recognize adoption until 1926, a legislative change attributed to pressure from child rescue organizations following World War I. Adoption was allowed under ancient Roman law but had all but disappeared in western European systems until the early twentieth century, partly due to the fear that the "bad blood" of an illegitimate child could spoil a family's pedigree. The Catholic Church opposed adoption, not just for illegitimate children but for orphans as well. One historian offered a particularly nefarious reason for the church's stance—adoption would have allowed childless couples to designate an heir, removing the opportunity for the church to collect their inheritances upon their deaths.

In the absence of a recognized legal structure, creative arrangements labeled "apprenticeships" or "wardships" were not uncommon, but they failed to bestow the rights typically granted to parents. Practical work-arounds would offer little hope to a foster parent who had grown attached to a charge of the Foundling Hospital, in any case; the governors refused on principle to accept offers to care for a foundling. As a matter of policy, children were to be removed from the care of their foster family no matter the circumstance. The burden on the family would be too great, the governors claimed.

More likely this stance was motivated by a belief that foundlings needed to be brought up separately from children born of respectable parents, not raised as their equals. The belief that the illegitimate child occupied the lowest echelon of society was so ironclad that it too was written into the hospital rules:

foundlings should be often reminded "of the Lowness of their Condition, that they may early imbibe the Principles of Humility and Gratitude to their Benefactors."[13]

It became apparent to me that the governors viewed foundlings as chattel, a commodity to be managed and raised for the benefit of society. It would have been contrary to the true intent of the Foundling Hospital—the aim of providing able-bodied hands for domestic service or war—to allow a foster family to keep a child for themselves. Indeed, these children were quite valuable! The governors were authorized by law to receive funds for the apprenticing of the children: boys were shipped off to captains, bookbinders, or farmers, while girls were sent into household service. Jonas Hanway, a founding governor and a persuasive advocate for the hospital, even quantified their value, meticulously calculating the gain a foundling provided to society—a whopping £176 per child (equating to tens of thousands of US dollars by today's standards). Even if these young foundlings had a chance to be raised in an atmosphere of love and tenderness, the governors would not allow such valuable assets to be given up easily.

When the day finally arrived for the governors to take possession of the charges they purportedly valued so highly, little thought was given to how a five-year-old child should be introduced to institutional life. By all accounts, the day of separation from foster families was horrific. The entry into the institution was conducted with total disregard for the sensibilities of the little children parting from what were in some instances loving foster families, leaving behind the joy and contentment of the only homes they had ever known. It must have been heartbreaking for these children to be given up not once but twice before the age of six.

Accounts show that the impact of that tragic day would remain seared in the memories of foundlings throughout their lifetimes. In the late 1990s, researchers at the University of London's Thomas Coram Research Unit interviewed twenty-five children who had been raised in the Foundling Hospital between 1900 and 1955; in 2011, the Foundling Museum launched an oral history project, both efforts focused on memorializing the experience of being raised as a foundling. Echoing my mother's narrative of the day, these experiences were uniformly traumatic. Young children would journey with their foster mothers to the Foundling Hospital, dressed in their Sunday best. Many were not told where they were going or what would happen to them when they arrived. Some were unaware that the woman who had raised them was not actually their mother.

Where are we going?
Will I be coming home for supper?
Will I see you again?

Their questions would go unanswered. Perhaps it was too painful for the foster mothers, or maybe the matrons who ran the institution looked down upon providing more information than was necessary. Whatever the reason, the parting of a foster mother and her charge seldom amounted to more than a pat on the head and a reminder to be a "good girl" or a "good boy."

Then, with the swish of a skirt, she would be gone.

Admission day for Dorothy started a bit differently. She was anxious and afraid, but unlike the other children, she knew what was going to happen to her. It had been a common occurrence for Louise Vanns to issue words of warning: "You just wait till you get to the Foundling Hospital, my girl!" The smallest infraction would invoke the refrain.

Dorothy lived in constant fear of the Foundling Hospital.

She didn't know where or what it was, only that it was a terrifying place.

On May 27, 1937, the day that her foster mother had warned her about finally came. They set off alone, just the two of them, walking into town before boarding a bus from Hadlow to the small village of Berkhamsted, a trip that took more than two hours, longer than Dorothy had ever remembered traveling. The final leg of the trip was by taxi. After driving through Berkhamsted, they started up a steep and narrow lane. The houses thinned and soon gave way to a large field dotted with cedar and beech trees. At the end of the field, the taxi made a sharp left turn and stopped in front of a gate. Identical small brick cottages stood on each side of the driveway, and a man emerged from one to open the gate, allowing the taxi to pass.

Just beyond the gate was a road that cut through an open field, and Dorothy got a better look at the buildings she had seen from outside the fence. The compound, enclosed by iron railings topped with ornamental spikes, contained regimented rows of two-story brick buildings with evenly spaced white-trimmed windows. The buildings were connected by covered archways held up by smooth concrete columns. At the center of the compound stood an imposing chapel with four tall columns, larger versions of the ones that adorned the walkways, and a steeple that loomed over the road, casting a wide shadow below. As the taxi slowed to make its way around the chapel, Dorothy's anxiety overwhelmed her, and she vomited on the floor of the car.

Passing between the two massive pillars that framed the institution's heavy oak doors did little to calm Dorothy's fears. None too pleased with the mess that the little girl had made, Louise Vanns showed little emotion as she pushed her charge into a wood-paneled auditorium with arched ceilings. After a cursory goodbye, Louise left, and a woman in a blue dress and white apron told Dorothy to wait with a handful of children who were seated on chairs along a wall. Earlier in the day a coach had crisscrossed the countryside, picking up foundlings who had reached the age of five, unceremoniously depositing them at the Foundling Hospital steps. Dorothy never learned why she'd traveled separately from the other children she joined, sitting shoulder to shoulder, legs dangling over the polished parquet floor. Some passed the time by gazing around the room, mouths agape as they surveyed the expansive arched ceiling; others sat with heads lowered, quietly weeping, terrified by the unfamiliar surroundings.

Eventually a portly woman with short brown hair and a round puffy face shuffled toward the children. She called out a list of last names.

From that day forward, no adult would use the first name of a foundling. The children would only be referred to impersonally, as Jones, Smith, or, in Dorothy's case, Soames.

"If I call your name, stand up and come with me!" the heavyset woman bellowed. She steered them through the door and corralled them into a small group.

"I am Nurse Rance. I'm in charge of you now, and what I say goes," she snarled. "You're mine now. Do you understand? Mine!"

She led them up a flight of stairs and down long corridors that must have seemed endless to the exhausted children. Next they were herded into a washroom, their clothes stripped from their bodies by another unsmiling woman, ordered into tubs two to three at a time, and scrubbed from head to toe. After a thorough washing, they stood naked and wet, some whimpering, others inconsolably sobbing, crying for the women they knew as their mothers. Nurse Rance, oblivious to their plight, took a pair of scissors and, one by one, grabbed each girl and roughly chopped off her hair down to the roots. By the time she was done, nothing but jagged clumps of hair would remain.

As I stumbled through my mother's words, I couldn't help but summon horrible images of shorn prisoners shuffled into steel-barred penitentiaries where they would languish for a lifetime, my jaw locked against descriptions of institutional protocol that would be considered wildly abusive today. There were no hardened criminals at the Foundling Hospital, only innocent children.

At first I could only read a few pages at a time. Eventually I became consumed, studying the pages over and over, my clients' projects sitting untouched in my in-box. I was struck by my mother's insights into what had happened to her all those years ago.

> Our hair and our foster mothers were not our only losses once the iron gates clanged shut behind us. We lost our individuality, our identity, our freedom, our voice and virtually all contact with the outside world.

Suddenly a memory surfaced, this one from my own life. I was young, not much older than my mother had been when she entered the Foundling Hospital. It was the day of a school dance, and I was nervous, anxious that no boy would notice me. I grasped a pair of scissors and looked into the mirror, thinking of a TV star with the beautiful feathered hair that was all the rage in the 1970s. I began to cut.

Snip.

Snip.

Snip.

The results were hideous, disastrous. I began to cry as I looked into the mirror, taking in the sloppy and uneven clumps of hair.

As the volume of my wails increased, my mother rushed in. It didn't take long for her to see what I had done, and only a matter of moments before she was on the phone with a local hairdresser.

It's an emergency!

She was insistent; they must help her daughter. She wouldn't take no for an answer. She scooped me up as I continued to sob, distraught at what I had done, and whisked me off to the hairdresser, saving me from the certain judgment of my peers.

I have few memories of my mother soothing me, easing a pain or hurt. That day, she was my hero.

All those years ago, there had been no one to comfort Dorothy. Freshly shorn, she was handed a set of clothes, russet brown, a color chosen centuries before, a symbol of her lowly status, a daily reminder of her poverty and shame. She was to wear that uniform, in successive sizes, almost every day for years.

The next stop was the infirmary, where the children would sleep until assigned to a dormitory.

"Now get in your beds, and I don't want to hear a peep out of any of you," Nurse Rance barked. "If you need to go to the lavatory, I will bring you a chamber pot. No one is to get up for any reason, or you'll have me to reckon with."

Dorothy and the other girls dutifully climbed into their beds. As the lights went out overhead and the room darkened, Dorothy could feel her anxiety growing. There was no one to turn to for consolation; the room was suspended in a tense silence, the children too numbed by grief and fear to cry out, not comprehending what had happened to them. But for Dorothy, the anxiety became too intense.

Sometime in the night, lying awake in the darkness of the strange new place, I called for a chamber pot, not because of a need but, I believe, seeking reassurance, a test to see if I would be taken care of.

Nurse Rance lumbered through the shadows toward Dorothy and tossed a chamber pot down next to her bed. Dorothy's bare feet made no sound as they touched the floor and she straddled the porcelain receptacle. She squatted there in the semi-darkness, the steely eyes of Nurse Rance glaring down at her, but her body refused to cooperate. She tried again. It was no use. The chamber pot remained empty.

That was when Dorothy received the answer to the question she had been posing—whether she would be taken care of, what her life would be like at the Foundling Hospital.

Nurse Rance thrust her fist into Dorothy's small abdomen. "Don't you ever do that again!" she roared.

Dorothy's eyes were wide open with fear. Breathless, clutching her stomach to ease the pain, she watched the back of Nurse Rance's stubby legs recede from view.

The memory of that day haunted my mother, but not because it was the worst day of her childhood. Instead, it was a warning of what was to come. As she would reflect years later, "no time had been lost initiating me into the Foundling Hospital system."

8

HOPE

*B*_{ird}.

It took just one missing four-letter word for me to know that my mother had Alzheimer's.

We were having lunch in the main dining room at the Beach and Tennis Club in Pebble Beach. Members paid thousands of dollars for the privilege of dining on garlic-roasted artichokes and freshly harvested Dungeness crab legs while gazing out the panoramic twenty-foot windows that overlooked Carmel Bay and the seventeenth hole of Pebble Beach's famous golf course.

My parents and I had come to a certain unspoken truce. I agreed to come home once a year, and they agreed to complain a bit less about my indifference. As usual, conversation between the three of us was a struggle, so we passed the time studying the menu or looking out into the bay, searching for a seal or an otter that might be frolicking among the kelp forests that grew just off the jagged shoreline.

As the waiter took our order, my mother began pointing out

the tall windows as if to alert us to something interesting that we needed to see.

"Look over there, see, it's a . . . it's a . . ."

"What is it?" my father asked.

"See right there, it is that thing, over the water."

"Mom, there are a lot of things to look at out there. What are you pointing at?" I asked.

The waiter looked at her and then at us, unsure of how to proceed. She continued to point, her brow furrowed as her frustration increased.

"What is it, Mom, a seal?" She shook her head. "An otter?" I watched her as she continued to struggle, as if the word she was looking for was just on the tip of her tongue.

"Is it a bird?"

I could see a vague look of recognition cross her face. "Yes, yes, that's it. It was what you said. It was flying."

"A bird?" I repeated.

"Yes." She hesitated. "That."

The word *bird* was no longer part of my mother's vocabulary. Other words soon followed.

Lettuce.

Plate.

Telephone.

Next were numbers, and then concepts. Soon after the bird incident, we were in a small café grabbing a snack to tide us over as we were waiting for my father. I looked into my wallet to see if I had enough cash, and my mother looked at the bills in my hand quizzically. She pointed.

"What is that for? It's that thing, what is it, that you use for . . . ," my mother stammered.

"Are you asking how much money I have?" I responded. It hadn't occurred to me that her question was more basic.

"No, that, what is it? I think that, well it must be, I have seen it before, I think . . ." She continued to talk about what was in my hands in garbled sentences.

"Money? Is that your question? Is this money?" I held up my hand. She stared at the crumpled green bills without a hint of recognition. "This is money, Mom. *Money*. We use it to buy things." Her face remained blank, expressionless.

As I watched her words and numbers slip away, I knew that it was my last chance to ask her about Dorothy Soames. But it was only a matter of time before she was placed in an Alzheimer's care facility. By that point, even if I had wanted to know more, it was too late.

I did want to know more, it turned out. It was during one of my visits to that health-care facility that my curiosity about my mother's past was initially piqued. My father and I were waiting outside my mother's room when he casually mentioned that she had never graduated from high school.

I was stunned. "What do you mean?" I peppered him with questions. *What about the Royal Academy of Music in London, where she learned to play the piano? Why didn't you tell me before?*

His mumbled answers only led to more questions. I wondered if it was just an issue of semantics. "Do you mean it was called something different in England?" My father just shrugged, then tilted his head and gave me a small, wry smile, as if he'd shared the punch line of a joke I should have been in on. He didn't elaborate, and I didn't push, perhaps silenced by years of conditioning that the past was off-limits. And then he too was gone.

But after I started digging into the details of my mother's life at the Foundling Hospital, I finally understood. It all seemed so obvious, in hindsight. Of course foundlings didn't go to the Royal Academy of Music in London; they didn't get accepted to Oxford or Cambridge; they didn't attend college, or even high school. My mind raced to my own childhood, the endless stream of lessons and tutors, the anxiety I still felt over the smallest of failures. Suddenly the script had flipped. My mother hadn't raised me in the image of her childhood, but in a warped, dystopian version of what she imagined a proper British upbringing to be. The reality of her own educational experience had been molded by a tribunal of paternalistic decision-makers two centuries before.

The governors believed from the outset that raising a child beyond his or her station would be cruel, leading to an over-educated adult too discontented or proud to perform servile tasks or accept the low wages befitting his rank. In 1757, they said as much in the lengthily titled *Regulations for Managing the Hospital for the Maintenance and Education of Exposed and Deserted Young Children: By Order of the Governors of the Said Hospital.* The foundlings, the regulations specified, were to:

> learn to undergo, with Contentment, the most servile and laborious Offices; for notwithstanding the Innocence of the Children, yet as they are exposed and abandoned by their Parents, they ought to submit to the lowest Stations, and should not be educated in such a manner as may put them upon a Level with the Children of Parents who have Humanity and Virtue to preserve them, and the Industry to Support them.[14]

The fear underlying the purple prose was that educating children conceived in sin would risk undermining the very structure of British society. If they were taught to write and use arithmetic, the foundlings could become bookkeepers and accountants, even clerks. They might one day consider themselves equal to legitimate children. The hierarchy needed to be preserved; it would be unjust to allow a foundling to rise above the children of righteous parents. A local satirical paper captured the sentiment in the 1750s with a few lines of verse:

The Hospital Foundling came out of thy Brains
To encourage the Progress of vulgar Amours,
The breeding of Rogues and th' increasing of Whores,
While the Children of honest good Husbands and Wives
Stand expos'd to Oppression and Want all their lives.[15]

The breeding of Rogues and th' increasing of Whores. The phrase, while satirical in nature, was starkly illustrative of the savage public opinion of illegitimate birth. While the hospital had been sanctioned by a king, its governors had to remain vigilant, careful and deliberate in their choices, ever aware that the obstacles that had almost prevented the opening of the Foundling Hospital could threaten its continued existence.

They stayed true to their stated objective—to raise children for necessary but lowly service—and that goal was reflected in their regulations. For boys, that meant "making Nets, spinning of Packthread, Twine, and small Cordage" so that they could be sent to "Sea or Husbandry."[16] The girls were also productive, engaging in "common Needlework, Knitting and Spinning; and in the Kitchen, Laundry, and Household-work, in order to make them useful Servants to such proper Persons as may apply for them."[17] No time was wasted, and the foundlings were pushed to be as productive as possible. I came across research that calculated exactly *how* productive foundling girls had been, based on the number of items produced in a given year. It seemed an odd endeavor to me, this study undertaken by a PhD student from the University of Hertfordshire in 2015 as part of her dissertation, but the results were revealing. For example, just twenty-five foundling girls produced more than 6,400 garments and household linens in a single year, ranging from towels and table-cloths to bibs, aprons, and night caps.

The governors did allow one exception to their unremittingly practical curriculum: the instruction of reading and writing when required, enough to prepare the foundlings to be good Christians, able to read and quote the Bible. At some point instruction was added to the curriculum allowing for reading and writing beyond the Bible—perhaps because these skills would make the foundlings more useful to their masters. As I read up on the hospital's history, I saw no reason to intuit any shift in the governors' worldview in these developments—their focus remained that of preparing the children for a life of service, an endgame that hadn't changed in the almost two hundred years between the institution's founding and my mother's tenure there.

So my mother learned to sew with exacting precision, first practicing her stitches on raw mushrooms, then making clothes for foster children and mending foundlings' uniforms so they could be worn over and over again. Her fingers would ache as she practiced straight, neat stitches, and soon became callused from so much time spent darning socks and hemming clothes. Another task was scrubbing and shining the hospital's long hallways, which the girls would make a game of, one girl wrapping herself up in a blanket while the others pulled her around until the floors shone brightly enough that they could avoid punishment.

My mother was given no homework or exams, and never received a school certificate or diploma. Critical thinking and independent thought were discouraged, and even practical skills—how to buy a bus ticket or make change—were neglected. Many children would leave the Foundling Hospital having never touched money at all.

There was one exception. Foundlings were taught to carefully pen their ABC's, a cane waiting for those who were not up for the task. Hours were spent training the young children to write with precision. It was widely reported by former foundlings, this emphasis on handwriting; but in all my research, I never discovered why it was so prized. Perhaps, I surmised, a lady's maid might be required to write a letter on behalf of her mistress, or create name cards that would be placed on dinner tables at society parties.

My mother's handwriting brought her praise in her adult life, strangers often commenting on it when she signed her name or filled out forms. Our home was filled with placards, always in her precise, masterful calligraphy, with instructions on how to adjust the thermostat, fill the birdfeeder, or find the spare key. And each year the inside of our family's annual Christmas card contained a season's greeting penned in her own hand. Somewhere along the way she'd learned to draw, too. One year the card was imprinted with an intricate pear tree complete with a partridge, done in black ink and created with one continuous stroke of her pen.

My mother's talents seemed endless to me. She could play the piano, and wield a paintbrush as skillfully as she could a calligraphy pen. She accompanied me effortlessly as I played concertos by Vivaldi or Handel. A still life she'd painted hung in our dining room, just a simple bowl of fruit, but I would always marvel at how she'd captured the smooth texture of an apple, the way the light reflected off its speckled reddish skin.

As I sifted through the stacks of books and records in my office, I wondered, more than once, how a foundling raised to scrub floors and darn socks learned to play the piano, and to create art that fit in seamlessly with the expensive tapestries and paintings that hung on our walls. I would find only some of the answers as I plunged into the Foundling Hospital's history.

FOR TWO CENTURIES, thousands of children like Dorothy Soames were raised to mend socks and clean chamber pots, to work in factories or be sent to sea. Music, art, and literature were luxuries reserved for the wealthy. But oddly, not long after opening its doors, the Foundling Hospital would become an epicenter for England's greatest painters, writers, and composers.

While the hospital was founded with the blessing of a king and a royal charter, it had been met with an insatiable demand from the very day of its opening, and funds were needed, desperately. Enter artist William Hogarth, who had become a member of the hospital's board of governors in the years after he painted *A Rake's Progress*. In 1746 he devised a plan to ease the hospital's financial problems and advance a pet project of his own: proving to the world that England's artists could compete on the world stage. At the time there was no academy in which artists could display their craft, and the halls of the Foundling Hospital seemed an ideal location. Members of the public would come inside, stroll through the halls, view the paintings and sculptures, and perhaps be more likely to offer financial support to the hospital, and artists would get a venue to show off their skills.

Soon the walls of the institution were adorned with dozens of works created by London's most sought-after painters: Sir Joshua Reynolds, Thomas Gainsborough, Allan Ramsay, Richard Wilson, and Francis Hayman. John Michael Rysbrack, hailed as one of the most important sculptors of the time, donated a marble relief depicting the allegorical figure of Charity carrying a child. In an unexpected turn of events, the Foundling Hospital became the first public art gallery in England, and London's elite flocked to view the work.

In the wake of this success, a committee of artists was established. Meeting at the Foundling Hospital each year on Guy Fawkes Day, they dined on fine foods while laying the groundwork for larger exhibitions. Their ambitions would eventually culminate in the creation of the Royal Academy of Arts in London, where the work of nearly every significant artist in Britain would be displayed throughout the 1800s. The school and museum still stand today on Piccadilly.

The foundlings saw little of the majestic art hanging in the governors' halls. A few paintings were placed in the children's dining area, likely for the benefit of the benefactors who occasionally came by for visits. Mostly the children were confined to colorless dormitories and classrooms with simple furnishings and plain walls. Nor, at least during the early years, were they invited to share in the musical performances that followed the display of paintings and drawings at the Foundling Hospital.

In 1749 the German-born composer George Frideric Handel joined the ranks of the leading artists associated with the cause, premiering his *Foundling Hospital Anthem* in the hospital's chapel, at an event attended by the Prince and Princess of Wales. To conclude the *Anthem*, the composer borrowed from his own work, pilfering a chorus from another majestic oratorio—Handel's *Messiah*.

Handel had performed *Messiah* several times, in Dublin in 1742 and on five occasions in London between 1743 and 1745, but the piece had failed to achieve widespread acclaim. On May 1, 1750, he offered another performance of the oratorio to benefit the Foundling Hospital. This time, it was such a success that a second concert was arranged a fortnight later. After that, attending performances became an annual tradition for London's upper class, raising significant funds for the hospital while securing the financial and historical success of the oratorio. Indeed, without the Foundling Hospital, Handel's *Messiah* may have been relegated to obscurity instead of becoming acknowledged as the enduring Baroque masterpiece it is today.

Over time, the hospital's governors grew eager to stake a claim to the success of *Messiah*, eventually submitting a petition asking Parliament to vest the property rights of the oratorio to the institution upon Handel's death. Though the composer declined to approve the scheme, he continued to attend rehearsals and performances of *Messiah* in honor of the hospital even after becoming virtually blind.

Handel's most famous work may have been the last piece of music he heard. In April of 1759, he collapsed during a rehearsal of the piece for a benefit concert that was to be held at the Foundling Hospital, and died a week later. The Foundling Hospital held a memorial concert for him (with an admission fee of half a guinea), anticipating such a large attendance that gentlemen were asked to come without swords and ladies without hoops under their skirts.

While Handel had refused to relinquish the rights to *Messiah* during his lifetime, he did honor the Foundling Hospital's role in popularizing the oratorio by gifting a pipe organ to accompany the children as they sang in the chapel. His legacy at the institution was tended to by a blind organist named John Stanley who continued to conduct annual performances of *Messiah*. Despite the widely held view that poor children should not be taught to sing or play instruments, Stanley urged the governors to provide musical instruction to the foundlings, and he succeeded. Going forward, the foundlings would be trained to sing and would perform in the chapel on Sundays. As London clamored to hear their sweet voices, the governors realized that the performances might "be of great use to this Charity by adding to the Fund for the support thereof."[18]

While further cementing its reputation as a cultural center for the enjoyment of society's elite, the Foundling Hospital would allow the children to experience the joy of music and song. Yet reminders of the hospital's true purpose were never far away. The hymns chosen for the foundlings to sing were focused on their plight, with lyrics that hammered home the disgrace of illegitimacy:

> Wash off my foul offence,
>   And cleanse me from my Sin;
> For I Confess my crime, and see
>   How great my Guilt has been.
> In Guilt each part was form'd
>   Of all this sinful frame;
> In Guilt I was conceiv'd and born
>   The Heir of Sin and Shame.[19]

Londoners cared little about the children's shame as they gathered to hear the young voices, filling the pews and coffers of the Foundling Hospital. But what must the children have thought, practicing and performing hymns that might have provided a respite from their harsh existence but were accompanied by stern reminders of their disgrace?

Like the children in that early choir, Dorothy Soames too had been taught to sing at the Foundling Hospital. Perhaps those memories made it too painful for my mother to raise her voice in song as an adult. Despite her musical inclinations, I can't conjure even one memory of my mother actually singing—no lullabies drifting me off to sleep, no sing-alongs to the radio in the car. But I do remember Handel's *Messiah* ringing out on our living room record player. Each Christmas its chorus would echo through the hallways of our home. Was my mother thinking of the Foundling Hospital when the glorious harmony of its *hallelujah*s wafted into the kitchen, mingling with the aroma of roasted turkey and her freshly baked bread? After dinner she would sit quietly on the living room couch, her hands folded, eyes closed, unfazed by the occasional skipping of the needle on the well-worn vinyl.

Maybe one day I'll find out how my mother learned to play the piano, an act that seems now like a rebellion against the men who stood in judgment of her beginnings, believing her to be unworthy of music and of art.

I did manage to find out, however, why she loved to read.

Our house was filled with books, stacks everywhere, with a dedicated library that my mother stocked with a full set of the *Encyclopaedia Britannica*, dictionaries, novels, and children's books. On the weekends my father sat at the round table in the middle of our library, reading briefs or preparing for his next trial. I would lie on the hardwood floor nearby, thumbing through an atlas or reading a book that I had taken from the shelf. Once I had read them all, we took weekly trips to the local library. The librarians knew me by name, greeting me with smiles as I asked for recommendations. I would stack the books on my bedside table, and at night, when it was time to turn out the lights, my mother would whisper to me as she tucked me in that I could stay up *all night* reading if I wanted to. I often did.

When I was young, before the bitter arguments, the slammed doors, and raised voices, she would read to me herself. These were some of the few times I can remember my mother touching me. I would climb under the covers of her bed and snuggle close to her warm body as she held a book in front of us. She always chose a classic—my favorite was *Little Women*, but we also read Dickens. As she read aloud from *David Copperfield*, she betrayed no hint of her connection with its author. I'm not sure she knew of it herself. It's unlikely that she read Dickens as a child, but I know that she had encountered his name every day, when she and the other children filed into the dining hall and took their place at long tables according to assigned teams, each with a corresponding color: Hogarth (green), Dickens (yellow), Coram (red), and Dorothy's team, Handel (blue).

She must have wondered who these men were, why each held such a revered status in the Foundling Hospital's history. Perhaps she never knew that her life, and more aptly, the lives of the foundlings who'd come before her, had inspired the author to pen some of the stories that would bring him his greatest and most enduring fame.

In the 1840s Charles Dickens lived just around the corner from the Foundling Hospital, and he took an interest in the institution soon after his arrival in the neighborhood, renting a pew at the hospital's chapel so he could hear the foundlings sing, or wandering the grounds and watching the children go about their daily chores. Dickens was evidently inspired by what he saw there, making unmarried mothers and children raised without parents frequent themes in his works, most notably in *Oliver Twist*. Other works featured the Foundling Hospital more prominently. *Little Dorrit* includes a character who grows up there and is named Tattycoram in homage to the hospital's founder, Thomas Coram; in *No Thoroughfare*, two foundlings are given the same name, with disastrous consequences.

I added a copy of *Oliver Twist* to the pile of books on my desk. I was familiar with the story as a child, but at the time, I hadn't known of the author's connection with my mother's past. Like "Dorothy Soames," the main character's name hadn't been

carefully chosen by loving parents, but was instead foisted upon
the child by an uncaring stranger; in this case, Mr. Bumble, a
fat, choleric man who was head of the institution where poor
Oliver Twist found himself. Mr. Bumble notably boasts that his
foundlings were named in alphabetical order:

> The last was an S,—Swubble, I named him. This was a T,—
> Twist, I named *him*. The next one comes will be Unwin,
> and the next Vilkins. I have got names ready made to the end
> of the alphabet, and all the way through it again, when we
> come to Z.[20]

Was that how my mother had been named—the letters a
stroke of fate based on the order in which she had been received?

My own name had been chosen carefully, or so I had been
told.

"You were named after the emperor Justinian," my mother
had explained. "Your name stands for justice and law." She took
great pride in the fact that I had gone on to become an attorney,
frequently reminding me of the aptness of my name.

"What about my middle name?" I'd asked. "Why did you
choose that?"

My mother hesitated before responding. "It means Is-A-
Belle," she said. "'Belle' is French for pretty, like you." At the
time her words rang hollow, uncomfortably colliding with a lifetime's worth of criticism of my appearance. Decades would pass
before the true reason behind her choice would be revealed.

As I finished reading *Oliver Twist*, I was struck by the hope-
fulness of its ending. Dickens's works are filled with stories of
fallen women in tragic circumstances, and *Oliver Twist* is no exception. Oliver's mother is unmarried, her lover dead. Nancy is
a member of Fagin's gang, and her noble acts of goodness only

underscore the tragedy of her short, vice-filled life. Even the innocent and transcendent Rose, Oliver's aunt, has a mysterious past, a "stain" upon her name which she vows to "carry . . . into no blood but [her] own."[21] But Dickens provided a happy conclusion for the titular hero, at least, in having Oliver adopted by the kindly Mr. Brownlow.

While Dickens received inspiration for his most famous character from the children raised at the Foundling Hospital, it is unlikely that the hospital's charges were given enough instruction to read the tale of *Oliver Twist*, hearing the author's name only as they ate their meager meals in a setting reminiscent of a scene from the book itself. Reading wasn't a priority for future servants and laborers, and most teachers required only rote recitation of their charges. Even if a child was a motivated reader, there was little opportunity, as books could not be taken from the classroom.

For Dorothy, the gift of reading would come from unexpected sources. One was a short, matronly woman named Miss Douthie, her gray hair plaited and wound into a flat bun on each side of her head. Unlike the other teachers at the Foundling Hospital, she filled her classroom with color and activity, creating a place of learning and imagination. During the holidays, she set up a miniature village complete with Santa Claus arriving in his sleigh. Though she didn't ask Dorothy to stay after class or give her any individual tutoring, Miss Douthie believed it was every child's right to learn. Sometimes she would become frustrated, forming the fingers of her right hand into a claw and thumping them up and down on a child's head, her voice rising and falling with whatever the girl was failing to comprehend, as if to push the knowledge into the little girl's brain. The children knew instinctively that Miss Douthie's methods were not born from anger or judgment. She didn't care that Dorothy and the other girls were destined to change linens, cook meals, and scrub floors. She did something no other teacher did, taking the time to actually teach her students, correcting them, and prodding them to get every word right as they read aloud.

Dorothy had never experienced the sense that an adult cared about her success. And once she learned to read, she was hungry for more. Maybe Miss Douthie would have allowed my mother to take a book from the classroom, but Dorothy didn't dare ask an adult for a favor. Instead she started to steal books from the library, a light-filled space with arched French windows overlooking the playing fields, typically off-limits to the children. Three of the walls were lined with glass cabinets filled with donated books, and when no one was looking, my mother would slip into the library, hide a book in her knickers or under an apron, then sneak it back to the dormitory to tuck it under her mattress. If she'd been discovered, she would have been beaten and branded a thief, but the risk was worthwhile, and she managed to steal moments here and there, reading pages that filled her with wonder and provided a glimpse into a life outside of her sequestered world.

One day she found a book that spoke of a land she had heard of only through whispered asides with other girls and conversations overheard in the hallways. The story started on a river that was grander than any Dorothy could have ever imagined, one that spanned farther than the eye could see and flowed for thousands of miles. It was about a young man who, at the age of nineteen, operated a flatboat for $8 a month, traversing the Mississippi, carting farm goods, corn, salt, pork, and other commodities. Dorothy soaked up the stories of this strange and foreign land and the young man who was born in a one-room log cabin. She followed his progress as he worked as a laborer, taught himself the law, and then rose to become the sixteenth president of the United States, eventually emancipating millions of people held in bondage.

To a young girl whose life had already been laid out before her, who was seemingly in bondage herself, it was difficult to imagine that there could be a place where someone poor and insignificant could become great. Her heart leapt at the thought that there might be hope, that maybe she could escape her fate in a place called America.

9

FEAR

My antidote for pain was anger, and I ingested it often.

While depression weighed me down like a fifty-pound anchor, anger propelled me forward. It gave me the strength to investigate corporate greed and government corruption, the thrill of discovering injustice masking my fear of taking on powerful interests. But my anger served another purpose—it protected me. It was a shield I used to repel my mother's criticism and keep her at arm's length. And so I nurtured it.

I fueled my rage with mental lists of her wrongdoings. I had decades of practice stoking my resentment toward my mother, and the anger became an integral part of my identity, buttressing my narrative that she, not I, was to blame for our family's dysfunction.

Some of her behaviors were colorful, eccentric, such as her habit of licking the cat. "She likes it," my mother protested when I scowled with disgust. "She thinks I'm her mother!" Or her certainty that extraterrestrials communicated through crop circles in fields of wheat. These offenses against the norm were harmless. There were times when she cornered my friends, forcing them to watch her crop-circle videos, or one-offs like flying to England to meet with local "croppies," characters who delighted her with stories of alien encounters she believed even after the true perpetrators (two jovial men in their sixties) revealed how they had created the circles with little more than two wooden boards and a piece of string.

The suicide threats were more disturbing. She left one on my voice mail in the middle of my law school exams.

"I can't live anymore."

This wasn't the elegant and contained voice that she saved for those outside the family, but the frenzied one, wild and unrestrained, at least an octave higher than the one she used in public.

"Why do you do this to me? Why are you so *mean*?!"

On it went, different versions of the same message: *I'm going to just end it all! What have I done so wrong? Why are you so cruel?!*

I was never worried that my mother would follow through on her threats. I had no basis for my belief, only an instinct. Or perhaps I had grown wise to her pleas for my attention. Her threats usually followed a phone call I had ignored or an unrequited invitation to visit.

I played one of the messages for a friend who'd come over to study, watching closely as his eyes grew wider, his expression providing little doubt of his opinion of the call.

I asked anyway. "That's not normal, right?"

"This is anything *but* normal," he said. "Your mother is crazy."

I felt calm hearing those words, if only for an instant, seeing my own world reflected as it felt to me instead of refracted through what sometimes felt like Alice's looking glass.

But those moments were fleeting, and it was difficult to hold on to the truth that my mother needed help. In moments of clarity I would try to persuade her to talk to a professional, but inevitably we would become locked in a battle of blame, one she would usually win.

The last time I tried, I was home from Berkeley for the weekend. My mother and I were in the guest bedroom that had once been my sister's room. It was furnished simply and elegantly, with the two twin beds from my childhood bedroom, their flowered comforters replaced with matching coverlets made of thick fabric, a pale peach intertwined with gold brocade that my mother had hand-stitched herself. The beds were near a set of bay windows overlooking the garden, and as we spoke, my eyes remained fixed on a willow tree whose cascading branches had once served as a secret fortress for my childhood play.

My mother's eyes were lowered as she listened to me make my case. Our conversation seemed to last for hours, the room eerily still. I heard myself presenting evidence as if I were a skilled lawyer instead of a twenty-year-old college student.

Everyone sees a therapist.
It will make you feel better.
It's just nice to have someone to talk to.
Everything you tell her will be strictly confidential.

I'd started going to therapy during high school, when my bouts of depression made it abundantly clear that I needed some help, and at Berkeley I'd made use of the services available on campus. I used every argument that I could think of, but my mother continued to sit in silence, and so I improvised. I felt a desperate sense that the outcome of this conversation could fix or doom our family.

109

"If you love me, you will get help."

My ultimatum was delivered calmly. But my mother remained silent.

"Mom, did you hear me? I am begging you—if you love me, you will get help."

There was a long pause before she answered. I could hear her slow breaths as she considered my words. She looked up at me and said simply, "I'll do it."

The relief I felt was instant, and it spread through my body like a drug. I was empowered with the knowledge that we might never be a perfect family, but there was hope. That's all I can ask for, I thought.

That night I fell into a dreamless and fitful slumber.

The next morning I found my mother perched on a stool pulled up to the wood-block table that sat in the middle of the kitchen. One hand rested lightly on its edge as she stared into a thickly glazed mug, while the other slowly stirred the plain scorching hot water she drank each morning. She looked up at me. I had seen that look before, and I instinctively recoiled as her eyes began to narrow.

"I have thought about it, and I'm not going to talk to anyone, not ever. Don't you see? *You* are the problem," she hissed. "We would be a happy family if it weren't for *you!*"

And so I made lists.

I am four. I'm at a birthday party. It's my party. There is a piñata. I can see the brightly colored papier-mâché, purples and pinks spinning as children smack it with a stick. I see the smiles on the other children's faces, but I am sobbing. I look up at her leering down at me. I've done something wrong. I can see it in her face, in her disapproving eyes. It's my fault. The party is ruined.

I am eight. She picks up my Fisher-Price dollhouse and pitches it across the room; miniature beds and tables and tiny plastic figurines hurtle through the air. I remain motionless as the house hits a wall and breaks in two.

I am ten. She is telling me that she should have been famous—like Albert Einstein or Elizabeth Taylor—but it had all been taken from her. The pitch of her voice rises. The look in her eyes frightens me. I lower my gaze and focus on the thick grooves around her mouth set in by her nervous twitch.

I am eighteen. We leave a restaurant because she feels slighted by a guest and has become inconsolable. I remember the look of the maître d' as we rush toward the exit, his eyes wide and lips curled in disapproval.

Other memories came back even more clearly.

There is a searing pain in my ear, but we have a guest, a classmate of mine from boarding school who missed his connection because the airport was fogged in. I'm holding my hands to my head, hoping the pain will recede. I am begging my mother to take me to the emergency room. "Mom! Mom! Please, please, make it stop!" I'm screaming, but she tells me to lower my voice. "Shh! Our guest will hear you! Be quiet!" I'm stunned by her dismissal, as my mother was always at her best during our childhood illnesses. She tells me that we can't go, it will embarrass my fifteen-year-old classmate. We have to wait. "He won't care!" I protest, but my words are unpersuasive in the face of her need to maintain appearances. I cry myself to sleep. The next day, when she finally takes me to the doctor, I am told that I was lucky. My eardrum had almost ruptured. I see the look of concern cross the doctor's face as she delivers the news, and I imagine a mucous membrane spurting out through my ear canal like a small explosion. The white paper from the doctor's table crinkles under my hands as I clutch the cold metal underneath.

There is a cat that shows up at the back door, hungry and afraid. Each day I lie on the driveway, motionless, speaking softly, coaxing it until the feral creature trusts me. It takes months, but the once-wild cat eventually curls up next to me at night, purring contentedly, loving me unconditionally. Until the day it vanishes, and my mother says that it was dirty. It had to go.

I see my mother's face. It is contorted as she violently flings the coffee table on its side, blanketing the Oriental rug with glittering shards as the glass top shatters. I don't know why she is angry, but my father tries to calm her down, tells me to go to my room. When I come out hours later, I am told that my mother has gone shopping in Los Angeles for a few days. She shows up a week later without any shopping bags.

On the list it went, no matter how small the offense, my ever-increasing tally of comforting transgressions, offering me the proof I craved. But none of it was ever enough to silence the voices in my head. *What kind of daughter am I, not returning my mother's phone calls? Perhaps I should visit more often. Maybe if I hadn't used that tone of voice . . .*

Sometimes I secretly wished that my mother had hit me or cut me with a knife. A single bruise or scar would suffice, giving me the evidence to once and for all prove that it wasn't all my fault.

But as I became more immersed in my mother's past, I came to understand a truth that had the potential to topple one of my most deeply held views.

Perhaps none of it was really her fault, either.

THE THINGS I read about life at the Foundling Hospital sometimes reminded me of a scene out of *The Handmaid's*

Tale. I had devoured the dystopian novel in college, captivated by the descriptions of Gilead, a fictional authoritarian regime where the Commanders, men of power and wealth, impose their theistic views upon subjugated citizens. Treated like chattel, females are assigned roles based on how they can best serve society. The protagonist, Offred, is a handmaiden, charged with bearing children to populate Gilead in the face of widespread infertility. She is renamed and forced to dress in a habit of red cloth, the fabric chosen to reflect her utility as a fertile female. When she goes out, she dons a white bonnet and walks alongside other handmaidens, always traveling in pairs, communicating in whispers and careful not to upset the Wives, the barren women dressed in blue who control the handmaids' daily lives. But they are most afraid of the Eyes, who can exact swift punishment for any perceived disloyalty to Gilead.

Unlike the rules imposed on Margaret Atwood's characters, the strictures governing every aspect of Dorothy's life were real.

The elite men chosen to oversee the Foundling Hospital had laid out their expectations for the foundlings' lives in a series of rules dictating the minutest aspects of their upbringing: from their clothing ("in a Manner proper for Labour") to the time they should rise ("Five o'clock in the Summer, and Seven in the Winter"), be out of the ward ("a Quarter of an Hour after"), begin work ("Half an Hour after Five in the Summer, . . . Seven in the Winter").[22] On it went, days filled with order, each moment accounted for in the endless cycle of established routine.

Over the next two centuries the world that surrounded the Foundling Hospital would be transformed: the industrial revolution would herald in an era of innovation and new technologies, Queen Victoria would reign for six decades, a king would abdicate the throne for his love of an American divorcée, and in Germany, a new leader named Adolf Hitler would come to power.

But life at the Foundling Hospital remained grounded in practices adopted centuries before.

The children were separated by gender, the boys on one side, girls on the other, thirty to a dormitory. Dorothy's shared living quarters amounted to a military barrack—a long rectangular room furnished only with row after row of small iron beds topped with thin mattresses, each girl assigned to a bed based on her height. Other than the beds, no other furniture was allowed, nor was there any decor to soften the prisonlike setting—no colorful bedspreads, no pictures on the walls. A set of plain windows overlooked a flat gray roof. Each morning at the exact same time, Dorothy would wake and put on her brown serge dress—the color chosen as a reminder of her station in life. On Sundays she would don a white apron and "tippet" (a scarf-like stole worn over the shoulders), and perhaps a cap atop her dark brown hair, cut the same length as that of every other girl at the institution, just above the earlobes, with bangs covering her forehead.

Next, she would line up with the other girls from her dormitory and march to the washroom, grabbing her toothbrush and standing quietly in front of the water basin.

"Taps on!" the dorm supervisor would roar. In unison, each girl leaned forward, turned on the water, and waited.

"Brushes under!" The girls would place their toothbrushes under the cold stream of water that sputtered out of the taps.

"And . . . brush!"

The line of girls would begin cleaning their teeth on cue. Back and forth, up and down, the collective sound of brushing echoing off the tile walls, until they heard their next instruction.

"Rinse!"

"And taps off!"

The room would grow quiet as the spigots went dry.

"March!"

The orders heralded the start of a day that would be spent obeying their superiors—the women, each dressed in blue with a white cap, who enforced rules that had been etched in stone. The girls left the washroom, always in twos—crocodile formation, as it was called at the Foundling Hospital. It was a phrase that I would come across often. In attempting to discover its origin, I found a reference suggesting that the phrase was derived from an ancient Indian warfare technique called *makara vyuha*. The *makara* was a legendary sea monster—a crocodile, in modern terms—and *vyuha* means an arrangement of troops. How the expression made its way to a home for illegitimate children in a country thousands of miles away is a mystery, although England's colonial presence in India seems a viable link. Regardless of its etymological trajectory, the phrase's military roots had certainly been preserved. The children were required to maintain the formation in complete silence, under the watchful eye of their supervisor. Down the stairs they would march, through the hallways, and into the oak-paneled dining room, where each would take her place at one of the long tables according to her assigned team, always in the same order—first Hogarth, then Handel, followed by Dickens and then Coram.

In the large hall, the girls would stand soundlessly. There were no whispers or rustling of skirts. The room would be eerily still as they awaited their instructions.

A teacher's voice would break the silence. *Pray!*

For what we are about to receive, may the Lord make us truly thankful, the girls would respond on cue. *Amen.*

Sit!

Row upon row, dozens of girls with the same haircut and identical garb would simultaneously turn and sit down, almost without a sound.

Begin!

They would consume their meals in silence, hearing only the clinking of their cutlery, the no-talking rule strictly enforced.

For the children in my household, meals were generally quiet affairs, particularly when we ate in the formal dining room, at a table that could easily seat a dozen guests. My mother sat at one end of the table, my father at the other, my sister and I in the middle. My parents rarely spoke. To fill the silence, my sister and I created a secret language, just a few words here or there, many based on swear words in French or Spanish. "You're a *merde*-head," my sister would quip, sending us both into uncontrollable fits of laughter. My parents would smile quietly at our disobedience.

A foundling would not be so lucky. A girl caught talking would be moved to a special table—the "odd table," as it was called. Later she would likely be caned, an example of the importance of obeying the rules. Day in. Day out. Breakfast, dinner, and supper would be eaten in total silence, except on Christmas Day, when as a special treat, the girls were allowed to talk at the table. In the years they would spend at the Foundling Hospital, not once would they sit down to a meal with an adult.

At the end of the meal, on cue, the girls would bow their heads and pray in unison:

For what we have received, may the Lord make us truly thankful. Amen.

Stand up!

March!

After breakfast, it was time to defecate. They knew their instructions—produce a solid. Each morning at the same time, a nurse gave them two pieces of paper and then stood over them, waiting until each had performed to her satisfaction. She would inspect the results. Only she could authorize a flushing, and if her examination of the contents of the toilet bowl dissatisfied her, the offending foundling would be sent to the infirmary for a dose of syrup of fig.

There was little unscheduled time, perhaps a short break in the playroom—an ill-fitting name for a large blank space that held nothing other than rows of tables and chairs, with lockers on one wall where the children could store their meager belongings. Even then, "we were always under watchful eyes, free to talk and play games, but not too loudly or roughly," my mother remarked. And lest they forgot, the reminder was displayed prominently in large letters on the wall above them:

> THE EYES OF THE LORD ARE IN EVERY PLACE,
> BEHOLDING THE EVIL AND THE GOOD.

The monotony and silence of endless days, their rhythms more akin to those of a prison than a school for young children, must have been excruciating. The foundlings' time was spent moving from place to place, obeying their superiors, or attending daily services in the chapel (twice on Sundays). *Get up. Get dressed. Line up. Brush. March. Pray. Eat. Poop. March. Eat. March.* Day in. Day out. Unchanging, and all to be done in silence with complete self-control, no whispering, no laughing, and most important, no mistakes.

Any deviation from the rules, no matter how slight, was swiftly addressed by a staff member tasked with guaranteeing that order be maintained. This staff member would most often be female. While setting hospital policies was exclusively the province of men, enforcement and the day-to-day care of the foundlings fell predominantly to women. Selected not for their knowledge or training in education or child-rearing but whether they were "Persons of good Characters, . . . unincumbered with Families of their own, [and] professing the Protestant Religion," few of the staff members had relevant experience.[23] A matron (also called the headmistress) oversaw the raising of the girls as well as the management of the female staff—the teachers, cooks, and "nurses." (The latter term was in keeping with the name of the institution, if not its mission, as "nurses" did not provide medical care. Instead they supervised the children, policing them as they brushed their teeth or made their beds, marched from place to place, and ate their meals.) A master oversaw the male foundlings, who lived in a separate wing, strictly sequestered from females.

Life for the staff was dreary, strict, and dull. There were rules regarding behavior, requirements that staff members obey commands without dispute. During much of the Foundling Hospital's history, the female staff could not leave the premises without permission, and visitors were discouraged. All staff were subject to strict curfews and forbidden from drinking or gambling. While some of the most restrictive rules seem to have been relaxed by the 1900s, the staff remained cloistered away from the outside world along with their charges. In the early years the women who worked at the hospital were young, typically under the age of forty, but by Dorothy's time they were primarily older and childless, their chances of finding other employment long since passed. "In all my years at the school I can't remember ever receiving a friendly comment, a solicitous inquiry or a compliment," my mother recalled.

> When the staff spoke to us it was never in a personal way. Usually it was in an authoritative voice, primarily to command, instruct or rebuke. I suspect that the staff was chosen selectively, able to turn us into the obedient, unquestioning, submissive servants we were destined to become. It is clear to

me now that the entire system was designed to prevent opportunities for us to deviate from our destinies.

Not trained to work with children and deprived of fulfilling lives of their own, the joyless, indifferent staff was ill-equipped to meet the needs of parentless children and relied instead on punishment to enforce the strict rules. Canings and beatings with leather straps were common, administered at a whim for the most minor of offenses, such as talking in line, inattention, or dropping a piece of food at mealtime.

Physical abuse was widespread, not just accepted but expected. Each classroom was equipped with a cane. Miss Abbott, one of Dorothy's teachers (called "mistresses" back then), had a reputation for being "cane happy." A short, birdlike woman with black hair and scrawny legs, she was so slight in stature that her cane seemed longer and more solid than her torso. My mother remembered her eyes bulging behind her glasses as she lashed her students' palms until they sobbed.

Other staffers preferred a wooden ruler or a hairbrush, always with a side of verbal abuse, often referring to a child's illegitimacy. The children were constantly reminded of their shameful beginnings:

You wicked child!

You're a disgrace, lucky to be alive!

One nurse was known for choosing her favorite form of punishment, not so much for the method but the timing. She administered her floggings in the evenings, and only after the girls had removed their undergarments in preparation for bed, allowing her weapon of choice to land on bare skin. During the day, if a girl displeased her, she would take a pen from her pocket and write the child's surname on her apron, marking an extra tick if the child misbehaved again. Just before lights out, she would call each name, one by one, and flog the girl on her bare bottom, the number of hits corresponding to the marks on her apron.

Reading about the horrors that my mother endured as a child, it was hard to know which was worse—canings that yielded bruises that lasted for days, or the insults and rigidity that left a lifetime's worth of emotional scars. My mother, like the other foundlings, was caught in an endless loop of punishment and suffering, with no chance of reprieve. The staff of the hospital were either ignorant of or indifferent to the impacts of their beatings, but modern psychological research has connected this kind of childhood neglect and abuse with a victim's inability to exercise self-control; their capacity to obey instructions is significantly hampered due to trauma or abuse. In other words, the more you beat a child, the less likely she is able to control her own actions. And so, from the outset, the Foundling Hospital created an exacting, unsparing, rigid environment where infractions and abuse became inevitable, leading to beatings that would make children more likely to act out, leading to yet more beatings, escalating in frequency and intensity. The studies piled high on every available surface in my office, their certainties reframing all I thought I'd known about my mother.

Some staffers were more vicious than others, evoking terror simply by entering a room, taking pleasure in the very act of inflicting pain on a child. In my mother's time, that would have described Miss Woodward, one of the youngest instructors at the school. Unlike the other staff members, who were typically heavyset and dowdy, Miss Woodward was tall and slender, her wavy ginger hair cut in a stylish bob that framed her pretty round face. But the girls were not fooled by her appearance. They knew that just beneath her elegant veneer, she harbored a fury that would rise, wild and uncontrolled, triggered by even the slightest of infractions or, even more frightening, with no provocation whatsoever.

Not a day passed that Dorothy wasn't filled with anxiety and dread that Miss Woodward would be lurking just around the corner, waiting, ready to batter her small body with whatever instrument might be handy. Her fear wasn't unreasonable. The worst beating she endured in her years at the Foundling Hospital was at the hands of Miss Woodward.

Dorothy had been in crocodile formation, marching alongside another girl on the way to class. Miss Woodward was in the front of the line, on a tirade, berating the girls as she often did, when Dorothy muttered in a barely audible voice, "Oh, shut up." Dorothy hadn't thought Miss Woodward could hear her, but she was wrong. Miss Woodward grabbed Dorothy, pushing her roughly into a nearby classroom. Miss Abbot, who was leading a class, quickly stepped aside, clearing a path for Miss Woodward to thrust Dorothy over the desk. Miss Woodward grabbed the cane that was always handy in each classroom, pulled down Dorothy's knickers, and beat her, thrashing her with such a fury that a purple-black mass of bruises remained for weeks.

Dorothy did her best to hide the damage from the other girls. She also made sure to steer clear of the infirmary, knowing all too well the dangers of allowing a doctor to discover signs of a beating. A doctor might ask questions, perhaps express concern, cause trouble for the staff, which was certain to elicit another beating. But Dorothy also hid her bruises because of the shame she felt, her belief that the beating had somehow been her fault. "I was embarrassed on weekly bath nights," she wrote years later, "believing that my black and blue buttocks were a reminder to everyone that I was a bad girl."

There were six white porcelain bath tubs, three on either side of the bathroom, serving two or three upper dormitories, and we bathed two to a tub. The so-called "nurse" in charge, the always grim faced, matronly, bespectacled Nurse Knowles, in a dark blue dress, white apron and cap, made no comment as she stood there, arms folded over her oversized bosom, watching while we bathed, and I was sure that she thought the beating was well deserved.

But the pain and bruising Dorothy experienced that day was not the worst that Miss Woodward could dole out. The most terrifying episode was yet to come, when Dorothy was unaware that she had done anything wrong—and it came without warning.

Dorothy was in class, sitting quietly, hands folded, when Miss Woodward strolled into the classroom and nodded at the teacher, who seemed to be expecting her.

"Soames, come with me," she instructed.

Dorothy made her way up to the front of the class, panicking. What had she done? While no stranger to punishment meted out at the hands of the hospital's staff, she could not recall an incident that would have precipitated Miss Woodward's unexpected visit.

Miss Woodward ordered Dorothy to go put on her swimsuit. Dorothy looked anxiously at Miss Woodward, who was known for pushing unsuspecting children into the pool as a teaching technique. She was so feared that some of the girls would try to hide in the toilets rather than attend gym class. Dorothy had just begun to learn to swim, and had never ventured past the shallow end of the pool. When they entered the pool area, the strong smell of chlorine wafted through the indoor enclosure. She padded quietly behind Miss Woodward until, without warning, she felt herself being lifted in the air and flung toward the deep end of the pool. Dorothy screamed as she was propelled through the air before she plunged into the water.

Unable to swim, she struggled to stay afloat, thrashing helplessly. As she came up for air, she was just able to make out the image of Miss Woodward holding the wooden lifesaving pole that normally hung on the wall by the side of the pool. It had a large canvas loop on the end, and she was pointing it in Dorothy's direction. "I naturally thought my punishment was over," my mother recounted in her manuscript. But Miss Woodward had something else in mind. She began poking Dorothy with the pole, pushing her under the water, bringing her up just long enough for her to gasp for air, and then forcing her underwater again. Dorothy was certain that she was going to die.

The next thing she remembers was lying next to the pool, dripping wet, prostrate on the cold concrete. As she struggled to catch her breath, she looked up and saw Mr. Bland, the music teacher, and Nurse Major, a dormitory supervisor, standing close by, chatting casually with Miss Woodward. They would occasionally glance over at Dorothy as they spoke. She had never seen them at the pool before and was certain that they had been invited there by Miss Woodward to watch Dorothy's punishment, a diversion from their otherwise dull and predictable days.

After that Dorothy lived in constant fear of Miss Woodward, certain that she would eventually die by her hands. And so, on cold nights when she felt afraid, she did the only thing that was in her power: she prayed. Kneeling in the dark quietly, to avoid the ever-watchful eye of the dorm supervisor, she would clasp her hands together, rest her elbows on the thin mattress that sat upon her small iron bed, and beg God to save her from Miss Woodward.

Oh Lord, please help me stop misbehaving and stop Miss Woodward from punishing me.

Night after night she would pray, unaware that one day her prayers would be answered. But relief would not come soon, and in the meantime she would have to suffer a punishment even worse than Miss Woodward's beatings—all because a man with an umbrella thought he knew best.

IF YOU VISIT Westminster Abbey, where Queen Elizabeth II was crowned and Princess Diana mourned, you will see a memorial to Jonas Hanway in the north transept, just after you enter through the Great North Door. Unveiled in 1788, the monument boasts a relief of Britannia doling out clothing to orphans, a coat of arms with three demi-lions rampant, and a heroic inscription singing the praises of Hanway's contributions to the poor:

> The helpless INFANT nurtur'd thro' his Care.
> The friendless PROSTITUTE shelter'd and Reform'd.
> The hopeless YOUTH rescu'd from Misery and Ruin.
> And train'd to serve and to defend his Country.
> Uniting in one common Strain of Gratitude.
> Bear Testimony to their Benefactor's Virtues:
> THIS was the FRIEND and FATHER of the POOR.

Indeed, Hanway's concern for the welfare of Britain's children is thoroughly documented. In 1756 he became a governor of the Foundling Hospital, rising to vice president of the institution in 1772. He founded the Marine Society, the world's first charity dedicated to seafarers; still in existence today, the charity helped prepare thousands of poor boys, many of them orphans, for a life at sea. He then founded the Magdalen House for penitent prostitutes, and advocated for the better treatment of chimney sweeps. Also known for his policy work, Hanway successfully lobbied for a law requiring the registration of poor children and another increasing wages for apprentices.

Jonas Hanway was a colorful character in London society. After a trip to Paris, he began carrying an ornate umbrella with him wherever he went. Its canopy was said to be pale green silk on the outside and straw-colored satin on the inside, and small fruits and flowers were carved into its ebony handle. At the time, umbrellas weren't used in London—at least not by men, as they were considered effeminate, a sign of weakness of character or, worst of all, of being too French. Hanway's umbrella was particularly disliked by operators of hansom cabs, the two-wheeled horse-drawn carriages that frequented London's streets. An umbrella was a threat to a cabbie's bottom line; a pedestrian caught in the rain might well forgo cab fare if he could stay relatively dry without the added expense. When hansom cab drivers saw Hanway, they would pelt him with rubbish. One driver reportedly tried to run him down with his carriage, at which point Hanway learned yet another use for his umbrella: to give the driver a solid thrashing. A known eccentric who cared little for the opinions of others, Hanway went on using his umbrella, and he is credited today for making the object one of London's most iconic symbols.

When he wasn't helping children or chasing off hansom cab drivers, Hanway was writing. Pamphlets had become an essential form of political discourse by the middle of the eighteenth century—the most famous of these was *Common Sense*, in which Thomas Paine advocated for the independence of the Thirteen Colonies. Hanway embraced this form of writing, producing more than eighty printed works in his lifetime, most of them pamphlets.

Hanway regarded himself as a great thinker, with much to

offer on how to improve British society. He wrote, among other things, on the operations of the Foundling Hospital, using his intimate knowledge of its workings to provide a detailed mathematical accounting of the financial gains achieved by putting foundlings to work. He also published writings on other subjects: religion, immorality, petty thievery, prostitution, how to create domestic happiness, the relationship between servant and master, and the advantages of eating bread. He was particularly passionate about his opposition to the drinking of tea, which was gaining popularity in London. In *An Essay on Tea: Considered as Pernicious to Health, Obstructing Industry, and Impoverishing the Nation*, he assailed tea drinking as an epidemic, claiming that it caused scurvy, weak nerves, and early mortality, and reduced the overall productivity of Britain's labor force. These problems were worsened, he believed, because people drank tea at a higher temperature than human blood.

More disturbingly, Hanway had an equal antipathy toward Jews, and wrote a lengthy pamphlet opposing their naturalization. "Was there ever such an instance of the depravity and corruption of men, as among the *Jews*?"[24] he asked, cautioning that to accept them into British society would be to "commit a *violence*" on Christianity.[25]

The impact of one of Hanway's pamphlets is still felt today. In his 1776 *Solitude in Imprisonment: With Proper Profitable Labour and a Spare Diet*, he advocated for solitary confinement—placing a person alone in a dark room with only bread and water. I ordered the pamphlet from a publishing company specializing in "forgotten" books. The text was difficult to read—the print tiny, the old-fashioned type a jumble, and the language arcane. But as I became accustomed to the strangeness of the language, the words' meaning began to take shape. Hanway considered himself a devoutly religious man on an important mission to eradicate evil, wherever it might be found. This mission was for him an urgent calling, one that required swift action. And in this fight against the destructive forces that could poison human nature, he had identified solitary confinement as a powerful tool that could fundamentally shift human behavior toward piety. The "idea of being excluded from all human society, to converse with a man's own heart," Hanway believed, "will operate potently on the minds and manners of the people of every class."[26] To him, solitary confinement was not cruel but compassionate, a practice that would "restore the prisoner to the world and social life, in the most *advantageous* manner; and that he may, in due time, teach what he has learnt, and hand down *virtue* instead of *vice* to posterity."[27]

With these words, which he penned as mindfully as those regarding his beliefs in the dangers of tea and the benefits of bread, Jonas Hanway took my mother from me.

DOROTHY WAS EIGHT when she was first locked in a closet. When the hospital opened in the mid-1700s, such a punishment would have been unheard of. In those early days, children were rewarded for good behavior. They were given a silver thimble, a pair of scissors, gingerbread, or even a special hat for a job well done, perhaps for perfecting a new sewing stitch or fashioning a particularly sturdy piece of cordage—a practice adopted not as a kindness but based on the then-current economic axiom that incentives increased productivity. This isn't to say that, in the hospital's first years, a foundling wouldn't receive a slap across the head or a switch across an outstretched palm following a cheeky comment. But records reveal a sinister development the year after Hanway, who was considered one of the hospital's most influential governors, published his pamphlet on solitary confinement. On January 29, 1777, the governors ordered "a plan and estimate of the expense of fitting up a place for the solitary confinement of children who may misbehave."[28] Once the confinement area had been built, it was referred to as the Dark Room, the Lock-Up Room, or, most often, Prison. The first to receive this punishment were children as young as eight, and they were sometimes locked up for as long as a week. The room was also used to confine apprentices who had already left the hospital but been returned by their masters due to bad behavior.

Hanway was not alone in his views, but his voice was powerful, and his ideas took hold. He is credited by some for the widespread adoption of solitary confinement in penal settings, and even for bringing the practice to the United States. Ironically, another notable supporter of the Foundling Hospital would be one of the most eloquent critics of the practice. In 1842 Charles Dickens traveled to the United States, visiting a prison just outside of Philadelphia. He walked away appalled at the conditions, describing the "hopeless solitary confinement" as "cruel and wrong," believing it to be a punishment "which no man has a right to inflict upon his fellow creature," its

> slow and daily tampering with the mysteries of the brain, to be immeasurably worse than any torture of the body; and because its ghastly signs and tokens are not so palpable to the eye and sense of touch as scars upon the flesh; because its wounds are not upon the surface, and it extorts few cries that human ears can hear; therefore the more I denounce it, as a secret punishment which slumbering humanity is not roused up to stay.[29]

I assume it unlikely that Dickens was aware that the brutal treatment he found so objectionable was being used at the Foundling Hospital. I certainly found no proof of it. Perhaps, if he had known, he would have stepped in to put an end to the cruel practice.

The "Prison" used to lock up children no longer existed by the time Dorothy was born. In the 1920s the hospital, under financial stress at that time, sold its land to a developer who wished to turn the area into a market (it would later become New Covent Garden Market, where the fictive Eliza Doolittle sold flowers in *My Fair Lady*). The governors bought back a small strip of land and constructed a new building to serve as administrative headquarters, containing re-creations of many of the hospital's original rooms—the Court Room, the Picture Gallery, and the Committee Room. This building is where the Foundling Museum is housed today.

The children were temporarily relocated to an old convent in Redhill before the hospital's primary campus was moved ultimately to the small town of Berkhamsted in 1935, two years before Dorothy's arrival. There is no record of a special room for solitary confinement on that property—but that didn't stop Miss Wright, the matron of the Foundling Hospital during Dorothy's time there. My mother seemed to remember every last detail about her:

> Dickens himself could not have created a headmistress any more joyless and forbidding than Miss Wright. Her graying hair was parted in the middle and pulled back into a bun, the sides professionally set in a series of waves framing her long face and nose. She kept her arms close to her primly-clothed thin body and her walk and bearing were almost stealthy; I couldn't imagine her swinging her arms, even slightly. Her

pursed lips never parted into a smile; a hearty laugh would have been unimaginable.

Miss Wright patrolled the hallways, looking for the slightest infraction. She eschewed canes and rulers, instead carrying a leather strap. She would enter a room with an air of importance, her steely eyes gazing expectantly as the girls rose to their feet.

But for Dorothy, Miss Wright preferred solitary confinement over the strap, and for the next several years Dorothy would endure being locked up in windowless rooms time and time again. Hanway had been wrong, it turned out—the solitude did little to stop her from getting into trouble.

It was no secret that Miss Wright picked on Dorothy more than the other girls. She considered her to be unruly, speaking out of turn, defying orders. Dorothy was precocious, and to Miss Wright, her lively personality was evidence that she was a "bad seed." It seemed an almost daily event for her to be on the receiving end of Miss Wright's leather strap, or locked away in a dark cupboard, closet, or storeroom for hours on end. Only sometimes would Dorothy be given bread and water. On the luckier days, she would be locked in a room with windows.

On one occasion, she had been shut away in a storeroom for hours with nothing to eat when she came upon a tin of chocolates. As the hours wore on and the pangs of hunger intensified, she could no longer control herself. She opened the tin and shoved the chocolate into her mouth, one piece after the next, until the tin was empty. This infraction earned Dorothy a sound beating to top off her confinement. She was also branded a thief, a label that followed her until the day she left the Foundling Hospital.

My mother never lost that ability to eat a box of chocolates in a single sitting. My father would buy them for her, always the iconic California-based See's Candies, a pound of assorted chocolates filled with marzipan, cherries, or nuts. She would disappear into her bedroom, get under the covers, and devour the treats with childlike joy, sometimes going through the entire box. Perhaps, as I like to think, she was imagining Miss Wright's face as the rich candies melted in her mouth.

I thought about what my mother endured in that storeroom as I reviewed psychological studies on early childhood abuse. The research exploring the effects of forced isolation on a living creature is startling. It was easier for me to connect that way, to process what had happened all those years ago in the context of clinical studies and three-inch thick textbooks. Unlike my family history, the research was transparent.

In the 1950s the psychologist Harry Harlow conducted animal studies on the impact of solitary confinement, placing monkeys in a "vertical chamber apparatus" that isolated them from any outside interactions. The results were horrific. After only two or three days of isolation, Harlow reported, the monkeys would "assume a hunched position in a corner of the bottom of the apparatus. One might presume at this point that they find their situation to be hopeless."[30] The reaction of the monkeys was so pronounced that Harlow nicknamed his apparatus the "pit of despair."[31] His experiments demonstrated that a perfectly happy monkey could be placed in the apparatus and, after only a few days, emerge hopeless, broken beyond repair. Unsurprisingly, his methodology was eventually condemned as unethical and inhumane.

My mother did not enumerate the number of times she was locked in a closet, a cupboard, or a storeroom, and the files I unearthed at Coram don't list her infractions. I tried to imagine myself in her place, sitting in the dark, alone and afraid. But somehow I couldn't conjure up the fear she must have felt.

Maybe my inability to empathize stemmed from fears of my own. What would replace the anger I had nurtured so passionately and for so long if I were to release it? My go-to mental image of my mother featured a sharp, critical voice, curled lips, nervously darting eyes. Even after her death, my psychological fallback was to review the list of wrongs she'd committed against me, buttressing my anger lest it subside ever so slightly. But the more I learned about her life, the harder it was for me to remember that familiar picture that lived within me. Instead, I began to see a small girl with features like mine, pale skin, a sprinkle of freckles, and smooth brown hair, huddled in a corner, alone in the dark.

That little girl named Dorothy did the unthinkable, performing a feat Harlow and Dickens could hardly have imagined—she managed to survive the darkness. Her fear of her captors was powerful, but her desire to escape the dreariness of her existence was stronger. She did not let them break her. Instead, she would defy her fate, taking every opportunity to be what she should have been all along: a beautiful and curious child.

And so, when it snowed and the girls were forbidden to leave the building, Dorothy would sneak outside just to stamp her small feet in the freshly fallen powder, or feel the wet snowflakes as they landed on the tip of her nose. And sometimes at night she would slip out of bed and crawl through an unlocked window onto the landing next to the dormitory. Shivering in the cool night air, she would tilt her head up and gaze at the stars. And there, underneath the expansive universe, she dared to hope.

10

LONGING

It was an annual ritual I dreaded—searching for the perfect Mother's Day card, one that would meet my mother's approval without being dishonest. I spent what felt like hours whittling down the options, placing cards that were too sentimental back on the shelf as I shifted from foot to foot.

Gifts, no matter how carefully chosen, were even more complicated. Whatever I'd brought my mother would be inspected, perhaps turned upside down as she sought a label, always finding something to disappoint. She wouldn't necessarily say that she didn't like my gift, but I could see it in her face.

Later, as I looked back at decades of holidays and birthdays, at gifts that went unused or ended up in a pile for Goodwill, I wondered if I'd misunderstood. Perhaps it wasn't disappointment that I saw in the dullness of my mother's eyes. Maybe it was simply too painful for her to hold a gift dearly, to truly cherish it, lest she become careless and let it slip from her grasp, never to be seen again. The feverish way she ate through those boxes of chocolates before they could be taken from her came back to me then with a different meaning.

I don't know what they told Dorothy the first time she received a gift from a mysterious stranger. A package would arrive once or twice a year, unexpectedly, or at Christmas, sometimes on her birthday, identifying marks always removed. Sometimes the gift was simple: a doll, a toy, a spool of yarn. Other times it was extravagant—a colorfully embroidered knitting bag with wooden handles, a delicate brooch, or her favorite, "a small black and white exquisitely carved ivory container in the form of a penguin that screwed open around in the middle. It was about two and half inches high. The eyes were two rubies. Real ones."

As an adult, with only a child's memory to inform her, my mother remained convinced that the rubies were real—the deep red, the way they sparkled in the light.

The only people Dorothy knew outside the wrought-iron gates that enclosed the Foundling Hospital's grounds were her foster parents, but the gifts were not from them. They had little money to spare and were indifferent to her welfare. She did see her foster mother from time to time, on "Mum's Day," when foster mothers were allowed to visit their former charges. The date was announced in advance, creating a buzz of anticipation among the foundlings who longed for any contact with the outside world. It didn't matter that the visits were short, an hour or two; the children looked forward to the day, some making gifts to present to their "mums." Dorothy once made a potholder for her foster mother, stitching together scraps she found lying about in sewing class.

While they knew in advance that the big day was coming, the children were not told whether they should expect to see their foster mothers. When the day finally arrived, the foundlings would assemble in the playroom. As they waited anxiously, one or two girls would peek out the door, listening for footsteps along the long corridor. The first to spot a teacher with a clipboard in hand would shriek with excitement, "List! List!" As she entered the playroom, the girls would continue to cry out as they clamored around her, begging her to reveal the names of the children whose foster mothers had come to visit. Dorothy longed to hear her name called out, but her recollections revealed the pain the day also brought:

> I remember how deeply depressed I felt when my name was not on any of the lists. . . . In spite of my difficult relationship with my foster mother, when she came to the school it was the most exciting day of the year for me. I knew she would inevitably criticize me or hurt my feelings in some way, but she was the only person I had in the world, my only connection to the outside world. . . . Too often, after a brief conversation, she spent most of the time talking with the other mothers nearby, and I never dared to interrupt her.

Dorothy was luckier than some of the children. Among the ranks of the waiting were those who, after being dropped off at the Foundling Hospital at the age of five, would never see their foster mothers again. Never told that their foster mothers would not be coming, they too would sit quietly, eager to hear their names called, only to be disappointed time after time. It was a cruel practice, raising a child's hopes only to dash them with the recitation of the List.

Dorothy continued to receive gifts, and over time she learned the identity of the mysterious stranger behind them—the sender was her "real" mother. I don't know when or how she discovered the truth, but it was probably the way that foundlings learned about most things—clues picked up from conversations between staff members overheard in the hallways, or gossip passed from one girl to the next. The staff rarely spoke to the children except to instruct or discipline, and questions were considered impertinent, likely to result in a whack across the head. But Dorothy soon learned that having a "real" mother was special, something that set her apart from her peers, though she had no way of understanding what it meant.

By design, foundlings were separated from society and told little about the outside world. The first permanent location of the hospital was in an isolated area of London known as Lamb's Conduit. The area was sparsely developed at the time, but it was not remote enough to prevent the curious from visiting. The site became a novelty of sorts, a diversion for the wealthy, who would come to see the foundlings, dressed in their matching uniforms, march from place to place. Many came just to watch the children sleep or eat. But the governors were strict, and soon limited the children's interactions with outsiders, fearing that the visitors might corrupt the children's morals and prevent them from being properly equipped for the life that awaited them. When visitors were allowed, the governors urged "that no familiar Notice may be taken of the Children, lest it should encourage them to forget the lowness of their Station."[32]

For well over a century the governors restricted access to the foundlings, and their isolation was only intensified when the children were moved to Berkhamsted in 1935, two years before Dorothy arrived. While not far from London, the new facility was more secluded, with few houses nearby. The foundlings only left the compound for short supervised walks on Sundays. Indeed, the governors' efforts to isolate the children were so effective that the townspeople grew concerned that the children did not actually exist, forcing the hospital to hold an event, marching the children along the fence line for all to see.

With little outside contact and supervised by adults who rarely engaged them in conversation, the children had to create their own understanding of the world. Many failed to grasp basic concepts about family structures, the difference between foster and biological families, or that members of a family had the same surname. Even in their early years, while they were being fostered in the countryside, many did not know whether the children they were playing with were foster brothers and sisters who would one day join them at the Foundling Hospital or their foster parents' children whom they might never see again. One foundling discovered that his foster mother had raised twenty-six other foundlings the day she first visited him at the hospital on Mum's Day.

Dorothy would have lacked any clear comprehension of what it meant to have a family, so it's hard to imagine what she thought about her connection to this mysterious biological mother who sent presents. But she did make it clear that these presents provided solace on some of her darkest days. Her birthday was particularly difficult, "a long, aching day" as she later described it. But she recalled feeling special on birthdays because, while some of the girls received gifts from their foster mothers, none of the girls she knew had ever received gifts from their real mothers. Yet questions about her mother remained unanswered. *Who was she? Why couldn't Dorothy meet her? Why hadn't she visited?* The answers were left solely to Dorothy's imagination and the uninformed chatter of her fellow foundlings, for the identity of Dorothy's mother was a closely guarded secret.

Her mother's name wasn't all that was being concealed from her, however. Something else was being kept from Dorothy, something that might have comforted her, even given her hope.

Dorothy's mother had been regularly writing, asking about her, begging to see her.

Lena Weston had sent the first handwritten letter a few weeks after she had left her daughter in the care of the Foundling Hospital:

March 28th, 1932

Dear Sir,

I would very much like to hear how my Baby is getting on, would you kindly write to me and say if she is quite well, as I should so much like to hear. The particulars of the child I enquire for are as follows. Taken into the Hospital March 2nd, 1932. Female child, alphabetical number O.

Yours truly,
Lena Weston.

A typed response was dispatched promptly:

30th March, 1932

Dear Madam,

I am in receipt of your letter of the 28th instant and am glad to tell you your little girl is quite well and is settling down nicely in her new surroundings.

I hope you will get on well.

Yours faithfully,
Secretary

The next month Lena sent another letter, this time enclosing £3 with a request that it be credited to her daughter's account. A response was dispatched the same day her letter was received:

1st June, 1932

Dear Madam,

I am in receipt of your letter of the 31st ultimo and am glad to tell you your little girl is quite well.

Thank you for sending £3, which amount I have placed to her credit in the Savings Bank.

Yours faithfully,
Secretary

I wondered what had happened to the funds placed in the savings account. There was no indication either in the files or in my mother's manuscript that it was spent on Dorothy, or that she had any knowledge of an account having been opened on her behalf. The letters continued, requests for information about Dorothy's welfare arriving month after month. Then, a little over a year from the day that she had left her child at the Foundling Hospital, Lena made a bold request:

March 25th, 1933

Dear Sir,
    I am writing to know how my little Girl is getting on, and also would you kindly state if I have a privilege to visit the child.

Yours truly,
Lena Weston

The reply was immediate, and it made no mention of Lena's request:

28th March, 1933

Dear Madam,
    I am in receipt of your letter and am glad to tell you your little girl is quite well.

Yours faithfully,
Secretary

I double-checked my files to see if perhaps I had missed an earlier response, one that had addressed Lena's request. Finding nothing of the kind, I continued on to the next letter in the file:

March 29th, 1933

Dear Sir,

I have received your letter of Tuesdays date informing me that my little Girl is quite well, and I thank you for letting me know.

I should also like you to tell me if you could in my case grant me just the favour to see her, if only for a few minutes. I should not cause you the slightest expense and I hope inconvenience for just this favour.

Yours truly,
Lena Weston

This time, Lena's request was directly addressed:

30th March 1933

Dear Madam,

I am in receipt of your letter. I am very sorry, but I cannot permit you to visit the child. We explained this to you when the child was admitted here.

Yours faithfully,
Secretary

Years would pass before Lena asked to see her daughter again, in a desperate bid attempted only when the world was on the brink of war. But she did continue to ask after the welfare of her child. Sometimes the letters were accompanied by gifts or a few pounds to be placed in the account in Dorothy's name.

Almost without fail, institutional replies would be sent the same day they were received—brief, typed letters, rarely more than a sentence or two. Almost all contained the same phrase: *Your little girl is quite well.*

A few letters contained brief descriptions of Dorothy's health. In 1936, when Dorothy was four, the secretary of the hospital wrote to Lena informing her that "the little girl has developed measles." At the time, measles was a dangerous disease, with a vaccine nearly thirty years away. That year, nearly six hundred people died from the disease in London alone, yet the secretary concluded his two-sentence typed letter with the reassurance: "There is however no cause for anxiety."

I had held Lena's letters in my hands, the paper delicate and worn with age, varying in size and color from blue to a faded, yellowing white, as if she had used whatever paper she could find. My mother's manuscript made no mention of these letters, and as I parsed through the documents, it occurred to me that in all probability, she had never seen them. In 1977, when I was eleven, she had visited London to see her files for herself, taking a journey similar to my own in an attempt to understand the past and how it had shaped her. I have no childhood recollection of her sojourn, and certainly wouldn't have been told about its purpose. It wasn't unusual for my parents to take trips abroad from time to time, leaving me and my sister with babysitters. She must have had high hopes, I imagine, but her trip to London would be less fruitful than mine.

Upon her arrival, she was told that privacy rules would prevent her from seeing her files. "I was told that the files were now held in the London Metropolitan Archives and that I would not be able to view them until I was 110 years old! This sounded suspiciously like a denial," she wrote. "The age limit was once 100 years, until a former Foundling had the audacity to live to be 109. Since I was not sure I could hang on that long, I was obliged to settle for the alternative—a summary of the file at the discretion of a 'social worker' on the Coram Family staff." I don't know what the summary contained, but the irony was unmistakable. The rules that barred my mother from seeing her files are still in place today, enacted to protect the identity of relatives who might still be alive. In a ridiculous twist, the obstacle preventing my mother from accessing her own files may have been the fact that she herself was still among the living. I was allowed to see the files only after I had provided proof that the people mentioned in the records were now dead. The application in which Lena detailed her desperation, the reports and interviews with her pastor, doctor, and brother, revealing the pressure those around her exerted on her to give up her child, the dozens of letters she sent asking about her little girl—I can only assume that my mother saw none of this.

As I thumbed through my grandmother's letters, I felt her love for her child in every bend and curve of her rough, inelegant, and sometimes illegible handwriting. I wondered whether things would have been different for Dorothy had she known of their existence. Knowing about the letters wouldn't have stopped her foster mother from criticizing her, kept Miss Wright from locking her in a closet, or prohibited Miss Woodward from beating her with a cane. But maybe knowing that someone out there cared for her would have given Dorothy some solace when she huddled in her bed at night, or in the corner of a closet, alone and afraid. She would have to find comfort elsewhere, and it would come at a high price.

MY MOTHER HAD no friends in her adult life, at least none that I knew of. From time to time a letter would arrive with a European postmark from my mother's "friend from Europe." But no neighbors stopped by for a cup of tea, no girlfriends tagged along on shopping expeditions. Occasionally she would mention a woman's name, referring to her as a "friend." It was rare that I would hear the same name twice. Sometimes I would ask my father what had happened, where a particular "friend" had gone. His response was always characteristically vague: "You know how she is."

This isolation fit the profile for a child raised with an absence of early attachments, I learned. The University of London researchers who interviewed adults raised at the hospital echoed much of what was already known about the daily experiences of foundlings—the harshness of institutional life, the rigid discipline preparing the children for domestic service. But through their interviews, the researchers also uncovered something surprising. Given the children's seclusion from the outside world and emotional isolation from the adults who managed their care, the researchers expected that friendships might have formed among them, as a refuge from the horrors of daily life at the Foundling Hospital. Instead, close friendships were the exception rather than the rule.

The regimented atmosphere emphasized group activities, allowing little time for personal bonds to form. But the researchers cited the dullness and invariability of the children's daily routine as a central reason why the children didn't create meaningful bonds with one another. A former foundling, a seventy-five-year-old man who went on to join the army, remarked that "funnily enough there weren't close friendships. It was odd because we just knew each other. We were all doing the same thing. There was no excitement. There was nothing to talk about."[33]

Another former foundling, ninety years old at the time of her interview, recollected that she always wanted a special friend "but it didn't really do to make friends particularly with one person. . . . I suppose I thought there's no good making a friend because they'll be taken away anyway."[34]

While the University of London study attributed the lack of friendships to the sameness of the children's daily lives, research conducted by John Bowlby, a British child psychiatrist, revealed a more consequential explanation for why children raised in institutional settings have difficulty forming attachments with others. His groundbreaking conclusions provide invaluable insights into the workings of the human mind and would lay the groundwork for the sea change that resulted in the Foundling Hospital finally shuttering its doors in 1954.

For Bowlby, bonds established—or lacking—at a young age would affect the ability of a person to form healthy and meaningful attachments throughout life. The reasoning behind his claim was both simple and profound—early attachments are based on a need for survival. For an infant, toddler, and young child, closeness to his or her mother is quite literally a matter of life or death. No primary caregiver means no food or shelter. But the repercussions of this biologically necessary attachment go deeper. If a child has a caregiver who is reliable and dependable, Bowlby maintained, the world seems secure, and the child can thrive. Without that security and nurturing, a child cannot grow to trust others or form healthy attachments.

Harry Harlow, the researcher known for his experiments on the effects of solitary confinement on monkeys, attempted to replicate the results of Bowlby's so-called attachment theory by taking monkeys from their mothers at birth. The question he sought to answer: Can you raise a healthy child without love? An early experiment involved taking infant monkeys away from their mothers within hours of their birth. The monkeys were fed meticulously, and were healthy and "disease free without a doubt," Harlow remarked, but in many other ways "they were not free at all."[35] They would sit and rock, staring into space while sucking their thumbs. When confined with other monkeys their age, they chose to stare at the floor of their cages rather than interact with their peers. In another of his experiments, monkeys were confined but given a choice between a "mother"—a cylinder of wood covered with a sheath of terry cloth or a wire mesh that held a bottle, emulating lactation. The monkeys spent far more time clinging to the terry-cloth "mothers," who offered them a bit of comfort, than to the wire mesh that gave them the nutrients they needed to live.

The need for nurturing, for love, trumps the need for food, Harlow's experiments showed. Without tenderness and security in early childhood, the ability to form meaningful and healthy attachments is irrevocably damaged.

Reading about Harlow's experiments, I couldn't help but wonder whether my relationship with my mother conformed to the dynamic he had discovered. She never lifted a hand to me, and at least on the surface, she dutifully cared for me. I received an excellent education and had all of my needs tended to. And while I diligently curated a mental list of my mother's failings, I knew intuitively that it wasn't a broken coffee table or a dollhouse smashed into tiny pieces that had severed our bond irreparably. While beyond the norm, these events could not explain why I recoiled from my mother's touch, finding even the brush of her hand against mine unbearable. Learning more about childhood bonding, how a lack of touch could shape a child's view of the world, it seemed more than possible that the fate of our relationship had been sealed in those first few months following my birth, before conscious memories could form. Perhaps my mother, who had received no love as a child, had been unable to hold and cradle her own tiny infant in her arms.

It wasn't surprising that the foundlings, raised to distrust, deprived of their basic instincts to bond with others, did not seek comfort from one another. Their constant togetherness did produce something unique, however, as I learned from the pages of my mother's manuscript: a special language that allowed them to keep secrets from the staff and at times stave off some of the abuse they received. "Skit," for example, was short for *Quick! Someone is coming. Stop whatever rule you are breaking!* "Hatch up" meant to pretend, and "glish" meant to look forward to. But more often the words of this secret language reflected the foundlings' isolation, and the punishing culture that existed among the girls. "Monk" meant miserable, and to "dob up" was to hand over food to a bully.

The girls used another term that would lead to one of Dorothy's most painful ordeals during her time at the Foundling Hospital—"Coventry." To be placed in Coventry meant that none of the other children would speak to you, for days, a week, or even longer. Dorothy never found out why she'd been placed in Coventry by one of the senior girls, but it was one of the worst ordeals she experienced during her time at the Foundling Hospital. For a week no one would look at her or speak to her during the stolen moments between classes or meals, when the girls would typically talk among themselves.

> Next to Miss Woodward's abuse, it was emotionally my most painful experience at the school. It was devastating. From the moment I woke up and all day long the pain was with me.

Feeling that she'd do anything to stop the agony of solitude, she made a choice—a choice to bargain, using the only currency she had. One by one, she gave them all away, the gifts that had come from her real mother and were her most precious possessions. She gave away the toy, the doll, the brooches—and the ivory box with its rubies that sparkled in the light. While they would disappear from her grasp, she would remember them for a lifetime.

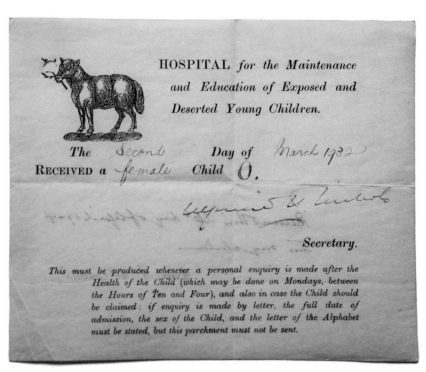

HOSPITAL *for the Maintenance and Education of Exposed and Deserted Young Children.*

The *Second* Day of *March 1932*
RECEIVED a *female* Child O.

Secretary.

This must be produced whenever a personal enquiry is made after the Health of the Child (which may be done on Mondays, between the Hours of Ten and Four), and also in case the Child should be claimed: if enquiry is made by letter, the full date of admission, the sex of the Child, and the letter of the Alphabet must be stated, but this parchment must not be sent.

Receipt given to Lena for her daughter, March 2, 1932 *Courtesy of Coram*

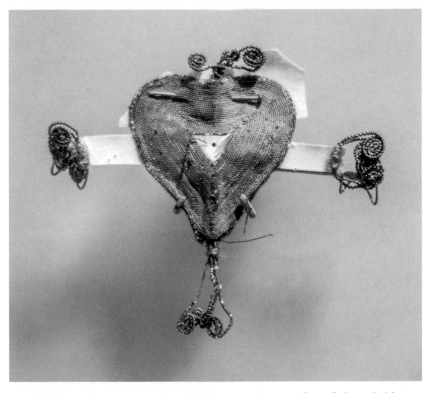

Eighteenth-century token left by a mother to identify her child
© *The Foundling Museum, London*

Portrait of Captain Thomas Coram, founder of the Foundling Hospital, by William Hogarth (1740)
© *Bridgeman Images*

Foundlings pose for a publicity shot on opening day of the Berkhamsted Campus, 1935

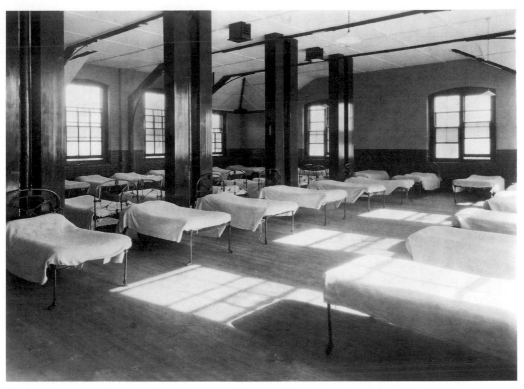

Foundling Hospital dormitory, circa 1930

Foundlings pretend to prepare a meal for the camera, circa 1930

Foundlings line up for inspection

Foundling Hospital campus in Berkhamsted, circa 1940

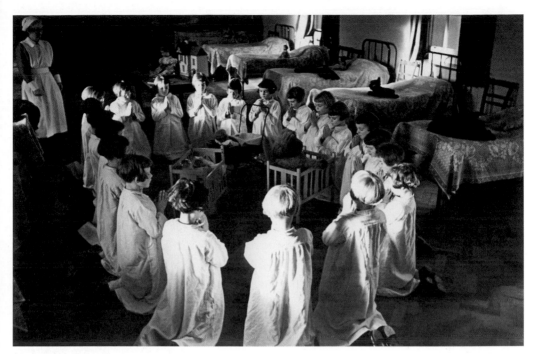

Foundlings pose with toys that were taken away afterward, 1941 *Felix Man/Stringer/Getty Images*

Foundlings pray before a meal, 1941 (Dorothy is present but not pictured)
Felix Man/Stringer/Getty Images

TELEPHONE 110.

At Home
9 to 10 a.m.   5 to 6-30 p.m.
Wednesday evening excepted.

RECEIVED
FEB 6 1932
Ans

Drumrossie,
Wellington,
Shropshire.

To whom it may concern.

I have been Medical Attendant to the Weston Family for
years and have always had a great respect for them all.
Miss Lena Weston keeps house for her brother who has a
small farm outside Wellington. I have never heard the
slightest hint or suggestion of any moral turpitude in
her character, in fact the recent lapse came as a great
surprise to me, and from what I know of her I am pretty
certain it will never happen again.

George Mackie
M.B.

4/2/32.

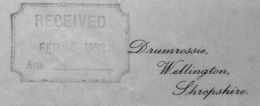

A physician assesses Lena's virtue,
February 4, 1932 *Courtesy of Coram*

MVR   S

30th March 1933.

Dear Madam,

        I am in receipt of your letter.
I am very sorry, but I cannot permit you
to visit the child. We explained this to
you when the child was admitted here.

                Yours faithfully,

                Secretary.

Miss Lena Weston.

Foundling Hospital denies
Lena's request to see her
daughter, March 30, 1933
Courtesy of Coram

Reference № 0.

March 2nd 1932.

Dorothy Soames

Rushmoor Lane Farm.
Nr. Wellington.
Salop.

RECEIVED
- 4 SEP 1939
Ans.................

Sept 2nd 1939.

Dear Sir

In the event of war breaking out, I would like you to consider my application for the custody of my little Girl. I feel that I could give her greater protection in this country district than would be possible elsewhere. At the moment it looks as if we are likely to be subjected to a certain amount of air raids.

Yours truly,
Lena Weston

The Secretary.

Lena asks for her child back as war breaks out, September 2, 1939
Courtesy of Coram

The Foundling Hospital chapel in Berkhamsted, 1941 (Dorothy, left centre) *Hulton Archive/Getty Images*

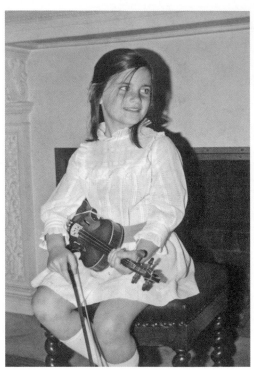

Dorothy the day after she was
reclaimed, age twelve

Justine at around age twelve

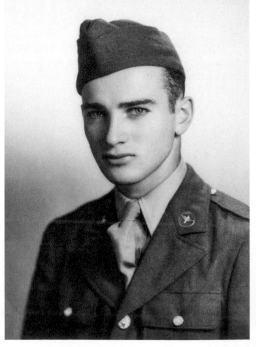

Eileen, aka Dorothy,
in San Francisco, 1962

John during World War II

11

HEALING

It was a clear day, and the view of the golden-brown hills canopied with oak and hickory trees should have been breathtaking. I was seventeen, in my third year at Thacher, a prestigious boarding school located on the outskirts of Ojai, a hippie-chic town nestled in the foothills of California's Los Padres National Forest. My feet felt like lead as I made my way up the narrow path past the tennis courts and pool. I climbed a set of stairs that opened onto the courtyard near the dining hall, a particularly good vantage point for gazing out over the valley. But I was too tired to notice the view. Instead I headed toward the infirmary for the third or fourth time, my face wet with tears, hoping that this time, the nurse would believe me.

"You're depressed, and that's what's making you tired," she had said when I'd first come in, complaining of exhaustion.

"No, that's not it—I'm depressed *because* I'm tired," I snapped, but she sent me away, unimpressed with my argument. My symptoms only worsened.

This time, I didn't wait for the unsmiling nurse to speak.

"I need to see a doctor," I insisted. "There's something wrong with me." Perhaps the urgency in my voice got through, or my condition had deteriorated to the point that I was visibly ill, but she finally arranged for me to be taken into town to see a doctor. He examined me only briefly before declaring that I had mononucleosis.

I was placed in the infirmary, quarantined from my classmates. The nurse made perfunctory visits to check in on me, but I spent most of my time alone, fading in and out of sleep. When awake, I was listless, tangled in starched white sheets, staring at the sage-green walls.

"Please call my parents," I finally pleaded with the nurse one night. "Tell them to come get me."

"Nonsense, you are staying right here," she responded, convinced that I was somehow trying to avoid getting back to classes.

I don't know how I found the strength to sneak into her apartment later that day. Cell phones were years away from making their way to the general public, and you needed a long-distance code to use the school's phones. The nurse lived on campus, as did most of the faculty, in a small apartment attached to the infirmary. I waited until I was alone in the building and there'd be a good chance she had gone out for dinner. Her apartment was sparely furnished, and I quickly found the phone. When I heard my father's voice on the other end I cried out, "Dad, please come get me!"

He must have driven all night, because he was there by morning. He barely spoke two words to the nurse when he arrived. Instead he lifted me into his arms and carried me outside, placing me gently in the back seat of his car. Overwrought with exhaustion and emotion, I threw up all over the seat. He cleaned it up without complaint, and we headed home.

Our family pediatrician confirmed the diagnosis, adding that it was the worst case of mono she had ever seen. I had an enlarged spleen, she added, which could have ruptured. My condition had become serious, and I was very ill.

For the next several weeks my mother nursed me back to health with broths made from meat and fresh vegetables that she simmered on the stove, stroking my hair to comfort me when I was frightened by my fever-borne hallucinations. She rarely left my side, and when she did, she placed a small brass bell in my hand, wrapping my fingers carefully around it, whispering to me that she would come running, that I didn't have to be alone. My mother's tenderness as she nursed me back to health seemed boundless.

I hadn't appreciated my mother's kindness all those years ago. Perhaps I was too weakened by fever, although I suspect that resentment had already taken too strong a hold of me, repelling not just her criticisms but any affection she may have had to offer. I viewed her actions with suspicion, questioning her motives. I certainly didn't conclude that her ministrations were inspired by love.

But it may well have been love that filled each spoonful of warm broth she fed me during those long weeks. Or perhaps the root of her fleeting gentleness came from the sickbeds she had experienced as a child.

DR. RICHARD MEAD customarily arrived at the Foundling Hospital in a gilded carriage drawn by six horses with two running footmen, strolling into the building with a gold-headed cane in hand. An eighteenth-century physician was rarely seen without his cane, its hollow perforated head filled with aromatics to stave off contagions that spread through the air. The "vinegar of four thieves" was a favorite concoction, consisting of a white wine vinegar steeped in herbs such as wormwood, sage, and rosemary and believed to guard against the plague. A physician might use the cane to make a dramatic entrance, striking the floor with its heel to release the cane's protective odor.

Mead's cane was an exemplary model, having been given to him by Sir John Radcliffe, the personal physician to King William III. With his gift, Radcliffe started the tradition of passing on the gold-headed cane to England's greatest physician of the time, and "gold-headed cane physician" came to mean a doctor at the peak of his profession. Six physicians would own this particular cane, which, after 134 years of service, was retired and entrusted to the Royal College of Physicians in London.

As Dr. Mead entered the hospital, passersby might have stopped to stare. After all, he was physician to King George II, Queen Anne, and Sir Isaac Newton. A key advisor to the royals, he counseled the British government on how to contain the plague during an outbreak in the 1720s. Highly celebrated and sought-after, his fees were so exorbitant that only the wealthiest could afford him. But foundlings received his services for free.

One of the original supporters of the Foundling Hospital, Dr. Mead was in attendance when Thomas Coram presented the Duke of Bedford with the royal charter opening the facility in 1739. After that, he took on the role of personally looking after the foundlings, advising on which medicines should be kept in stock and how to improve the children's care.

Dr. Mead was joined in his efforts by other notable physicians including Sir Hans Sloane, who succeeded Sir Isaac Newton as the president of the Royal Society, the oldest scientific academy in continuous existence in the world. Sir Sloane's practice was lucrative, allowing him to become an avid collector of art, coins, medals, books, and manuscripts—a haul he eventually bequeathed to King George II. Sir Sloane's collections, which included animal and human skeletons and dried plants, became the foundation for both the British Museum (the world's first national public museum) and London's Natural History Museum.

With London's finest doctors to look after them, the foundlings received superior medical care, particularly given their lowly station in society. The diseases that struck the children included scarlet fever, measles, dysentery, the "itch" (scabies), and scrofula (a tubercular condition of the lymph glands), but the most pernicious was smallpox, the "speckled monster," as it was called, likely the single most lethal disease in eighteenth-century Britain. While knowledge of how disease spread was rudimentary at the time by modern standards, it was understood that limiting contact with those who had fallen ill could reduce contagion. The hospital was merciless in this task, screening children prior to admission and rejecting those who appeared ill, regardless of the fate that would befall them, whether they would be left to die of their illnesses or relegated to a life of starvation on London's streets. Those who fell ill after being admitted would have their clothing and bedding destroyed and be placed under strict quarantine. The practice of separating the sick from the well became an essential part of the hospital's medical care—and one that would have terrifying consequences for my mother almost two centuries later.

To its credit, the hospital also implemented lifesaving medical protocols that were ahead of their time. With a smallpox vaccine decades away, the institution carried out an inoculation program wherein the virus itself was inserted into the skin. The practice was controversial, and Dr. Mead, one of the leading physicians advocating its use, was reported to have fought a duel to defend it as a course of treatment. His convictions were based on a groundbreaking trial of the inoculations performed on a group of prisoners held in the Tower of London; ordered by Princess Caroline of Ansbach, a smallpox survivor herself, the trial paved the way for the treatment to become recognized as an essential lifesaving procedure.

Although Mead died in 1754, his innovations continued to save lives. By 1756, at a time when smallpox mortality was at its peak, 247 children had been inoculated at the Foundling Hospital, and only one had died of the disease.

But inoculation methods were far from settled, and doctors administered a wide range of treatments, some controversial, even dangerous. Sir William Watson, appointed as the Foundling Hospital's physician in 1762, developed a plan to identify the best method of treating smallpox. Like his colleagues, he had already made his mark on history, not in the medical field but by virtue of his work identifying and controlling electricity. A leading member of the Royal Society, he approached his experiments with enthusiasm. In 1747 he laid twelve hundred feet of wire across the new Westminster Bridge over the river Thames, and with the help of a Leyden jar (a metal-sheathed glass jar capable of storing an electric charge) and volunteers from the Royal Society, he used the river to complete an electrical "circuit" (a term coined by Sir Watson himself), his theory proven when the volunteers felt shocks in their wrists and elbows. He continued the research over the span of several weeks, extending the circuit up to four miles and onto dry land, demonstrating both that electrical conduction was nearly instantaneous and that it could occur via the earth. Twenty-five volunteers participated, with venison pastries and French wine compensating them for their discomfort at receiving the occasional electrical shock.

When Watson was finished experimenting with electricity, he turned his attention to children. He was a man of insatiable curiosity, and after adding the study of medicine to his endeavors, he decided to investigate the multitude of "treatments" being used to allegedly improve the effectiveness of smallpox inoculations. Some physicians had their patients refrain from eating meat prior to receiving their inoculations, others prescribed laxatives or the ingestion of poisonous substances like mercury and antimony (used today in batteries and flameproofing materials). As a scientist, Watson was skeptical of the findings of his colleagues, yet understood that he needed a large group to study how inoculations best worked. His appointment as the Foundling Hospital's physician gave him access to the ideal human laboratory. The children ate the same food, wore the same clothes, slept in the same dormitories, engaged in the same activities. Their lives were virtually identical—a perfect petri dish for his experiments.

Watson began to undertake his inoculations in a series of carefully controlled tests. One group of children received mercury and jalap (a laxative) prior to inoculations; another senna and a syrup of roses (also a laxative); and some only the inoculations. The pretreatment of mercury and laxatives provided no additional benefits, he concluded.

Watson's experiment was the first study on inoculations resembling a modern clinical trial, with an explicit study design and methodical quantification of the results. The ethics of conducting experiments on parentless children without their consent did not appear to be considered, and the uniformity of the foundlings' upbringing allowed for other experiments as well. Some of these were undertaken by a Dr. William Cadogan, a respected physician who became a governor and house physician for the Foundling Hospital. Like Watson, he experimented on the children in attempts to improve inoculation methods. He also recognized the advantages of uniformity in developing a broader base of knowledge on proper methods for child-rearing. In *An Essay upon Nursing and the Management of Children, From their Birth to Three Years of Age*, based on his observations of the foundlings, he wrote about the effects of cleanliness, food and clothing, even how long a child should be breastfed. His conclusions were considered as revolutionary at the time as Dr. Benjamin Spock's insights on child care would be in the twentieth century. In writings that would be translated into French and German and reprinted for the American market, Dr. Cadogan rejected many prevailing views of the time, such as the belief that infants should be tightly swaddled: thus bound, he argued, an infant's "Bowels have Not Room, nor the Limbs Any Liberty," which might lead to swelling, and even "Distortions and Deformities" of the body.[36]

Dr. Cadogan also believed that child-rearing should not be left to the "Unlearned," but should be based on rigorous "Observation and Experience."[37] The key mistake of the past was entrusting the task to "Women, who cannot be supposed to have proper Knowledge to fit them for such a Task, notwithstanding they look upon it to be their own Province."[38] Instead, husbands should take a more active role in child-rearing. Not long after his essay was published, mentions in hospital records regarding "feminine advice" on child-rearing began to disappear.

When Dorothy arrived in the 1930s, the children continued to receive excellent (if sometimes experimental) medical care. The infirmary was spacious and bright, equipped with a well-stocked pharmacy, and the children had access to high-quality optical and dental services. As my mother recounted years later, it seemed that every possible medical procedure was used to maintain a foundling's health. She recalled a series of ultraviolet treatments on account of her "natural pallor," to no apparent effect. Even the staff in the infirmary was notably superior to the grim "nurses" who patrolled the institution's halls and enforced its rules. Chosen for their training and skills, the infirmary's staff members were kind and attentive. They would make a fuss over the foundlings, chatting with them and allowing them to speak to one another. As a result, Dorothy was always delighted to be admitted to the infirmary. Jaundice, mumps, chicken pox, whooping cough, or measles—whatever the cause, it was a special treat to be sick.

As my mother nursed me back to health all those years ago, she never mentioned the women who had tended to her when she was a child. But I have to think that the tenderness she received on those days and nights when she had a sore throat or was weak with fever might have stayed with her as she nursed me back to health. It was the only training she ever received in caring for others.

When I traveled to London to view my mother's records, I took the short train ride to Berkhamsted to see the institution where she had been raised. Passing through the large black gates, I saw for myself the fields where she once played. Since the 1950s, the campus has been known as Ashlyns School. A secondary day school for children over the age of eleven, this self-described progressive learning environment places a high value on student engagement, with students "actively encouraged to make choices, knowing that they are in a safe and supportive environment." I visited on a school day, and the grounds were filled with energy as small groups of teenagers strolled through the hallways, books in hand, chatting casually, laughing, unaware that similar behavior in the past would have brought a swift and painful rebuke. I wandered through the area that had once been the infirmary, a bright room lined with windows, with a large door that led to a courtyard. I learned that on warm days the nurses wheeled the children through the door, allowing them to be outside, if only for a short time. I imagined my mother there, breathing in the fresh air and feeling the sun on her face.

Early medical practices and theories left their mark at the Foundling Hospital in many ways, especially when it came to views on exposure to the elements. In the 1700s it was generally held that fresh air, particularly during the colder months, could be harmful to a child's health. But Dr. Cadogan believed that infants should be taken outside every day, no matter the weather, and that children should be free to roam, even proposing that they do so barefooted. Exposure to "all Weathers" would produce healthy and strong children, he believed.[39] The Foundling Hospital's daily practices reflected this belief—windows were opened and closed according to the direction of the wind, and it was considered particularly important for boys to work outside, to make them hardy.

The Berkhamsted grounds where Dorothy was raised were well suited to preparing children for a life of physical labor. When the hospital relocated to the site in 1935, the property spanned over two hundred acres. The facilities themselves were likewise expansive and modern, with large rooms and long hallways, an indoor swimming pool, and a gymnasium. I wondered what visitors thought, decades ago, when my mother was housed there. From time to time distinguished supporters would visit the facility, men dressed in suits with stylish top hats, women sporting the latest fashions—wool skirts with silk blouses, brooches pinned to their collars, fine hats perched atop expertly coiffed hair. The foundlings would be paraded out onto the field and lined up in military formation, dressed in white linen tippets and aprons adorning their plain brown frocks, their uniformly cut hair topped with white peaked caps. They would stand quietly, each awaiting their turn to meet these strange and wonderful visitors who would stroll the grounds, see the state-of-the-art infirmary, hear of the outstanding medical treatment the children received, delight in the expansive fields, the gymnasium, and the pool. The cruelty of the Foundling Hospital was tucked away, belied by slick parquet floors and freshly painted walls.

The bright and airy infirmary where the children were nursed back to health and the well-kept grounds where they marched and played were created not to provide parentless children with a positive learning environment but to build strong bodies well suited for inevitable lives of service. Recreation and exposure to fresh air were not diversions but an integral part of a regimen to strengthen foundlings' bodies, making them better soldiers, seamen, or scullery maids.

In the early years, foundlings even received a weekly immersion in cold baths. While I found no mention of the practice during my mother's time at the Foundling Hospital, she described being sent outside in all weather short of snowstorms. If it rained, the children would huddle under the colonnades to stay dry.

But when the weather was fine, the activities that strengthened their bodies for hard work also provided a break from the cruelty of their existence. Sent outdoors for rare unsupervised moments, the children would spend their time charging around the mowers, getting covered with grass. There was no structured play time at the Foundling Hospital, but a few toys could be found, perhaps donated by a local charity, allowing them to jump rope or play with tops and marbles. Dorothy's favorite activity was rounders, a game that somewhat resembles baseball, played with an old bat and any ball they could find.

Each summer the children were sent off to a camp in Folkestone, an industrial port town on the English Channel. The camp was basic, comprised of row after row of white canvas tents in a field. But for six weeks, dressed in lightweight khaki uniforms, the children would be granted a hiatus from their captivity as they slid down hills, picked wildflowers, and splintered off into smaller, haphazard groups, a respite from the crocodile formation that dominated their daily lives. These were some of my mother's happiest memories as a child, moments when she experienced rare glimpses of joy as she watched small lizards scamper up an old fence or breathed in crisp sea air while playing carelessly in the fields. But those days would be cut short as an army mobilized along the border of Poland. Soon Dorothy would need the memories of those carefree summer days to sustain her during dark and lonely nights, as the skies above England erupted in battle.

12

WAR AND ISOLATION

I don't remember if it was the siren or my mother's piercing screams that woke me. I must have been four or five at the time, and that night remains my earliest recollection of my mother. I rushed to my parents' bedroom and saw her hunched over in a white nightgown. Her hands were shielding her ears from the siren's relentless pulses, and my father was beside her, his arms encircling her, murmuring in her ear. The siren stopped abruptly, and my mother's howls became quiet whimpers.

"Go back to bed," my father told me when he saw me in the doorway. "It's all right. She just had a nightmare."

He explained the next day that the loud sounds that had rung out into the night came from an air raid siren left over from World War II. We passed by it almost every day, a tall wooden pole topped with plain slate-gray speakers and indistinguishable from an everyday utility pole, but I hadn't known what it was. The sirens had been installed after the Japanese had attacked Pearl Harbor, my father told me. There were fifty of them at the time, located in various places around San Francisco. They would warn of an attack if the Japanese air fleet made it to California. Of course, an attack hadn't been the reason the alarm sounded that night. It was just a malfunction, a technical glitch, no cause for concern.

The sirens are still there, now used to alert San Franciscans of impending disasters—should an earthquake trigger a tsunami, for instance. There are more than a hundred sirens now, sitting atop their nondescript poles, scattered throughout the city. Most residents pass them by without noticing the utilitarian pieces of urban architecture. I only understood why they so terrified my mother after learning what had happened to her in the infirmary all those years ago.

AT 4:45 A.M. on September 1, 1939, Germany invaded Poland. One and a half million German troops spilled across the border as Luftwaffe planes crisscrossed the skies, bombing Polish airfields.

The next day, Lena Weston asked that her child be returned to her care.

September 2nd, 1939

Dear Sir,

In the event of war breaking out, I would like you to consider my application for custody of my little Girl. I feel that I could give her greater protection in this country district than would be possible elsewhere, at the moment it looks as if we are likely to be subjected to a certain amount of air raids.

Yours truly,
Lena Weston

When the Foundling Hospital opened in the mid-1700s, it was not unusual for parents to reclaim their children before they were discharged. According to historian Ruth McClure, the first recorded request occurred in 1742, and others soon followed. At first, children wouldn't be returned unless their parents had paid for past upkeep and posted security for the child's future care. In 1764 the rules were relaxed, and the hospital encouraged parents to reclaim their children without a fee, provided the parent be proven "of such Character, and in such a Condition to Maintain" their child.[40] A notice of the new policy was placed in a major London newspaper, and forty-nine children were reclaimed in that year alone. While not insignificant, the count was small when compared to the thousands of children in the care of the hospital in the early years of its operations.

The process was not always straightforward, for any mother (and they were usually mothers) who wanted her child returned to her had to provide proof that it was hers. Since all children were renamed upon admission, it was common for women to affix a token to the infant for identification, usually an everyday object—coins with distinguishing nicks, buttons or pieces of fabric, rings, bottle tags, a carved ivory fish. Some mothers left tokens that gave voice to their despair—short notes on the backs of playing cards declaiming the "cruel separation," or engravings on heart-shaped tokens: "You have my heart, though we must part." The token would be stored away, sealed, only to be opened in the event that a claim was made.

In 1758 the hospital began providing a receipt for a child who was left in their care, stamped with the full name of the institution at the top—"*Hospital for the Maintenance and Education of Exposed and Deserted Young Children.*" The form included places to identify the sex of the child and its date of admission

(*The* _____ *Day of* _____, RECEIVED a _____ Child), as well as some legalese:

> NOTE.—*Let this be carefully kept, that it may be produced whenever an enquiry is made after the Health of the Child (which may be done on Mondays, between the Hours of Ten and Four), and also in the case the Child should be claimed.*

In 1853 Charles Dickens wrote about the receipt in a magazine article titled "Received, A Blank Child," depicting the Foundling Hospital as a place where what he called "blank children" would be "trained out of their blank state to be useful entities in life."[41] In his eyes, the utilitarian value of the institution was clear. But he did warn the mother who had "previously rung the porter's bell to obtain . . . admission of her child," to be "particularly careful in preserving this parchment."[42] For without the receipt, they might never be reunited.

Dickens frames the parchment in practical terms, but I have to imagine that like me, he was struck by its transactional language.

The receipt Lena Weston was given was almost indistinguishable from the one Dickens had written about a century before, and heeding his advice, she kept it, preserving it carefully, hoping that someday the piece of paper would enable her to see her child again. But the language on the receipt was disingenuous and misleading—the Foundling Hospital had long since discontinued its practice of encouraging the reunification of foundlings with their mothers. Throughout the nineteenth century, the hospital received petitions from mothers, and sometimes fathers, too, seeking reunification. Most of those requests were denied. The following letter was a typical response:

It is very natural that you should feel hurt at the decision of the Governors, but you are mistaken as to the grounds of that decision. There is no charge against either your character or that of your husband: the simple matter is this—the Governors think they can provide for the boy's future welfare better than you can. You should recollect that you have other children, who may for aught we know stand in the way of the Boy; at any rate you ought to feel happy that so great an interest is taken in your son's well-being. The decision of the committee is final.[43]

I wasn't able to make sense of why the practice changed so dramatically, from an initial encouragement of the notion of reunification to the rejections evidenced in the Foundling Hospital's files, but I came to suspect that the hubris evident in so many of the hospital's regulations had something to do with it. Men of great learning, stature, and power, the governors simply considered themselves best positioned to raise a child for the benefit of society. Perhaps over time they'd developed a loyalty to the institution itself, consciously or unconsciously making decisions designed to perpetuate its very existence. Whatever the reason, once admitted as an infant, a foundling would likely never leave the confines of the institution—at least not until he or she had been adequately prepared for a life of service, which during the eighteenth and nineteenth centuries could occur as early as eight years old.

The beginning of the 1900s brought a slight shift in attitude, with a 1907 annual report maintaining that the governors "reserved the right" to restore a child to her mother if they were satisfied that she could support the child. But in practice, little changed. Following World War I, the hospital came under pressure to allow parents to reunite with their children. In 1921 the bishop who headed the Church of England diocese in Canterbury gave a sermon acknowledging the importance of the Foundling Hospital in saving the lives of abandoned children, but stated that his belief was so strong "in the parent being the natural and proper teacher about God and Jesus Christ that [he] would never remove from touch with its mother any illegitimate child."[44] No matter how well a child might be cared for, he argued, "the little person will want the sense of someone lovingly interested in its welfare."[45] The same year, Dr. Bruce Low of the Ministry of Health was more forthright, questioning whether the hospital's methods for raising children were outdated entirely. The children at the hospital have "an institutional appearance and appear dull witted," he noted. They appear to "behave mechanically and the natural buoyancy of spirits of a young child seem to be totally absent."[46] The governors dug in their heels, vigorously disputing Dr. Low's account of the foundling experience—still convinced that the care provided by the hospital was superior to that which the parent of an illegitimate child could give.

That Lena's request arose during different circumstances may have provided her some hope that the committee might accede to her request. When she penned her plea to the Foundling Hospital eighteen years after the bishop's opinionated sermon, Europe was on the brink of war with Germany, Hitler's army was amassing, and the predictions of casualties were dire. The government had already begun stockpiling coffins. Its primary concern was safeguarding Great Britain's citizens, particularly its children, and a plan to protect them was set in motion. Named Operation Pied Piper, it was to become the largest and most concentrated mass movement of people in the nation's history. The principle was simple: move children out and away from cities that were likely to become targets of German air strikes and into the countryside.

And so, on August 31, 1939, the order was issued: "Evacuate forthwith."

The evacuation began the following morning. Over the next three days, approximately five hundred thousand children were sent to the countryside, with thousands shipped to Canada, the United States, and Australia. Over the course of the war, millions (mostly children) would be evacuated from Britain's cities.

For such a massive undertaking to succeed, the government needed the cooperation of its citizens. Marketing campaigns created by the Ministry of Health targeted mothers nervous about sending their children away. With slogans encouraging them to relinquish their children—"Mothers send them out of London," "Children are safer in the Country"—the government sent a clear message that cities, particularly London, were deadly places for a child to be.

In addition to encouraging city-dwelling mothers to give up their children, the British government needed families in the countryside to house the millions who would soon flee the cities. One area considered particularly ideal was Shropshire, the county where Lena Weston happened to live. Located near the Welsh border, the rural area continues to be one of England's most sparsely populated, with a prewar census showing only 244,000 residents in an area spanning nearly 900,000 acres. In contrast, London, which was less than half the size, housed a population of more than eight million residents at the time. Thinly populated farmlands were of little interest to the Germans as potential targets, and by the end of September 1939, the county of Shropshire had already taken in thousands of evacuees. Before the evacuation, local billeting officers interviewed and selected hosts who were often less than willing, requiring that they take in evacuees or face a fine. On evacuation days, children arriving at the train station would be lined up against a wall or on the stage at the village hall, and hosts were allowed to pick which children they would like to take in.

Many ended up on farms, like the one where Lena Weston lived. Scores of children arrived in her village, and seeing them would more than likely have stirred her yearnings to have her daughter back, to keep her safe and out of harm's way. While the Foundling Hospital was now on the outskirts of London, having moved thirty miles north to Berkhamsted a few years earlier, it would remain in the crosshairs of German pilots whose planes could reach speeds of several hundred miles per hour.

Most of the children evacuated to the countryside as part of Operation Pied Piper were separated from their parents. Their fathers were busy fighting the war, while their mothers stayed behind in the cities to eke out a living. But if Lena's request were to be granted, there would be no painful separation—only what would hopefully be a welcome reunion.

Lena's sought-after reunion would not be granted. On September 6, 1939, less than a week after thousands of children had been evacuated from cities, and just days after Great Britain declared war on Germany, she received her response:

Dear Madam,

I received your letter of the 2nd instant and am pleased to inform you that the little girl is quite well.

You may rest assured that all possible precautions have been taken to ensure her safety at the Schools in the event of air raids and you need have no anxiety as to her care.

Yours faithfully,
Secretary

A war would be fought in the skies above London, the likes of which the world had never seen. And as the battles raged, Lena would have for reassurance only the words of a nameless, faceless man that her little girl would be "quite well."

IN A MATTER of months, most of western Europe had fallen to the Germans. Hitler's forces invaded Denmark and Norway in April 1940, and Denmark surrendered in a matter of hours. The following month Germany launched invasions of Belgium, the Netherlands, Luxembourg, and France. Within a few weeks all but France had surrendered, and by the end of June, it too had collapsed.

With much of Europe under his control, Hitler set his sights on Great Britain. Prime Minister Winston Churchill knew what was coming, and tried to prepare an anxious nation:

> I expect that the Battle of Britain is about to begin. Upon this battle depends the survival of Christian civilization. Upon it depends our own British life, and the long continuity of our institutions and our Empire. The whole fury and might of the enemy must very soon be turned on us. Hitler knows that he will have to break us in this Island or lose the war. If we can stand up to him, all Europe may be free and the life of the world may move forward into broad, sunlit uplands. But if we fail, then the whole world, including the United States, including all that we have known and cared for, will sink into the abyss of a new Dark Age made more sinister, and perhaps more protracted, by the lights of perverted science. Let us therefore brace ourselves to our duties, and so bear ourselves that, if the British Empire and its Commonwealth last for a thousand years, men will still say, "This was their finest hour."[47]

Dorothy would never hear these powerful words that soothed a frightened nation as it prepared for war. The children at the Foundling Hospital were not given access to newspapers or radio broadcasts, and the staff never directly discussed the impending war with them. The children knew so little that, well after the war had begun, Dorothy recalled a member of the staff bursting into her classroom shouting, "They've sunk the *Bismarck*! They've sunk the *Bismarck*!" The *Bismarck* was the Nazi's "unsinkable" flagship, and a symbol of Hitler's intention to dominate Allied convoys in the English Channel and starve Britain into submission. Its sinking on May 27, 1941, was a great victory for Allied forces, and the news likely caused cheers to erupt throughout England. The girls at the Foundling Hospital, however, stared at the teacher blankly, having never heard of such a ship.

Nor were the foundlings likely aware that as the sun rose over England a year earlier, on July 10, 1940, German bombers had struck a shipping convoy in the English Channel, while more had attacked dockyards in South Wales. The Battle of Britain had begun. From July through September, the Luftwaffe bombed convoys, ports, factories, and airfields. Unsatisfied with the results, on September 7, 1940, the Germans changed their tactics, setting a new goal—demoralizing the British people through an intensive and relentless bombing campaign on its major cities. The Blitz (named after the German word for lightning) would leave more than forty-three thousand dead, and tens of thousands more injured.

Well before the first German plane flew into British airspace, preparations for the inevitable attack had begun: blackouts were underway, thirty-eight million gas masks distributed, four hundred million sandbags stacked around London's buildings. Landmarks that could draw large numbers of citizens were closed and Londoners were barred from using the city's famous underground.

The London Zoo euthanized its venomous snakes and destroyed its fish as tanks were emptied to conserve resources. Citizens prepared themselves by installing corrugated metal shelters that could be dug into a garden and covered with dirt, or, for those without a yard, a cage-like structure that could double as a dining table.

The raids were continuous and relentless, with incessant bombing lasting through the night. At one point, London was blitzed continuously for fifty-seven nights. The psychological damage of the raids was well documented—heightened anxiety, with coping behaviors including drinking, excessive bravado masking an underlying fear, even reports of an increased sex drive in women. Although it was rare that anyone sought professional help, priority being given to those with physical injuries, doctors reported increases in stress-related ailments such as peptic ulcers.

The Ministry of Health was particularly concerned about the psychological impacts on children—going so far as to make psychiatrists and child guidance experts available. The magazine *Housewife* provided advice on how to keep children safe and comforted during air raids. Ensuring that children received a good night's sleep was considered essential, and the magazine cautioned that it was "unwise to leave children in the bedroom of a bungalow or upper story of a small house when better shelter is available"[48]; instead, in areas where continuous raids were expected, shelters should be used as permanent sleeping quarters for any children. A child could not be stable, the article warned, if he was repeatedly woken at night; furthermore, there should always be an adult present, as "even sleeping children must never be left alone during a raid. . . . An extra loud explosion might wake them and they will find much comfort in a sleepy, indifferent murmur from a trusted 'grown up' saying that it is only a fight and that the English are winning."[49]

Anna Freud, the daughter of the psychoanalyst Sigmund Freud (who had died from cancer in Hampstead just weeks after the outbreak of the war), agreed that special care should be taken to protect children from the psychological impacts of air raids. Having fled Vienna with her family following the Nazi invasion in 1938, she remained in London during the Blitz, helping to set up housing for children who had not been evacuated or could not stay with their families. The children did not suffer too greatly, she concluded, provided that they were not separated from their mothers—and if they were, that the separation not be too abrupt. Ideally the children would be "in the care of their mothers or a familiar mother-substitute."[50] In looking after children separated from their parents, she kept siblings together, and organized local air raid patrol workers and firemen to take on the roles of mothers and fathers.

Anna Freud's conclusions were reinforced by the leading psychology experts of the time—Edward Glover, Melitta Schmideberg, John Bowlby, and Donald Winnicott. The air raids, while terrifying, weren't as psychologically damaging as separation from parental care.

At the Foundling Hospital, where the children had already been damaged by such a separation, there were no plans for evacuation. Blackout curtains adorned the windows, and storerooms under the kitchen were transformed into makeshift shelters. Each night, air raid wardens in olive-green uniforms and brimmed metal hats would make the rounds. Checking to make sure that no lights could be seen from the skies above, they would wander the grounds, reminding the children of their duty to keep the curtains closed. Dorothy, like many of the foundling girls, lived in fear that one of the children would be careless and cause a German plane to see some sliver of light, blasting them all into smithereens before they could be evacuated to the shelters below.

As the girls lay in bed in their dormitories on the second floor, they would hear the distant hum of planes, the sounds of air raid sirens wailing, the thumping of bombs growing louder as they moved closer—but no one was allowed to move, not until the school's alarm bell went off. The wait might be a few minutes, but to Dorothy it felt like an eternity. When the alarm finally rang, each girl would put on her cloak, pick up her gas mask and sling it over her shoulder, grab a blanket and pillow, put on her shoes, and line up in crocodile formation as if she were going to class, following the hospital's rigid evacuation protocol. Once in formation, the girls would be led by blue light (less visible to the enemy) down the staircase to the lavatories, where each would take turns using the toilets. Only when everyone was done would they proceed, walking, never running, to the air raid shelter. Escorted silently through the expansive corridors past the cloakrooms, Miss Wright's study, the dining rooms, and the kitchen, they would end their journey in the basement, where they would lie down on mattresses already set on the floor, alongside the host of cockroaches and beetles undeterred by the pink insecticide powder spread around the edges of the room.

There would be little sleep during the long nights, the mournful sound of the air raid sirens sending shivers down Dorothy's spine, filling her with fear of what would happen next. Of course, Dorothy couldn't see the German planes, waves of them, often described as bees buzzing in fury, or as clouds of insects that would blanket the skies, but she could feel their vibrations shaking the building. She soon learned to tell the difference between the chugging sounds of the German planes and the quieter whir of Allied planes. Each night she would hold her breath as the vibrations grew stronger, praying that her dormitory would not be hit. The sound of the bombs could be deafening, the sheer force of a single explosion creating shock waves with a velocity six hundred times that of a hurricane. One night there was a direct hit on the town's water tower, also knocking out the main water line. The Red Cross supplied the school with boiled water for several days until it was repaired. Dorothy remembered another nearby scare:

> One night a bomb was dropped that to this day, the tremendous thud it made remains the loudest sound I have ever heard. We were in the shelter and I was sure that the school had been hit, but it turned out that the bomb had fallen just across a lane from the school. I have no doubt that our school was the target, large and prominent as our school grounds were.

Eight-year-old Dorothy was justified in her fear, as was Lena; schools were particularly vulnerable to destruction, providing a large target for the Germans flying overhead. Once hit, a school was vulnerable to fire, its wood floors and walls serving as kindling, with large assembly halls providing a draft to fan the flames. One of Britain's worst civilian wartime tragedies took place when a school on the outskirts of London took a direct hit and the building collapsed, the rubble falling into the basement and killing close to six hundred people sheltered there.

Another night, no bombs fell, but the school was shaken, the glass in windows along the boys' side of the school shattered. The children emerged the next day to find that a German plane had been shot down on the playing field. There was no sign of a pilot, and the children were told nothing except to stay away, which, of course, they did not. They could see the plane from the playroom window, and when their keepers weren't looking, the girls would take turns dashing out a side door to look for small pieces of shrapnel for souvenirs. When it was Dorothy's turn, the only thing she could find was a piece of glass. She stashed it in one of her gym shoes (plimsolls, as they called them) in her locker. Later, forgetting it was there, she cut her foot on it and wound up in the infirmary.

The raids were constant, planes passing overhead and bombs exploding nightly. When the bombing subsided, the children would be marched back to the dormitories, only to return if another raid occurred. No matter how frequent the raids, the dormitory supervisors would line the children up to use the lavatory each time.

As the battle over Britain's skies intensified, the children and staff began to remain in the shelter throughout the night. Sleep didn't come easily for anyone, and in an uncharacteristic departure from the rules that prohibited entry into the dormitories during the day, children were allowed to take daytime naps.

One of the few stories my mother told me as a child maps back to this wartime period. I'd come down with chicken pox, and we were on the way home from the doctor, stopping at a neighborhood store for a Popsicle, our sick-day routine. As we passed the corner where the air raid siren had malfunctioned several months before, she said, "I was sick once, like you, when I was a little girl."

My mother rarely spoke of her childhood, and although I was still young, I knew that I should listen intently. She had been away, she told me, at a boarding school of sorts. An isolated anecdote with no context, it was a rare glimpse of my mother's upbringing, a brief retrospection that would happen from time to time and only added to the mystery of her past.

"It was during the war, the war against the Germans. If you were sick, you had to stay in the infirmary away from everyone else. When the sirens went off, everyone went to the shelter—except me. They left me there, in the infirmary, all alone."

Her eyes didn't stray from the road as she told me her story, and we drove the rest of the way home in silence.

As a young girl, I hadn't understood the full meaning of her words, but as I pored over the pages of my mother's manuscript and studied the hospital's wartime history, they came back to me with a vivid intensity. I recalled the history of medical treatment during the early years of the Foundling Hospital, how policies were put in place to isolate sick children no matter the cost. I'd visited the site of the former infirmary at Berkhamsted, walked the long hallways, past classrooms and dormitories, down some stairs to the kitchen just above the area where bomb shelters were once located. If something had happened during my mother's stay at the infirmary, no one would have been able to help her. Had she screamed, her voice would have echoed down empty hallways with no one to hear.

The secretary had told Lena that "all possible precautions" would be taken to protect Dorothy, and that she "need have no anxiety as to her care." But they were wrong. They didn't take care of her or keep her safe.

My mother would have nightmares decades later, when an air raid siren piercing through the night transported her back to a terrifying time in her life.

I had nightmares of my own to contend with.

When I was a child, they were always the same—a feeling of falling, my body sinking into the bed, my head heavy on the pillow. Then the bottom would give way, and I would careen into a deep abyss. Over the years, the falling sensation was replaced with something more sinister. I would see only black, a consuming darkness. I would scream, but no one could hear me.

I had always assumed that the screaming sensation was only

in my mind, but after Patrick and I married, I found out otherwise. "Sweetie, you're having a nightmare," Patrick would say, shaking me gently. I had been crying out, but through closed lips. He described the sounds I made as something straight from a horror film, bloodcurdling screams squeezed through a mouth that had been stapled shut.

In the course of my research into my mother's past, I came across an article in a psychiatry journal about a man whose Holocaust nightmares would wake him screaming in the night. But the thing was, *he had never been in the Holocaust*. Instead, he was the child of a Holocaust survivor. I was fascinated by the phenomenon, clinically known as the "epigenetic transmission of trauma." The article reported research suggesting that trauma might create a chemical coating on a person's chromosomes, a biological memory that could be passed down to the next generation. The theory is controversial, and the evidence circumstantial at best. But the same researcher had another theory, an interpretation that resonated with me—Holocaust survivors project trauma-related feelings and anxieties, and the child becomes a "reservoir" for the repressed grief of the older generation.

Either way, whether the transmission of trauma had occurred via an altered chromosome or within my troubled childhood home, my readings on the subject reinforced my early feelings that what ailed our family wasn't so easily described. Whatever lurked in the shadows, not conveniently identified like a bruise or an open wound, was real enough to cause my horror-movie screams.

Something else came to mind as I pondered the abuse my mother suffered, a sentence from her manuscript:

It was in my third year that the canes and leather straps came out and the angry words and detentions began, massively

177

augmented by the reign of terror of the gym mistress, Miss Woodward.

I hadn't put the pieces together before this moment.

While the treatment Dorothy received throughout her childhood was cruel, the true terror she experienced had not started until her third year at the Foundling Hospital. According to my timeline, that would have been after the war had begun—after Lena Weston asked for her daughter back.

When Lena wrote that letter, my mother had not yet been beaten so viciously that the bruises lingered for weeks. She hadn't been locked in dark closets, left alone for hours, or thrown into a pool and savagely shoved underwater with a stick. She hadn't been left in a deserted infirmary during the Blitz, one of the worst bombing campaigns the world had ever seen. Year after year, they'd told Lena that her little girl was "quite well." But she wasn't. And the little girl who was in fact far from safe, or fine, or loved, or cared for grew up to be my mother.

Perhaps there might still have been time for Dorothy at that critical juncture when Lena Weston sent her pleading letters. The damage of early childhood separation might have been irreparable, but I wondered whether the course of our shared destiny would have been altered if the pleas in those letters hadn't fallen on deaf ears. I remembered an article I'd come across during my research on Operation Pied Piper, about a boy who had been evacuated to the countryside during the war—"Happy Memories of a Shropshire Wartime Evacuee." When he was five years old, the boy had left the city for a farm outside Shrewsbury, just a few miles from Lena's farm. He'd been enrolled in the local school and spent his free time on the farm, collecting eggs or milking cows. For him, in the bucolic setting of Shropshire, far from the relentless bombing raids that terrorized London, the war was distant, something he only rarely heard about on the battery-powered radio.

What if they had given Lena her daughter back? Like that boy, Dorothy could have traveled to Shropshire, escaped the horrors of war and of the Foundling Hospital, and experienced the care of a loving mother.

Of course, that's not what happened. But fate sometimes offers surprises, and the war would bring Dorothy hope in the most unexpected of ways—in the smiles and generosity of strangers.

13

SUSTENANCE

Like the cross-section of an old oak tree, my childhood can be measured by the food my mother prepared. The early years betrayed no hint of what was to come, and my stomach was regularly filled with a generous array of British fare—thick slices of toast slathered with marmalade for breakfast, its tartness making my mouth pucker; or bangers, crispy brown from sizzling in a cast iron pan, served with a soft-boiled egg in a cup, still in its shell and perched on an ornately carved stand. "Gentle now, just a *tap tap tap*," my mother would remind me as I carefully removed the top of the egg to reveal the creamy yolk inside. Lunch was simple but nutritious: soups or canned sardines served with mayonnaise on bread, my mouth watering at the saltiness of the fish. Dinner was savory and substantial, thinly sliced steaks with sautéed onions or hearty stews with chunks of tender beef that melted in my mouth.

I was around six or seven when the British cuisine disappeared from our table, replaced by American foods made entirely from scratch. Baked macaroni and cheese, browned on top with soft, moist pasta underneath; scalloped potatoes dripping with butter; turkey with chunky cranberry sauce and herbed stuffing. To this day, these are the foods that I turn to for comfort when I'm feeling low.

Then, in the 1970s, my mother's views on food began to change. The health food craze was just gaining momentum, and my mother, as always, was ahead of the curve. Eggs and sausages were replaced with dry, tasteless puffed wheat served with unpasteurized milk. I detested the milk, the cream layer on top so thick it formed clumps over my cereal. Each day my mother now handed me a seaweed pill so large that it had to be broken in two, the sharp ends where the pill had been severed scratching my throat as I gulped it down. Gone too was anything that made food palatable—salt, sugar, spices, butter—her once aromatic cooking replaced by bland and flavorless fare.

I must have complained, perhaps refused to eat. In response, my mother instituted "Junk Food Day." Once a year, my father would take me and my sister to the grocery store, and each of us would be allowed to pick out any six items that we wanted. I would wander the aisles, looking for anything that would satiate my desire for sweetness and flavor: Cap'n Crunch cereal, pink-and-white frosted animal cookies, a tub of vanilla ice cream with nuts and swirls of chocolate. It was my favorite day of the year. Back home, I would eat it up greedily until my trove was gone. I was never asked to share, although I had learned at an early age that if you left sweets unattended, they would soon be gone, the wrappers in my mother's bedroom trash bin the only proof of their existence.

Her health food kick continued through my high school years, until it was replaced by a phase that came and went without explanation. I only discovered it when I came home from college for an unexpected weekend visit and, looking for a snack, found the gleaming white refrigerator empty except for a sturdy cobalt-blue enameled Dutch pot. My mouth instantly began to water as I recognized the stew pot that used to sit for hours on a burner, the low flames tenderizing beef, infusing carrots and potatoes with flavor. I opened it, expecting to see thick brown gravy and instead finding only pale gray globs of cold oatmeal. Later, my father admitted that the thick gruel was all my mother would eat for breakfast, lunch, and dinner.

Her crazes became more extreme over time, food becoming a salve for whatever ailed her, her newfound fervor akin to religiosity. The big blue pot filled with porridge was joined by a giant juicer the width of our kitchen counter with the look of an arcane medical contraption. Eventually she upped the ante, paying thousands of dollars to attend a "fasting institute" in Oregon in order to cure an inner-ear infection and cleanse her body of toxins. Fasting became a regular part of her regimen, and she would sometimes spend more than a week at a time without food, becoming so feeble she could barely speak.

Then, after years of jumping from diet to diet, she settled on the most harmful of them all, an extreme set of food beliefs she followed until shortly before her death—vegan raw foodism. This "living food" diet dated back to the 1800s, and was based on a belief that cooking made food toxic and, conversely, raw food staved off illness. Following its rigid doctrine, my mother refused to eat animal products, or any foods that had been processed or cooked. It sounds healthy enough—eating fruits and vegetables supplemented with a few nuts. But the danger of the diet is not what *is* consumed, but what is *not*. Following the dietary strictures, my mother refused to eat legumes, dairy, eggs, fish, or tofu, all of which contain proteins or other essential nutrients: calcium, vitamin B_{12}, and more. The press published reports warning of the dangers of extreme raw foodism, but my mother only became more dogmatic, so much so that near the end of her life, when our family was finally able to convince her to see a doctor, she was diagnosed with malnutrition.

My mother's obsession was certainly fueled by food crazes common in California, and could perhaps be explained away as an idiosyncratic behavior that was a sign of the times. Maybe she also used food as a form of control, the way I dug a fingernail into the palm of my hand to distract myself when my troubles consumed me. But as I delved into the history of the Foundling Hospital, I wondered if, just as a generous serving of macaroni and cheese had a comforting association with early childhood for me, my mother had found solace in an aching belly, the sharp pangs of hunger providing her with some familiar comfort I would never understand.

AS THE FOUNDLING Hospital got under way in the mid-1700s, eminent physicians were developing a diet meant to produce strong and healthy children who could withstand a life of service. Sir Hans Sloane, one of the doctors who oversaw care of the foundlings, believed that two out of three infants would die if they were not breastfed, and that those who survived might suffer from gripes (colic), green stools, or an irritated gut. Another one of the hospital's physicians agreed, rejecting practices of the day such as feeding an infant butter, sugar, or a "little roast Pig."[51] Although one of the governors lodged concerns that the nurses' "mental and bodily maladies would be communicated to their sucklings,"[52] in the end the advocates of breastfeeding prevailed. An elaborate system for hiring and overseeing wet nurses was instituted. If an infant would not suckle, Sir Sloane recommended that the infants be given breast milk by spoon.

The physicians also suggested that the children consume broths made of the "Flesh of full grown Animals, because their Juices are more elaborate"; that food not be sweetened as was the custom "with Sugar, Spice and sometimes a Drop of Wine"; and that foundlings be given good bread and cow's milk, but never boiled, as it makes it "thicker, heavier, and less fit to mix and assimilate with the Blood."[53] While the advice was wide-ranging, the central philosophy of providing nourishment to foundlings was summed up by Dr. Cadogan: a foundling "bred in a very plain, simple Manner . . . will therefore infallibly have the more Health, Beauty, Strength, and Spirits."[54] The doctor believed every child was born healthy and strong, but that such an advantage was lost due to nurses, aunts, and grandmothers, who had "been in the wrong, [and done] Mischief to Children . . . cramming them with Cakes, Sweetmeats, etc. till they foul their Blood, cloak their Vessels, pall the Appetite, and ruin every Faculty of their Bodies; as by cockering and indulging them, to the utter Perversion of their naturally good temper, till they become quite froward and indocile."[55]

And so the Foundling Hospital served small and plain meals. Breakfast might be bread and butter, gruel, or milk porridge. Dinner (the term used for lunch) would be rice pudding, or mutton and greens. The day would end with a light supper of broth, or just some bread and cheese. While foundlings following this diet in the eighteenth century were likely to have been malnourished by modern standards, they were well fed compared to other poor children of the time.

In the 1930s, the Foundling Hospital diet remained repetitive and bland. Dinners during my mother's time there might have consisted of mutton with white beans or steamed or boiled fish, its pungent odor filling the dining hall where the foundlings ate in silence. The food was largely unappetizing—boiled cabbage, lumpy rice, meat encased in yellow fat and gristle, and white margarine more useful for slathering on tiny hands to lessen the sting of a cane than for food. While early records of hospital practices make no mention of tea, likely due to Governor Hanway's strong objections to its consumption, by the twentieth century afternoon tea was commonplace, though simple, served with bread and treacle (molasses) or jam.

The staff dined on more appetizing fare: bacon, roasted meat, coffee, butter, and occasionally rich desserts. The adults' food was also more plentiful, and the children would take any opportunity to steal leftovers from uncleared trays left in a hallway. Always hungry, Dorothy clamored to be chosen when the kitchen requested volunteers to help shell peas or chop vegetables, popping a fair share in her mouth when the cooks weren't looking. Sometimes the kitchen would even reward volunteers with a dessert from the tastier menus offered in the staff dining room.

Conditions for the foundlings only worsened during World War II, as they did for the rest of Britain's citizens. Before the start of war, England had produced less than a third of its food and raw materials, importing millions of tons of essential goods each year. Knowing this, the Germans used air and submarine attacks to cut off the transport of food and other supplies; in response, Britain reestablished the Ministry of Food, an agency it had dissolved shortly after the end of World War I. Under the ministry, food supplies were stockpiled and moved away from potential bombing sites, and rationing was instituted to stretch the country's food supply in the event of war.

Civilians received tickets for rationed items such as meat, tea, butter, eggs, margarine, and cheese, to name a few. The amounts allowed in a week varied, adjusted by the Ministry of Food depending on projections of availability. One citizen's typical weekly ration might include an egg, an ounce or two of cheese, a few ounces of butter, margarine, and cooking fat, three pints of milk, four ounces of bacon or ham, eight ounces of sugar, and two ounces of tea, along with some soap, preserves, and sweets. Meat might be rationed by cost, the 1940 weekly allowance limited to a shilling and two pence.

While fears of bombing raids were never far from citizens' minds, Lord Woolton, who ran the Ministry of Food, quipped that egg rationing produced more emotion than the Blitz. Recipes abounded for dishes typically made with hard-to-get items— vinegar substituted for eggs, paraffin for cooking fat. Even the London Zoo, which had to care for the animals that remained in their care during the war, was forced to be creative, breeding their own mealworms to feed birds and animals and, when things got desperate, broadcasting a plea for acorns on the radio. Donations of acorns poured in at a rate of one ton per week, to be fed to the agoutis, squirrels, monkeys, and deer.

With supplies of most staples limited, the Ministry of Agriculture launched a massive campaign encouraging citizens to grow their own food. Soon private yards, school playgrounds, public parks, rooftops, and even the lawns outside of the Tower of London were being tilled and turned into the small farm plots heralded as "Victory Gardens." Following suit, the Foundling Hospital set up its crops on three acres adjacent to its playground, growing potatoes, leeks, and row upon row of carrots.

Carrots in particular were vigorously promoted, with jingles claiming that they could improve eyesight and safety during nighttime raids:

NIGHT SIGHT CAN MEAN LIFE OR DEATH—
EAT CARROTS AND LEAFY GREEN OR YELLOW VEGETABLES . . .
RICH IN VITAMIN "A," ESSENTIAL FOR NIGHT SIGHT.

CARROTS KEEP YOU HEALTHY AND
HELP YOU TO SEE IN THE BLACKOUT.

A CARROT A DAY KEEPS THE BLACKOUT AT BAY.

"DIG FOR VICTORY!" government posters declared. There were special efforts to entice children to eat the vegetables—carrots on sticks sold in lieu of the ice cream that had been banned by the government as an unnecessary luxury, and a cartoon featuring Doctor Carrot ("children's best friend"), his image appearing on recipes for carrot flan and carrot fudge. A particularly skilled British Royal Air Force bomber named John Cunningham fueled the fervor. During the German bombing raids of 1940, Cunningham, nicknamed "Cat's Eyes," racked up an impressive twenty kills, nineteen of them at night. Cunningham became a hero akin to a movie star, providing hope to a country beleaguered by war. How had he accomplished his seemingly miraculous feats? He ate an abundance of carrots, or so the nation was told. While it's true that a deficiency of beta-carotene can negatively affect eyesight, gorging on carrots will do nothing to enhance eyesight, night or day, nor will it help a pilot shoot down enemy planes from the sky. But behind the public story lauding the power of carrots, the British government was hiding a secret. Their scientists had developed a technology—on-board Airborne Interception (AI) radar—that allowed pilots to home in on German bombers with unprecedented accuracy, day or night. There is no evidence that the Germans fell for it, but the ruse is largely credited for propagating the enduring myth that carrots can help a person see better in the dark.

Dorothy didn't know the fanciful stories of how carrots may have protected her from enemy bombers. All she knew was that once the war started, she was hungrier than before. She was not alone. Her classmates, all longing to feel full, would hoard what little food they could scrounge, scraps from dinner hidden in their knickers, food stolen from food trays, or the precious "Sunday bun" served as a treat once a week, and on Miss Wright's birthday. They would stash the food under their pillows or in their lockers to avoid detection and, after a week or two of building their troves, would assemble well after dark on the chosen night to enjoy their magnificent feast. They greedily stuffed their mouths, not caring that the food was cold or the buns stale.

When their secret supplies were exhausted, they went in search of food elsewhere. The perfect target was just steps from the playground. The Victory Garden was strictly off-limits to foundlings, but that didn't stop Dorothy and her coconspirators from sneaking in unobserved through an unlocked gate and gorging on seemingly endless rows of carrots. They returned to their dormitory undetected, stomachs ready to explode. And explode they did. They hadn't been caught in the act, but the orange vomit splattered on the lavatory floor betrayed them soon enough.

Just as difficult as the scarcity of food was the foundlings' growing isolation. Many of the younger staff members, who were generally less cruel than those who had been worn down by decades of life at the hospital, were off serving in the war effort. While the hospital had never been a joyful place, the war years were particularly bleak. The only exposure to the outside world came on Sundays, when the girls were allowed to leave the compound for a walk, their standard uniform topped by brown felt hats emblazoned with the school emblem—a lamb with a sprig of thyme in its mouth. The emblem was a segment of the Foundling Hospital's crest, the full crest also depicting a young child lying naked and exposed below the lamb. The lamb was meant to symbolize innocence; the thyme, derived from the

Greek *thymus*, "courage," to represent strength. My mother saw something more sinister:

> What comes to mind is that the lamb seems rather appropri-
> ate. Weren't we Foundling girls penned-up sacrificial 'lambs,'
> raised and herded around like sheep, to be sacrificed to the
> (slaughter)houses of the rich?

Setting out in their brown felt hats, the foundlings would pass through the large iron gates that opened out onto Chesham Road. To the right was the town of Berkhamsted, but they rarely turned in that direction and, when they did, were never allowed to go inside shops or stop to peer into any of the shop windows. Mostly, they headed toward the sparsely populated countryside and the so-called Grumpy Man Woods, thick with brambles, where the girls were allowed to pick blueberries later used by the kitchen staff to make desserts.

What a sight they must have been, all those virtually indis-tinguishable girls marching silently in crocodile formation along a country road. Yet few people ever did see them—that is, until 1942, when everything changed.

HOW EXCITED AND frightened the girls would have felt the first time they encountered a group of soldiers mill-ing about on the side of the road, or saw a convoy material-ize out of nowhere, the gray- or olive-colored military vehicles trundling by one after the other. The vehicles were filled with Americans—but not the kind the children might have seen be-fore. Dorothy had seen and heard cartoon versions of Americans when the hospital played *Snow White and the Seven Dwarfs* for the foundlings in the school's auditorium. But these were the first flesh-and-blood Americans she had ever encountered. She was fascinated by their casualness, how they leaned against doorways and lampposts and talked louder and laughed more often than the English soldiers. Sometimes they would smile and call out to the girls as they went by, and Dorothy would giggle and try to catch a word or phrase to practice later. Adult smiles, friendly words, and approving looks were nonexistent in the foundlings' lives, and the brief encounters made an impression.

On one of the children's prescribed walks, an American serviceman even looked right at Dorothy and called out, "Hi, Freckles!" Though she hadn't realized that her freckles were so obvious, she was pleased to have been singled out. Dorothy and the other girls took to chanting out greetings and pleas for treats to the convoys rolling by. *Throw me some gum, chum!* In response the soldiers would fling sticks of American gum into the air to the arms outstretched below.

My mother's account of catching gum in midair as convoys drove by was already familiar to me, one of those isolated stories she had shared with me during my childhood. It was a scene she had described more than once, although without any hint of the deep secrets that surrounded her formative years. It was common for American soldiers to hand out the gum that was included in their meal rations, I learned. Always looking to make new friends, the Americans used the gum to forge bonds with the locals. But my mother clearly felt singled out by the gesture, seen as special somehow. I remember her eyes sparkling and her mouth curving into a smile as she recounted the small kindness. It was only in her written account that I learned that, if caught chewing a piece of contraband gum, Dorothy and her fellow foundlings would have encountered reprimands for indulging in the "disgusting American habit." The consequences were not much different in my childhood home, where gum was never to be found. On the rare occasions that a friend would give me a piece and I happened to chew it in front of my mother, she would be quick to make her displeasure known: "You look like a cow chewing its cud," she'd say, wrinkling up her face in disgust.

Dorothy didn't know why the Americans were in England, that they had come in 1942 to prepare for the Allied invasion. Nor was she aware that Germany had conquered most of Europe, or that the United States had entered the war after Japan attacked Pearl Harbor. She knew almost nothing about Americans, in fact, and the same could be said for the American GIs when it came to the Brits. The US War Department had attempted to school the more than two million servicemen passing through on the topic of cultural integration with a pamphlet titled *Instructions for American Servicemen in Britain*, some of it devoted to morale-boosting propaganda: "YOU are going to Great Britain as part of an Allied offensive—to meet Hitler and beat him on his own ground."[56] The publication was mainly focused on the practical considerations that would arise for servicemen in foreign lands, such as language barriers (a truck is a "lorry"), and advice on how to get along with the locals. One section cautioned Americans not to bring up the American Revolution. Another informed them that the reserved style of the British was not an indication of unfriendliness: "So if Britons sit in trains or busses without striking up a conversation with you, it doesn't mean they are being haughty and unfriendly."[57] Yet another warned against showing off, urging its readers to remember that, while the British might not know how to make a decent cup of coffee, "you don't know how to make a good cup of tea. It's an even swap."[58]

The Americans Dorothy encountered were stationed at the US Air Force base at Bovingdon Airfield, just a few miles southeast of Berkhamsted. Once a British Royal Air Force base, the airfield had been turned over to the Americans for use as an operational training base. Soon the base developed a level of fame, housing General Eisenhower's personal B-17 bomber and even hosting the occasional celebrity. Clark Cable came to visit, and so did Jimmy Stewart, William Holden, Eleanor Roosevelt, Bob Hope, and Glenn Miller. In September 1944 Bovingdon became the base for the European Air Transport Service, and thousands of Americans spent their last few hours on British soil at the Bovingdon air terminal before returning to the States.

For Dorothy, even before the Allied victory, the troops' presence was a bright spot in a long war, and that became particularly true on the day that Miss Wright made an extraordinary announcement during the daily assembly. An invitation had been received from the American officers at Bovingdon Airfield: twelve girls would attend the Christmas party at the base.

The girls were out of their minds with excitement. But Dorothy experienced a different emotion:

> Immediately the pain of exclusion and rejection engulfed me.
> I knew there wasn't a chance that I would be among those
> chosen to attend, naughty as I was and just an average student
> besides. . . . It was completely unimaginable that I would be
> selected.

To her astonishment, however, she heard her name called out. For a moment she saw her captor in a new light, momentarily forgetting the power of Miss Wright's belt or the terrors of an unlit storeroom, and for the first time thinking that there might be goodness under her forbidding exterior.

On the evening of the party, the chosen twelve assembled in the entry hall with its tall windows, large double entry doors, and polished oak parquet floors, waiting excitedly for their hosts.

Soon four military cars arrived to pick up the girls—for most of them, their first ride in a motor car of any kind.

As the convoy glided along in the velvety wartime evening, blackout curtains ensuring total darkness, no one in Dorothy's car uttered a sound. It was too magical for words, and anyway she was overcome with shyness in front of the uniformed American driver. The driver never spoke, which Dorothy assumed was customary when chauffeuring.

The motorcade pulled up to a set of open double doors that led to a large, brightly lit mess hall. The room was adorned with colorful decorations and a Christmas tree, and the girls were greeted by a jovial Santa Claus. An airman approached them, offering a tall, shiny cylindrical tin filled with hard candy. Dorothy reached in at his urging, gingerly taking only a single piece. The airman laughed, telling her to grab a handful, which she did. The candy would have been an extra-special treat, as wartime sweets were strictly rationed even for regular citizens.

The girls were divided up and seated at separate oblong tables, with about seven uniformed men to a table. For the next hour or so, a squad of American airman gave the girls their full attention, chatting them up and plying them with toys and food while cheerful music played in the background. Unaccustomed to conversing with adults or receiving any kindness at all, Dorothy found it almost impossible to talk. Every so often one of the airmen would say, "Are you *sure* you don't have a big sister?" and the small crowd of men gathered around her table would burst out laughing. When they tried to draw her out with questions, she would respond with barely audible monosyllables.

Soon a large plate of food was placed in front of Dorothy, food she had never even heard of—turkey, yams, cranberry sauce. But she was too embarrassed to eat much, being the center of attention for the first time in her life.

Dorothy didn't know that these men were training as bomber crews in preparation for the liberation of Europe, and that they would be instrumental in freeing those dying in concentration camps. She only knew that they were her heroes, and she later described the evening as a turning point:

> Never in my life had I been in the company of such friendly, happy, generous adults. . . . I'm sure there was no way they could possibly have known the enormity of the impact they were having on their subdued guest.

"It remains the greatest party of my life," she wrote. As I read my mother's words, I thought about her lavish parties, when workmen would come in and clear our expansive living room of its furniture, filling it instead with round tables soon set with white linen cloth, fine china, and crystal glassware. Then the caterers would arrive with an overabundance of food, generating leftovers that would last for days. As the host, my mother would be the center of attention, graciously moving from table to table, welcoming each guest personally. Perhaps she was trying to re-create what she felt that day, when the attention she received gave her a first glimmer of hope about what she might find outside of the walls of the Foundling Hospital.

Dorothy's luck was changing. The war had brought hunger and hardship, but also kindness from strangers, and an unexpected gesture from Miss Wright. She was soon to find relief from the cruelty of another staff member, the only one who had beaten her more brutally, terrified her more, than the hospital's headmistress—the ruthless Miss Woodward.

It happened on an ordinary day. Dorothy was outside in the yard with the other girls when she heard the news.

It must have been cold; the girls were wearing their cloaks.

William Hogarth, who had brought art to the halls of the Foundling Hospital, had designed the garments in the mid-1700s, and
the style had remained unchanged. They were made of the same
standard brown as the girls' daily uniforms, but their lining was
distinct—rich scarlet, a stark contrast to the dull colors of the
girls' usual wardrobe. I like to believe that Hogarth included the
splash of color as a small gift to the outcast children destined for
an achromatic life.

As the girls played outside, the news started to spread. One
girl ran over and whispered into another's ear, and on it went
until the play area was abuzz with the news.

Miss Woodward was dead.

There were questions, of course. *How did you find out?* The
staff was overheard talking about it in the hallways. *What did she
die of?* Something called leukemia.

> I'm not sure that any of us had known someone who had died
> and Miss Woodward's death became a subject of serious dis-
> cussion among the girls. Of course we wondered what hap-
> pened to people after death. I recall some discussion about
> fainting and dying and the difference between them and I felt
> reassured that there was no chance Miss Woodward would
> come back.

As more and more of the girls heard the news, and fears
of her returning from the dead were quelled, the energy and
excitement began to grow. Dorothy was not the only girl who
had been on the receiving end of Miss Woodward's ire—she
was the most hated teacher of them all. Spontaneously, a few
girls started to march defiantly around the yard. Someone else
yelled, "Hurray!" One little girl flung her cloak inside out over

her shoulders, revealing the deep scarlet lining. Then the next girl followed suit, and then another. They grew louder, more confident, and soon the girls were marching in a line, their scarlet cloaks ablaze in the winter sun, chanting:

Hurray! Hurray!
Miss Woodward died today!
Hurray! Hurray!
Miss Woodward died today!

The din grew louder as they circled the field in a scene reminiscent of *The Wizard of Oz*, a movie my mother and I watched together countless times—the Munchkins celebrating the miraculous demise of the Wicked Witch of the East. I imagined my Dorothy there, small but defiant, her arms swinging in unison with her classmates' as they marched through an empty field, overwrought with joy that Miss Woodward was undeniably and reliably *dead*.

It was one of the best days of Dorothy's life.

Hardly able to contain her delight, she left the other girls and ran into the building.

I remember racing up the staircase to my dormitory, though it was out of bounds during the day. I felt compelled to kneel at my bed and to thank God for taking Miss Woodward away. In cold dark nights I have several times knelt there asking Him to help me stop misbehaving and to stop Miss Woodward from punishing me. I could never have imagined that He would take her away forever, and I was not in the least sure that He had done so just for me, but I was glad that He had.

In the days that followed Miss Woodward's death, Dorothy felt a sense of freedom and relief, knowing she could walk along the corridors without fear of encountering Miss Woodward again. Her shrill voice in the gymnasium would become just a memory, and most important, Dorothy would never again be subjected to her brutality.

14

ESCAPE

When I opened my eyes, I could see the moonlight streaming in through the window near my bed. The pale light should have soothed me, but my heart was beating fast and hard, and my forehead felt unusually warm. Something bad was about to happen, but I didn't know what it was. Then I remembered. Soon I would be sent off to boarding school, as my sister had been a few years before. I should have welcomed the chance to leave—the arguments between my mother and me had intensified. But I was consumed with fear at the thought of leaving home, and I stumbled across the hallway into my mother's bedroom. My parents had slept in separate rooms for as long as I could remember—my mother cited my father's snoring as the cause. For a moment I stood quietly next to the bed. Sensing my presence, my mother opened her eyes.

"I don't want to go," I said simply. The look on her face gave me the answer I didn't want to hear.

I went to my father the next day, hoping he would help. I

should have known it was a fool's errand, but it would be years before I understood the essential part my father played in perpetuating our family's dysfunction.

There was a pecking order in our house, and my mother was always top hen. Nothing about that seemed unusual. When the two of us argued, or when my mother became agitated for any reason at all, my father would turn to me and say, "Let's be nice to your mother." It didn't matter who was right, or what had precipitated the argument. Deescalating the situation was the priority, and back then I accepted my father's role as peacemaker without question.

I adored my father, and while I kept my mother at arm's length, I always longed for more time with him. Once I had my own home, I often invited him to visit, stocking the fridge with his favorite foods, the ones he wasn't allowed to eat at home—pimento cheese and white bread with potato salad on the side. We would take the dogs for long walks and go out to dinner with my friends. In the evenings, we sat on the back porch watching the fireflies as I told him about the cases I was working on.

My mother put an end to the visits. I don't know what she said, but one day my father told me that he could no longer visit unless she came along. At first, my anger was directed in only one direction.

She ruins everything, I thought.

That perception began to evolve when even speaking to my father on the phone became a challenge. I would call home, crossing my fingers that he would answer, so I could talk to him without my mother on the line or in the background.

"I just want to talk to you," I would plead. "Don't put Mom on the phone."

Again and again I would beg, but it was as if the words had never even come out of my mouth. *Can't we talk for just a few minutes? Then she can get on the phone.* Without missing a beat, he would call out, "Mom, your daughter wants to talk to you! Get on the phone!"

If my mother answered before he did, I would simply hang up.

I pleaded with my father to stand up to her, for the sake of our relationship. In response, he came up with a sordid solution and set up a secret voice mail.

"Just leave me a message that you want to talk," he would instruct me. "I'll drive to the library and call you from there."

I called once but hung up, too ashamed that my father had asked me to do something so dishonest. I had trouble reconciling the father who wouldn't take a quarter from the phone company with the man who had asked me to lie to my mother.

For a while I just lived with the inconsistency, ignored it, but doubts tickled the back of my mind. He was a prominent attorney who represented powerful corporations. It was his job to stand firm. What would have happened if he simply spoke to me for a few minutes before turning the phone over to my mother? And why couldn't he simply say to his wife, "I am going to visit my daughter"?

The questions about my father's role in our family dynamics lurked in the back of my mind, their intensity growing, until the dam broke, and my anger came rushing out.

It happened in a crowded bookstore. I was living in Atlanta, and my parents were in town for a visit. They were staying at a nearby hotel, and my father and I had found some time alone under the guise of getting him a book for the plane ride home.

"Why do you always take her side?"

My voice was filled with anger, and too loud for a bookstore. I was distinctly aware of the looks from other customers, but I couldn't stop the feelings that had been stored deep inside from spilling out. I counted off each time he had taken her side, each time he had neglected our bond, and then broke down sobbing in the middle of the store, repeating over and over again:

Why didn't you protect me?

Why didn't you protect me?

My father grew quiet, and then he whispered, almost inaudibly: "Because I had it worse."

I have no way of knowing if my father was right on this score. Perhaps I should have felt more sympathy for his pain, but as his words sank in, I only felt anger rising in the back of my throat until it erupted in a scream.

"You could have left. But what about me? I was only a child!"

Growing up, I sensed that my parents' marriage was troubled, but the specifics of their interactions remain slightly out of focus, in the way that all childhood memories do. Raised voices would have only reached me as muddled vibrations through bedroom walls in any case, as I spent most of my time in my room, playing with my toys or reading books.

Many years later, I learned that my father had once tried to leave, going so far as to pack up the car and load my sister and me into the back seat. I was a toddler at the time, and don't remember what led my typically restrained father to take such a bold action. My mother must have done something terrible, but I only know what I've been told: that my father sat for a long time in the loaded car in the driveway before making a choice for his daughters. A broken mother was better than no mother at all.

As for his happiness . . .

In the vision of him I perpetually conjure up, my father is sitting alone in the living room, a newspaper folded neatly on a small table next to him. The room is quiet, and his shoulders are slightly hunched, his hands on his lap as he stares across the room at nothing in particular. Perhaps he was only resting, but I interpreted the silent hours spent in his well-worn leather chair as a symptom of a deep sorrow born of a joyless marriage. This is conjecture on my part, of course. By the time I was old enough to comprehend adult dynamics, I had moved thousands of miles away and had little insight into my parents' daily lives. I do know that when my mother was initially placed in a facility for the memory-impaired, she was housed in a small apartment that allowed my father to live with her. It wasn't long before a nurse found my mother hitting my father, and he was forced to move out. I will never know if it was the first time my mother had struck him, or simply the first time there had been a witness.

Sorting through some old files, years after my father's death, I found a handwritten letter he sent me in response to a long-lost letter of mine, its contents now forgotten. His note was uncharacteristically forthright on the subject of my mother, and painful to read:

> I was very pleased to get your letter today. I read it several times and have it firmly in my mind. Then I shredded it so that it would not get into the wrong hands.
>
> I am at the library so I can write uninterrupted.
>
> I am very sorry about the family situation. I love you very much and will always be there for you. But I need to explain something. I am 81 years old and want to live out the remainder of my life with as much harmony (at least less disharmony) as possible. I cannot turn my back on Mom.

He went on, pleading with me to make peace with my mother. I had been the lucky one, he claimed, not having endured the full force of her wrath.

"I am going to tell you again," he continued, "I love you and will always be there for you."

He would always be there for me. I felt such hope reading those words. I yearned for us to be close, cherishing each stolen moment we were able to spend together away from my mother's influence. His letter let me know that it was not to be:

> I wanted to come see you. But if I had told Mom that, she would have wanted to come also. So it was my consideration of you that caused me not to come.

His words stung, a firm reminder of the price that I paid for keeping my mother at a distance.

Looking back at our intractable family dynamic, petitioning my father not to send me away to boarding school was a peculiar stance for me to take. In a few years' time, I would be willing to go anywhere and do anything to be far away from my mother.

But seen from an adult perspective, the oddest thing about my request was the misguided hope that my father might actually help me. To do that, he would have had to do something he had never done—stand up to my mother on my behalf.

A few days later I was peering through the back window of a car as my father drove off, my mother standing at the end of our driveway, waving, tears streaming down her face.

I never questioned why he'd made me leave home against my wishes, not until years later, when I asked him point-blank why I had been sent away. His response was simple: "To get you away from your mother."

IN 1944, WHEN Dorothy was twelve, it was understood that in two years' time, she too would be sent away—leaving the Foundling Hospital in order to receive training in the domestic arts. Along with the other girls her age, she would be sent to Roselawn, part of the Foundling Hospital's Domestic

Economy School. There, she would receive rigorous training in "modern housewifery," learning to cook and clean. Though she would no longer be within the walls of the Foundling Hospital, she would continue to be isolated, forbidden to leave the premises except to attend church or run an errand. When her training was complete, she would be placed into a household as a maid or a cook.

For two centuries girls like Dorothy had been apprenticed as domestic servants while boys were sent away for a life at sea or became laborers. There were occasional exceptions—a few girls might be trained as milliners, and boys, who generally had more options, might be apprenticed as cheesemongers, butchers, or blacksmiths. The conditions of the apprenticeships were negotiated by the Foundling Hospital, the terms similar to indentured servitude; the masters agreed to provide training, food, shelter, and clothing in exchange for cheap labor. Foundlings could be apprenticed only to Protestants and could not be transferred to another master without the hospital's permission. And girls could not be apprenticed to unmarried men—nor to married men, unless their wives had seen the girl and expressed concurrence in the application. The age of apprenticeship varied over the years, sometimes dipping below ten but generally hovering around eleven or twelve, and ending between the ages of twenty-one and twenty-four.

Over the lifetime of the apprenticeship project, the hospital was continually under pressure to make its charges as productive as possible. In the 1760s, Parliament threatened to withhold all financial support. The need for a pool of able-bodied servants hadn't diminished, but the stigma against the poor, who were still thought of as lazy, immoral, and undeserving of public support, endured. The hospital continued to receive funding, in part due to the king's intervention, but over the following decade, various resolutions condemning the institution were passed on the grounds that the foundlings were unfit for useful labor. One resolution, which sought to reduce the costs of caring for the children, recommended that they be apprenticed by age seven or before, bringing swift opposition from the governors of the Foundling Hospital. A child apprenticed at such a young age would not be desirable, they countered, boys under the age of ten being unfit for service at sea, and girls likewise not yet able to perform tasks required by domestic service.

Once apprenticed, a foundling's fate would be forever set as a soldier or dressmaker, seafarer or chambermaid. Running away was risky. Many who tried were caught and returned to their masters, but not before they were punished. Those who eluded capture would encounter few prospects for earning a living without a legitimate apprenticeship. Most foundling apprentices would remain at the mercy of masters who were free to mete out physical punishment, provided it was used in moderation and left no lasting marks. There were few deterrents for a master who failed to abide by these loose standards, with historical accounts revealing ample claims of overwork, beatings, and sexual assault, and very few prosecutions. A wood screw manufacturer attempted to "debauch" a girl of eleven and had "debauch'd several other Apprentices," but no legal action was taken.[59] A prominent attorney forced a young girl's head between his knees while simultaneously beating her, a fact that was discovered only after she escaped to the Foundling Hospital, her body still "of livid colour, tho' 6 days had lapsed" since the incident.[60] The revelation did little to hinder the attorney's legal career, perhaps because it was not uncommon for girls to be sexually assaulted. The proof lay in the Foundling Hospital's own records, which contained pleas from young former charges begging to have infants born during these apprenticeships admitted to the Foundling Hospital. Even murder failed to move the dial for an abusive master. In 1771 a weaver named William Butterworth kicked his apprentice "on the Belly with his foot and broke her Belly that she could neither hold her stool or Urine," and then in the morning, "stood over her & made her eat it."[61] She eventually died as a result of her injuries. While Butterworth was charged and convicted with her murder, the judge reprieved him.

Despite the risks, and with pressure mounting to make useful citizens of foundlings more quickly, the governors allowed some to be apprenticed to the factories that had started to pop up across England. The placements would occur en masse, but historical records indicate that the governors did take their duty to protect foundlings from unscrupulous masters seriously, dispatching inspectors to check on the conditions. When the hospital apprenticed twenty-four girls to an embroiderer in Essex, Governor Hanway inspected the premises himself and found the children in good health and clean. But not all masters could be scrutinized, particularly those located far from London. The results could be catastrophic, as when charges of rape and beatings followed the apprenticeship of twenty-one girls to a screw maker in Stafford. Or worse, the case in 1765, when seventy-four children were apprenticed to a clothier in Yorkshire, and a year later twenty-two were dead.

By the time Dorothy arrived at the Foundling Hospital, young girls were no longer being sent off to factories to toil away under brutal masters. But Dorothy could still expect a hard life in domestic service. The thought of scrubbing floors and polishing silver for a wealthy family filled her with dread. As far as she knew, the life she'd glimpsed that night with the American GIs was beyond her grasp. She was trapped, her every movement monitored, with no chance for escape. A fence surrounded the school, and the exit was always guarded. Runaway foundlings existed in stories from the past—but usually they were apprentices who escaped once they'd left the institution, slipping off when a master had his back turned. Most were quickly found and returned, as the administrators knew to look first to the child's foster family after receiving a report of a runaway. Some would try again, but unless there were proven instances of abuse, the foundling would simply be returned to his or her master once again.

Dorothy had never considered running away. The chances of success were too slim; it had never been done. But on April 16, 1944, Miss Wright did something out of the ordinary. It was an insignificant decision, one whose consequences would change the course of Dorothy's life.

Once again, Dorothy had done something to displease Miss Wright. But Sunday services were about to begin, and Miss Wright had little time. Instead of securing Dorothy in the usual place, a closet or the storeroom near her office, she locked her in an upstairs washroom—a room with windows.

As Dorothy heard the key turn in the lock and listened to Miss Wright's footsteps fade down the corridor, she realized that she was alone, the building empty, with everyone across the courtyard in the chapel. It felt strange to be alone, but at least she wasn't in a windowless storeroom. Nor were German planes whirring overhead, as they had been the night she had spent in the infirmary. Dorothy stood with her back to the door, surveying the room, one wall lined with a row of white porcelain washbasins, two walls each containing a single sash window. She peered out the first window; she was on the second floor, and below the window was a sheer drop. The second window was more promising, looking out over a wide, flat roof. Dorothy inserted her small fingers between the sill and the window casing and yanked with all her strength. To her surprise, the window moved, opening an inch or two. With a bit more pushing, she was able to edge up the bottom half of the sash just enough to wiggle her small body through the gap.

Once on the roof, she tiptoed toward a row of four windows to the left, small bits of tar and gravel crunching under her shoes. To her relief, the first window she tried slid open. She hoisted herself through the window and dropped gently onto the parquet floors.

She hadn't thought about what to do once she escaped the washroom, and with nowhere else to go, she made her way to the playroom, where she waited for her classmates to return from services.

I found myself rooting for Dorothy, and equally surprised by her daring to take on the evil Miss Wright. I thought about how Miss Wright would react when she entered the room, what kind of punishment she might enact. Apparently, Dorothy was thinking the same:

> I . . . tried to imagine what Miss Wright's face would look like when she opened the washroom door to find I had escaped. But since Miss Wright was intolerant of even the slightest infraction, I was also highly apprehensive about what would happen to me. This was no small transgression but my most brazen act of disobedience ever, and I had to gasp at my own audacity. To my knowledge, no girl in the school had ever committed anything like it.

Dorothy feared the worst as her classmates filed in after church services had ended. A girl named Margaret took the seat next to her, and the two girls began to whisper, Dorothy keeping an eye on the door as she waited for Miss Wright to enter. Dorothy's mind raced as she imagined Miss Wright's anger at her impudence. She would be fiercely beaten, she thought. When Miss Wright finally did arrive, Dorothy froze, locking eyes with her grim-faced tormenter. She braced herself for the punishment that was certain to come, but after a brief disapproving gaze, Miss Wright continued on as if nothing had happened.

Dorothy was perplexed. There was no thrashing with a belt; she wasn't dragged from the room to be locked up in a windowless room, she wasn't told go to bed without food.

Nothing happened.

Bewildered, she returned to her conversation with Margaret, who was telling Dorothy about her foster parents, the Braithwaites. They lived near the river Thames in Chertsey, Margaret said, in a bungalow she called "Bob-Dor-Ree." Dorothy listened with envy as Margaret spoke of their kindness, and how happy her life had been, a stark contrast to her own early years with a belittling foster mother. Margaret had grown weary of being bullied by the staff, confiding in Dorothy that she longed for the warmth and kindness she had felt as a young child in Chertsey.

"I'm going back there," Margaret whispered. "I'm going to escape." She felt certain her foster parents would let her come home to live with them, if only they knew what it was like at the Foundling Hospital.

Dorothy was stunned at Margaret's confession. Margaret was pretty, with large blue eyes and a clear, innocent-looking face. Her short light-brown hair had a natural wave to it, swirling into a cowlick on her forehead. She was quiet, and always a good student who was not often in trouble. She didn't seem like a girl who would consider such a dangerous violation of the rules. But Dorothy wanted in.

In all my years at the school I had never heard of anyone even mentioning that they'd like to run away, or heard of anyone who had. It probably never crossed our minds, captive and dependent as we were. It wasn't that we were happy there, but simply that we had been isolated from the world since the age of five and this was the only world we knew.

Dorothy wasn't averse to taking occasional risks, as she'd just demonstrated, and Margaret seemed to have slowly come to some sort of breaking point. And so, in excited whispers, right there in the playroom under Miss Wright's nose, the two girls began to plan their escape.

Their first concern was food, but as they whispered, Dorothy and Margaret quickly came up with an idea. Each Sunday the children received a sweet bun, and if the two could manage to smuggle their buns out of the dining room, they could hide the contraband in their playroom lockers until they made their escape. The next obstacle was how they would get to Chertsey, where Margaret's foster family lived. They had no access to maps, but Margaret believed Chertsey to be just south of London. It would be simple, they thought, to walk to London, then continue south until they reached Chertsey. What they didn't realize was that Chertsey was directly south of the Foundling Hospital, while London was to the southeast. Walking to London on their way to Chertsey would add an extra twenty miles to their thirty-mile journey.

Nor did they consider that England was a nation still at war. In January 1944 Hitler had launched the final bombing offensive in retaliation for Royal Air Force raids on German cities. Dubbed the Baby Blitz, it did not compare to the relentless bombing endured in the early days of the war, but nonetheless it took the lives of approximately fifteen hundred people, injuring nearly three thousand more.

Now that they had a plan in place, the next step was getting beyond the school grounds. A low concrete wall surrounded the campus, topped with spiked iron railings five or six feet high. Leaving through the front gate was not an option, since that would require ringing a bell to alert one of the two gatekeepers, who would never open the gate for a foundling. They settled on a side gate adjoining the girls' playing field, used mostly by the hospital's secretary, Mr. Nichols. Dorothy had never interacted with Mr. Nichols, but she would see him go through the gate as he walked to and from his house nearby. The gate was secured by a heavy iron chain with a padlock. Dorothy noticed that in the morning he sometimes left the padlock hooked to the chain, unlocked. The two girls agreed that slipping through the gate offered their best chance of getting away unnoticed.

An escape route, a bit of food, and a general idea of the direction in which they needed to go . . . Neither girl ever considered the need for money; it simply wasn't part of their world. They had learned sums in class, sometimes using shillings and pounds as written examples, but had never actually laid eyes on a pound note or a sovereign coin.

The night before their planned escape, Dorothy was overwhelmed with excitement. It never once crossed her mind that they would get caught or lost along the way. Her only fear was that Margaret would change her mind and tell the staff about their plan, and there would never again be an opportunity to get away.

When morning came and Nurse Knowles, the dormitory supervisor, ordered the girls out of bed, Dorothy looked eagerly across the room at Margaret, hoping to catch her eye. She anxiously sidled up next to her on the way to the washroom, and to her great relief, Margaret whispered a conspiratorial affirmation.

The plan was on.

After breakfast, while the rest of the girls filed into the playroom, waiting for the go-ahead to proceed to their morning classes, Margaret and Dorothy lingered near the cloakroom. When the coast was clear, they grabbed their brown cloaks and, sweet buns in hand, stepped into the deserted hallway. They looked down the corridor, with several classrooms on either side, aware that a teacher could emerge from one of the doorways at any time. Steadying themselves and exchanging tremulous looks, the girls scurried down the hallway and opened the door to the outside. The next part of their journey was the most treacherous, or so they thought. They would have to walk down a path and pass through the very gate Mr. Nichols used each morning. If luck wasn't on their side, they risked encountering him on his commute. A more likely and even worse possibility was that Nurse Knowles might glance out her bedroom window, which overlooked the path leading to the gate, and spot them.

But Dorothy and Margaret scampered down the path and through the unlocked gate undetected—at least by the staff. Above them, in the playroom, their classmates stood in a row, noses pressed against the Palladian windows, silently watching with envy and admiration as the two cloaked figures made their daring escape.

As they scuttled away from the grounds, Dorothy was bursting with energy, exhilarated to be unsupervised and out of her prison at last. They walked past meadows, a few cottages, and a gray stone church where the white-haired vicar who often conducted sermons at the Foundling Hospital chapel waved at them tentatively. The girls waved back, unaware that the vicar would soon telephone the school to report the unusual sighting of two foundlings out on their own.

As they continued on their way, soon passing Bovingdon

Airfield, Dorothy remembered the kindness of the Americans, how special she had felt in their presence. The girls debated stopping but decided not to, suspecting that the Americans would have no choice but to return them to the hospital. Unbeknownst to them, D-Day was just weeks away; the base was in full swing, preparing for one of the greatest invasions in history.

When Dorothy and Margaret came upon a giant concrete drainpipe set up to block the road against a German ground invasion, they decided to rest. With aching feet and empty stomachs, they crawled inside the pipe and devoured their sweet buns before setting off again, making their way along the narrow lane, its banks thick with uncut grass and lined with leafy hedges. The morning was overcast and slightly chilly, typical for April, but Dorothy soaked up the feeling of newfound freedom.

After traveling another mile or two, the girls came upon a signpost with several arms, one of which indicated that it was twenty-five miles to London. The girls didn't know how long the journey would take, but the distance sounded daunting. The distances on the other arm posts were shorter, and they were discussing the options when they were approached by two middle-aged women, both dressed in country tweeds and woolens. Dorothy and Margaret stepped aside and waited for them to pass, but the women stopped and asked whether they could help. It was a question Dorothy was unprepared for; help was something no adult had ever offered. And so she blurted out the truth—they had run away from a place where they were beaten with canes and locked in cupboards. They needed to get to Chertsey, to Margaret's foster parents, who would take them in and save them from their horrible life at the Foundling Hospital.

The women had introduced themselves, but Dorothy retained only one of the names—Miss Hopkins. Miss Hopkins was familiar with the Foundling Hospital and had attended a choral concert there, she said. She also seemed to be sympathetic to their plight. "My nephew is quite unhappy at his school, too," she explained as she led the girls to her cottage.

Miss Hopkins's home was a simple two-story brick house surrounded by trees and shrubs, but what thrilled Dorothy was that it had a name—"Milestones." She hadn't seen the inside of a private home since she'd left her foster parents seven years earlier, and the charms of the old house weren't lost on her. In a small homely room off the kitchen, with floral-papered walls and a sideboard cluttered with decorative china objects and pictures, Miss Hopkins gave each of the girls a piece of cake along with some hot chocolate as she checked the train schedule. A train was leaving soon, she informed them. The girls finished their cake while Miss Hopkins busied herself in the kitchen, and the small group then made its way to the village of Amersham, six miles and a lifetime away from Berkhamsted. Miss Hopkins used her own money to purchase train tickets for the girls, helping them into a carriage where two female passengers were already seated. Asking one of the women to help Dorothy and Margaret change trains in London, she handed the girls two box lunches and some money. As the train pulled away, Miss Hopkins and her friend waited on the platform, smiling and waving. Already, the experience of running away had been more than Dorothy could have hoped for:

> To have met two perfect strangers who were willing to listen to us, to assist us, to take our side against the mighty Foundling Hospital was simply inconceivable. It happened at a time when children were truly supposed to be seen and not heard, when they had few rights, when adults routinely upheld each other against them. And as Foundlings we had no voice at all. How unbelievably fortunate I felt that day. Whatever one's

beliefs, a higher power must certainly have been watching over us.

As the train left the Amersham station, Dorothy and Margaret wasted little time in opening the box lunches, which were filled with savory ground pork pies, cakes, and fruit. Dorothy's mouth watered, her stomach churning with hunger, but she stopped herself before taking a bite. She looked up at the woman who had promised to help them once they arrived in London.

"Would you like something to eat?" she asked, pausing before helping herself. The fashionable woman smiled politely and shook her head.

Reading her description of this stranger seventy years later, I could sense my mother's awe, the way the image had imprinted itself on her twelve-year-old brain. Dorothy had never seen anyone like her. She couldn't guess the woman's age—she seemed neither young nor old. The stranger was "refined and elegant," her clothes "subdued" in color and of "high quality," my mother reflected. When she created the aristocratic persona that she later wore as an armor, was this the image in her mind?

Their hunger sated, Dorothy and Margaret turned their attention to the money that Miss Hopkins had given them. They tried to count it, but, having never seen money, had no idea how much it amounted to. They spent the remainder of the journey gazing at the small towns and rolling hills passing by, soon replaced by factories, businesses, and cramped housing complexes. Finally they pulled into an echoing covered train station.

They'd arrived in London, Dorothy realized. It was everything she had imagined, and she soaked up its energy. Her senses were heightened by the trains pulling in and out, the plumes of steam rising, the banging and clanging and commotion of people bustling from place to place. They followed the woman who had been asked to care for them, and soon the three were in a taxi on their way to another station. Their host said little during the taxi ride, but pointed out sights as they passed by. Trafalgar Square made a particular impression on Dorothy, with its endless flocks of pigeons, its massive bronze lions, and a fluted concrete column stretching into the sky.

When they arrived at Waterloo, their new friend gave them each a penny and sent them down a steep flight of stairs to use the toilets, past walls of shiny white tiles in the shape of bricks. The adults outside Berkhamsted continued to astonish Dorothy. She had not asked to use the toilets, yet an adult had anticipated her needs. She felt looked after, even cared for. The woman took them to the train platform and told them what time their train would leave, pointing out an enormous clock that hung over the cavernous station. Before Dorothy could thank her, she disappeared into the crowd.

When their train arrived, a uniformed attendant asked the girls for their tickets. Dorothy looked down and found that in her nervousness, she had twisted the ticket around her finger, rendering it unrecognizable. The attendant pointed them in the direction of the ticket booth. As Dorothy raced across the platform, she was ashamed of what she had done, and also frightened, not sure whether she had enough to buy a second ticket and lacking any real concept of how much money she had. She heard a shrill whistle as she piled all that Miss Hopkins had given her on the ticket counter. To her great relief, she learned that she had enough to buy a ticket, and money to spare.

The two girls traveled to Chertsey without incident. They had no address, but had assumed that Margaret would recognize the home where she had spent her first five years. Margaret remembered that it was close to a body of water, near Chertsey Meads. Dorothy asked a porter for directions, and soon the pair was walking along a footpath past humble houses, many partially hidden by thick hedges. They walked for an hour or more, Margaret scanning each house they passed. Then, somewhat unbelievably, they found it—the modest bungalow shielded by elderberry trees and large oaks where Margaret had spent her happiest years. She grabbed Dorothy's arm and shrieked. No one was home, so the girls sat down on the veranda and waited for Margaret's foster parents to return. Mr. Braithwaite worked at the Vickers-Armstrong factory where tanks were tested, while Mrs. Braithwaite worked in a canteen, providing refreshments to soldiers as part of the war effort.

Mr. Braithwaite turned up first. The restrained man showed little reaction at finding the two foundlings on the veranda, listening quietly as the girls told the story of how and why they had escaped.

His response was equivocal: "I have to tell your foster mother." Like many people at the time, the Braithwaites didn't have a telephone, and he set off to contact his wife. When he returned, it was clear that he had also called the school, which had insisted that the girls be returned as soon as possible.

Dorothy and Margaret were devastated.

They followed Mr. Braithwaite into the house. Dorothy scanned the room, reveling in its coziness and warmth. Comfortable upholstered furniture, pretty ornaments, and photographs filled the space, so different from the austere rooms of the Foundling Hospital. Soon Mrs. Braithwaite appeared. She was full-figured and motherly, warm-hearted and tolerant, just as Margaret had described. She was calm as she set up a bed for the girls to sleep in, seemingly unangered by their escape, although Dorothy detected a worried look on her face.

The next morning Mrs. Braithwaite prepared them a full breakfast that included, among other things, soft-boiled eggs in little china egg cups, something Dorothy had never seen before. On the way to the bus Mrs. Braithwaite even bought them fudge, despite the strict wartime rations on sweets, as well as knitting needles and yarn, perhaps to keep them occupied on the ride home. As the trio set off, Dorothy watched passengers get off and on the bus, captivated by their varied clothing and hairstyles. To her delight, they boarded a second bus—a red double-decker. Emboldened by the kindness they had received since their escape, Dorothy asked if they could ride on the top deck.

It may have been the rich fudge, or fear of what would happen when Miss Wright got hold of her, but just as Dorothy had vomited in the taxi before arriving at the Foundling Hospital years before, she vomited on the floor of the bus. Shortly after, Margaret did the same. This time, instead of a stern reproach, none of the passengers, neither Mrs. Braithwaite nor the strangers seated nearby, showed any displeasure, not even a frown. At the hospital, Nurse Rance would scold Dorothy if she threw up, but out here in the world not a word was said, even as they pulled into a depot and everyone disembarked to board a clean bus. Dorothy was mortified, overwhelmed with her own sense of badness, but amazed to find that she suffered no harsh words or punishment.

When the girls reached the Foundling Hospital, Mrs. Braithwaite quickly disappeared, and Dorothy and Margaret were ushered into Miss Wright's office. She scolded the girls, instructing them to return any unspent money from the funds Miss Hopkins had given them. Trembling in fear, Dorothy handed over what was left, convinced that Miss Wright would now follow through on her repeated threats to send her away to reformatory school. Miss Wright turned to Margaret and sent her back to the dormitory for the rest of the day. And then, instead of doling out an equivalent punishment to Dorothy, she simply told her to return to her classmates.

Dorothy was allowed to go on as if nothing had happened, but she was apprehensive and bewildered. She couldn't comprehend how she could have committed such a brazen act of disobedience and received no punishment whatsoever.

Scouring through Dorothy's files nearly three-quarters of a century later, I learned that the school did in fact take immediate action, dispatching a letter with a full repayment to Miss Hopkins.

20th April, 1944

Dear Madam,

The Matron of our Schools has reported to me the circumstances with regard to two of our girls who left our Schools at Berkhamsted without permission and wandered through Amersham in the hope of visiting their foster parents.

I am afraid your action in facilitating the travel of the two children to Chertsey caused our staff a great deal of anxiety.

At the same time the Governors appreciate very much your kindness to the children and direct me to send you the enclosed note for 20£ which they hope will cover the expense you were put to. The Governors feel they cannot allow you to be out of pocket over the matter.

You will be interested to hear that the children arrived back here safely yesterday.

Yours faithfully,
Secretary

Miss Hopkins's reply revealed a restrained irreverence, and I like to believe that, given the opportunity, she would have helped any number of foundlings to run away.

April 24th, 1944

Dear Sir,

I thank you for your letter of the 20th [illegible] enclosure, although I regret you thought it necessary to return the money, which could have been placed to your funds.

I accept your reprimand of my action, which I know is fully deserved—I can only say that a desire to see parents means a lot to me.

Yours truly,
M. Janet Hopkins

On her trip to England in 1977, my mother traveled to Amersham on a whim, hoping to find Miss Hopkins. She was able to find her number in a local directory, and to her surprise, Miss Hopkins answered the phone. My mother asked to stop by for a visit, picking up a cake on her way from the lone open shop in town. The offering seemed inadequate, considering the kindness that Miss Hopkins had shown all those years ago. But as my mother held Miss Hopkins's hands and expressed her gratitude, her concerns about decorum melted away. The two women sat by the fire in her small, comfortable cottage. They would stay in contact until two years later, when Miss Hopkins died.

Back in the spring of 1944, Dorothy knew that she had committed one of the worst offenses imaginable within the world of Berkhamsted. To me, her behavior was a remarkable act of bravery, a little girl standing up to an institution that had ignored the bounds of human decency. Dorothy didn't see it that way.

I felt ashamed, a terribly bad person, the worst in the school.
I wished that I could be forgiven and that I could behave like

other girls. I felt guilty, believing I had led Margaret astray and had got her into trouble. I had continual foreboding about my future. With my escape from the washroom and now from the school itself, I could see that my misbehavior was escalating at a frightening pace.

Yet there had been no reprimand, no beatings, no confinement in a closet, not so much as a slap across her head. Far from feeling relieved, Dorothy felt an unease about what would happen next, growing more anxious as the days passed.

A week later, on the morning of April 26, 1944, she was sitting at her desk during her arithmetic class when the door opened and Nurse Foley entered. She exchanged a nod with Mrs. Dadds, Dorothy's instructor, and then stood by the door, waiting.

"Dorothy, hand me your work and go with Nurse Foley," Mrs. Dadds instructed. Dorothy's heart sank. As much as she hated life at the Foundling Hospital, she feared reformatory school would be much worse. "I knew I wasn't coming back," she wrote years later. "It was the dreaded moment that I knew was coming. I was gripped with fear as I went out. I was sure the girls knew as I did that I was headed for reformatory school." But in characteristic fashion, she put on a show of bravery: "I walked out with my head up and an I-don't-care attitude in an attempt to hide my pain and humiliation."

As she stepped into the hallway and awaited her instructions from Nurse Foley, she was resigned to her fate. Her daring escape had been worth it, she thought, a magical adventure with sights, flavors, sounds, and treatment so different from the daily drudgery of life as she knew it. She hoped those memories would sustain her through the bleak days ahead.

Confirming Dorothy's fears that she would be leaving, Nurse Foley told her to go upstairs and have a bath; she would be up shortly with clean clothes. Dorothy was crestfallen, overcome with a deep sense of dread—until she heard Nurse Foley's next words.

"You're going home, Dorothy."

Dorothy stared up at Nurse Foley, uncomprehending. She knew she shouldn't question an adult, but she was too stunned by Nurse Foley's statements to stop herself.

"I don't understand," she blurted out. "I'm going home to live with Mrs. Vanns?" While she wasn't fond of her foster mother, Dorothy was relieved to hear that she wasn't being sent to reformatory school.

"No," Nurse Foley clarified. "You are going home to live with your mother—your *real* mother."

It took a few moments for the words to sink in. "In one second I had been in the depth of despair and in the next delirious with joy," my mother wrote, recounting the momentous day.

I'm not sure which emotion was the most intense, but nothing in my life since has come remotely close either way. But, as was normal in the presence of staff, I didn't utter a word or show a flicker of emotion, not so much as a gasp, so completely internalized had my feelings become in the presence of authority through the years of repression.

The one outward sign of the enormity of the impact the announcement had on me was that I took off like the wind along the corridor—fully aware but not caring that I was breaking the rules. I rounded the corner to the right, raced past the cloakrooms, careened to the left and flew up the wide staircase two steps at a time. By the time Nurse Foley caught up with me with a complete set of clothes in hands, I was already stepping out of the bathtub, having run the water and given myself a swift swish all over.

After her bath, Dorothy was given a small suitcase and taken to the playroom to empty her locker. When she opened the locker and saw her insignificant belongings, her plimsolls and perhaps a small toy she had made herself in sewing class, she was filled with guilt and anguish, remembering all of the gifts that her mother had sent—the knitting bag, the brooches, the ivory-carved container embossed with a penguin with ruby eyes. They were all gone, given away to curry favor with her classmates. What if her mother were angry? Dorothy's joy was replaced by a sudden worry that her mother wouldn't accept her or love her.

As she placed her few belongings into her suitcase, her class-mates filed in. The news had already spread: Dorothy had been "claimed," something that had never happened to any other girl, at least during the years that Dorothy had lived there. Seeing Dorothy, the girls rushed toward her, crowding around her, peppering her with questions, some of which Dorothy couldn't answer. *Where are you going? What is your real name?* Everyone wanted to see her, to touch her. Some were standing on benches, others kneeling on the table near her, hoping to get a better view. They were clamoring for her attention, arms outstretched, call-ing out her name, begging her to write them.

Write to me, Dorothy!
No, write to me, Dorothy!
Dorothy! Dorothy! Write to me!
Dorothy! Dorothy! Dorothy!

Dorothy had never felt so special in her life.

She had been told that her mother was to pick her up after dinner, which meant that Dorothy would have to walk, one last time in crocodile formation to the dining hall, sitting in silence for her final meal.

As Dorothy took one of her last bites of the tasteless food, Miss Wright entered the dining hall, motioning for Dorothy to follow her. Dorothy obeyed, walking quietly between the long rows of benches where the girls remained seated in silence, heads turned to catch a glimpse of Dorothy as she passed. She felt a moment of sadness as she passed under her classmates' watchful gazes. There was, after all, a bond between them, a shared experience that no one else would ever understand. Together they had huddled in a cold basement as German planes droned overhead, endured beatings and brutality, filled their stomachs with stale buns and stolen carrots, and shared in the joy of Miss Woodward's death, marching defiantly as one. These girls, who were not always kind, were the only real family Dorothy had ever known.

As she approached the door, Dorothy thought about turning around to wave goodbye, but she stopped herself, knowing Miss Wright would disapprove. With her head held high, she walked out of the dining room and down the long hallway toward Mr. Nichols's office, where she would finally meet her mother.

15

MOTHERS

I was seven when I found my mother standing in the hallway that led to her bedroom, motionless except for her hands. She was wringing them, twisting her fingers intently, her knuckles turning white under the pressure. Tears were rolling down her face, and she made no effort to wipe them away.

"Mom, what's wrong?"

She looked at me blankly, not realizing at first that I was standing in front of her.

"Nothing," she finally said, after a long pause. "It's just my tear ducts. There's something wrong with them, is all."

I knew she was lying.

"Mom, tell me what's wrong," I repeated, my voice trembling. I hadn't seen my mother cry before, and I would see her tears only a few more times during my life.

"It's nothing to be worried about. Someone passed away, a distant cousin, no one important," she replied.

I had never heard her mention a cousin, or any family member, for that matter. I knew better than to try to find out more.

Without another word, my mother turned away and went into her bedroom, closing the door behind her.

More than forty years would pass before I would learn the truth, that the tears she'd shed that day were not for a distant cousin, but for someone whose memory she had buried long ago.

LENA WESTON HADN'T given up on her little girl, not when the Foundling Hospital refused to let her visit, not when the governors denied her request to reclaim her daughter on the eve of war. She prayed for her daughter's safety and continued to write, month after month, year after year, always with the same question—*How is my little girl?* Without fail, she received the same reply: *I am pleased to tell you that your little girl is quite well.*

The winds changed in 1943, when she received a distressing reply to her query. Lena's letter, dated December 11, was no different than the ones she had sent before:

Dear Sir,

   I have sent a parcel for my little Girl and I shall be very grateful if you will please let me hear whether she is quite well.

   Yours truly,
   Lena Weston

But the response, this time, was unexpected:

13th December, 1943

Dear Madam,

   I have received your letter, together with the Christmas presents for the little girl, with which she will be very pleased.

   I am glad to say her health is quite good but she is rather

temperamental and difficult and it may be necessary to seek further advice regarding her.

Yours faithfully,
Secretary

The familiar but impersonal black typewriter marks revealed no further details about Dorothy's behavior, but to Lena, it didn't matter. Her daughter needed her. She had to act.

December 16th, 1943

Dear Sir,

I have your communication of Dec 13 and note the report you give of my little Girl. I think it would relieve you of additional concern and myself possible anxiety if you would kindly consider releasing Her to my care, and will you kindly take the necessary steps to bring this about. I am most grateful to you for all you have done for Her and for the courteous replies you have always given to my enquiries, may I therefore anticipate a reply from you in due course.

Yours truly,
L. S. Weston

For years, Lena had waited to hold Dorothy in her arms, to comfort her, only to have her dreams dashed time and again. This time, she received a response that gave her reason to hope:

21st December, 1943

Dear Madam,

I have received your letter of the 16th instant. If you really feel you would like to have the girl restored to you I will bring an application before the Governors.

I think you had better let me consult our Doctor and get a special report on the child's condition.

In the meantime perhaps you would kindly tell me what you have been doing these last few years and what you are doing at present and what facilities you have for looking after a child.

Yours faithfully,
Secretary

Having organized the documents chronologically, I could see that this last letter from the Foundling Hospital's secretary had been sent right around the time Dorothy was being chauffeured to Bovingdon Airfield for that special Christmas feast with the American GIs. It had been an extraordinary privilege to be selected, one of twelve among more than four hundred foundlings housed at Berkhamsted at the time. Why had Miss Wright bestowed such an honor upon Dorothy, a child who could not follow the rules, who was troublesome and difficult? My mother had attributed her good fortune to some heretofore hidden vein of compassion within Miss Wright. Perhaps the thought that a woman as cruel as Miss Wright had a bit of goodness in her had provided my mother with some comfort.

My review of the documents gave me a dimmer view of Miss Wright's motives; her lone act of generosity came as Dorothy's time at the Foundling Hospital was coming to an end. Perhaps Miss Wright realized that the child she had beaten and routinely locked in closets would soon be in the company of a loving adult who might not approve of Miss Wright's treatment of her daughter.

If there was kindness in Miss Wright's heart for Dorothy, it was not evident in the way she described her young charge in a

230

report prepared as part of the hospital's investigation into Lena Weston's request:

The Secretary has asked me to write to you with regard to Dorothy Soames.

He has, I believe, told you that we have found her increasingly difficult.

Dorothy is now even more disobedient and defiant and is, in consequence, a very bad influence in the school.

She adopts a very insolent attitude and manner, resents any authority and is very unwilling to conform to any rules of the school.

Her work in school is erratic depending upon her mood, and her power of concern seems to have grown less. She makes no attempt to do anything which she finds difficult and very rudely resents at such a time any offer of help.

She is a most tantalizing child and will scheme and plan to do all in her power to annoy anyone with whom she comes in contact. And yet Dorothy can be quiet and charming.

Friday evening (later)

Dorothy has had a bad afternoon, petty stealing (notepaper, etc.), followed by untruthfulness and the usual bad temper.

J.W.

Miss Wright's contempt oozed from each typewritten word. I felt protective of Dorothy—a parentless twelve-year-old girl could not deserve such wrath. But I also felt the sting of recognition: difficult, defiant, erratic . . . In my household, that meant never knowing whether my mother might fly into a rage at a moment's notice, or retreat to her bedroom to brood in the dark. In decades prior, Miss Wright's words might have comforted me, supplying me with the proof I craved that my mother was to blame for our troubled relationship. Instead, I was struck by the tragic irony of the report. The very traits Miss Wright found so intolerable had been forged by her own hand, and reinforced each time she raised her belt or bolted the storeroom door.

Lena had written back not long after she had received the secretary's letter asking about her ability to care for a child, informing him that she was a housekeeper at the family farm, and that she felt that she could "now look after the little Girl and give all the attention desirable for Her Welfare and upbringing." After that, there was nothing for Lena to do but wait. She wrote periodically, anxious to hear news as the hospital's investigation dragged on, until, two months after her initial request, she received the following response:

21st February, 1944

Dear Madam,

I expect you are wondering why you have not heard from me.

The fact of the matter is that the Governors have decided your daughter should have some psychology treatment and sufficient time has not yet elapsed to see whether it alters her disposition.

I will write to you again later and if we have a representative coming into your district. I will get him to call and explain the matter to you more fully.

Yours faithfully,
Secretary

Having grown familiar with Lena's determination, I wasn't surprised to see that she wasted no time in her response:

February 23rd, 1944

Dear Sir,

I arrived back five thirty Tuesday morning very sorry to give inconvenience, and I thank them very much for the kindness shown. I feel certain the Governors would not disagree just at the moment it is of national as well as private interest to get back to work, [illegible] all very late. I have received your letter this morning, when I brought the child to you at the commencement, I was very glad to receive your aid, and I know that you are disappointed that you cannot educate the child. I have been thinking the cause, you have in fulfillment your [illegible] to the highest degree, but our lives are not revealed to us, how we shall start or finish in life time time alone can only give the answer. I shall be glad if you will kindly let me hear the decision of the Governors at their meeting,

Yours truly,
L. S. Weston

I never found any records detailing the "psychology" treatment that Dorothy received, and my mother didn't mention it in the pages of her book-to-be. It's unlikely that any treatment administered in those years would have been accurate in its diagnosis or effective in its results. In the first half of the twentieth century, the field of child psychology was in its nascent stages. Behavioral issues were often attributed to breeding and considered to be moral problems, deserving of punishment rather than psychological care. At the time during which Dorothy's treatment purportedly occurred, the groundbreaking clinical work that would soon lead to a collective understanding of the harms of institutional child-rearing was under way. But the governors of the Foundling Hospital would not have been likely to embrace these new ideas, their approaches to child-rearing anchored firmly in the past.

Given what I'd come to know about the institution, I wondered whether there was anything wrong with Dorothy at all. She was described as troublesome, and having personally experienced my mother's mercurial ways, I could vouch for the possibility that their assessment may have been right. But it was equally plausible that Dorothy was simply bright and inquisitive, although perhaps a bit mischievous, as many children are. My own behavior as a "precocious" child, a term I learned at an early age as I explored my surroundings or interjected myself into adult conversations, came to mind as I pondered the question. My impertinent disposition was considered a sign that I was high-spirited and curious. Perhaps Dorothy was just like me—or, more aptly, I was like her. It was a comparison that I would have despised just months before, that any part of my mother might be contained within my own body. I also thought of some of Miss Wright's words, that Dorothy was defiant and challenged authority. These were traits we shared, except that where I was rewarded for my nature, Dorothy was labeled disobedient and savagely beaten and abused.

I felt a familiar wave of anger flash through my veins, but this time it was not directed at my mother. Instead, as I came to fully understand the implications of the decisions of powerful men long since deceased, the full force of my anger shifted course. Channeling my emotions into an internal scream, I hurled invectives their way, accused them of injustice, cruelty, sadism, all the while knowing that my anger was directed into the chasm of history. I heard only the echo of my own voice coming back at me in response.

What I read next did little to quell my anger. When Lena first reached out to the Foundling Hospital, asking for assistance in raising her daughter, she had to prove that she was a virtuous woman. With unrestrained hubris, the governors scrutinized her reputation, and only after a thorough investigation did they deem Lena worthy of their help. Over the ensuing years, her daughter would be subjected to abuses no child should ever suffer, but these failures would not spare Lena from going under the magnifying lens yet again. Still convinced that they provided the superior model of care, the governors dispatched a representative to Lena's home in the quiet farming community of Shropshire to investigate whether she could provide what they deemed to be an appropriate home for her daughter. I found the investigator's report in the Foundling Hospital files:

APPLICATION by LENA WESTON
FOR THE RESTORATION OF HER FEMALE CHILD, LETTER "O"
ADMITTED 2ND MARCH, 1932

With reference to the above application I beg to report that the girl in question, Dorothy Soames, No. 24090, is present in the schools at Berkhamsted and is reported to be a source of great anxiety to all the teaching staff and has always been a very bad influence in the school. Miss Wright is of opinion that she undoubtedly finds institution life very difficult and given the freedom and interests of home life would probably be a far better and happier child.

I had an interview with Miss Weston at Rushmoor Lane farm Salop where she has lived the past fifteen years with her brother. I pointed out to them that the Governors were anxious to give their sympathetic consideration to her application and informed them that the girl was rather difficult at school, but they felt convinced they would be able to manage her and they are fully prepared to accept all responsibility if the Governors decide to restore her.

. . .

The house consists of two living rooms and three bedrooms, but there is no bathroom and the house has oil lighting. The rooms are large but I found them not particularly clean and very untidy. For example at three o'clock in the afternoon the beds had not been made and judging from the appearance I doubt whether they were ever made.

Lena's financial situation would also be considered. Lena and her brother, Harry, were co-owners of a forty-five-acre farm with thirty head of cattle, which included twelve milkers and one pedigree Friesian bull, along with ten calves and yearlings, one breeding sow, and three horses. Lena's financial interest in the farm was surprising, given that her brother had kicked her out all those years earlier.

The investigator also sought out the same three men who had vouched for Lena's character when she first sought the assistance of the Foundling Hospital; instead of evaluating Lena's virtue, this time the questions focused on whether Lena could be a proper mother. Dr. Mackie, the Westons' family physician, attested that the Westons were "industrious people and although they lived in a rather untidy state," he believed they would be "kind to any child that went to their home and he saw no reason why the governors should not restore the child." The investigator spoke with Harry, who expressed the belief that "on the farm the girl could be of some help to them and that he did not think there would be any difficulty overcoming her peculiar ways." The report noted that Reverend Nock, who had also been interviewed at the time of Dorothy's admission, had since died.

The investigator also interviewed Lena, who expressed thankfulness "for all the Governors had done for her," crediting them for helping her out of a "great trouble as at the time her brother had a very serious quarrel with her regarding it, but he had now

forgiven her." The investigator noted that, from the "the manner in which she made this latter statement, . . . there was no
question of incest in this case." The report concluded with the
investigator's impressions of Lena, that she appeared to be "a
respectable woman but somewhat erratic and talkative."

As the investigation continued, Lena wrote often, eager for
news of whether she would be reunited with her daughter. And
then she received the letter that she had been waiting for.

19th April, 1944

Dear Miss Weston,

Referring to your letter of the 22nd March, the Governors
have further considered your application to have your daughter
restored to you and have decided to accede to your request. I
shall be obliged if you will kindly let me know when it will be
convenient for you to call and fetch her.

We can let her leave in the clothes she is wearing and you can
return these later.

I hope that the Governors' action will be for your happiness
and the welfare of the girl.

I may tell you that she has been exceedingly troublesome
lately, and the psychology treatment she has received does not
appear to have done her any good.

We can arrange for her to be ready on Friday this week, or
Wednesday or Thursday next week.

Yours faithfully,
Secretary

Further correspondence reminded Lena to "please bring with
you the parchment receipt given you on the admission of the
child," and she heeded the secretary's instructions. I had held

the original document, yellowed and frayed, when I first saw my mother's files. The "receipt," a simple form that had remained largely unchanged for over a century, reminded me of an old-fashioned IOU, as if its subject were an inanimate object instead of a living, breathing little girl. I don't know if my mother ever saw the slip of paper, but if she had, it would only confirm her convictions.

> Whatever was articulated about the purpose of the Found-ling Hospital, it is clear to me now that the entire system, every action, every rule, the regimentation and rigid disci-pline, the strict obedience enforced, the isolation, the si-lences, the punishments—all virtually unchanged since the founding of the Hospital in the 18th century—were for the purpose of training us to become superior, unknowing do-mestic servants. The distancing of the staff for instance, I feel sure, was instituted as part of our training as future ser-vants in the homes of the upper echelons of society, where no talking to or familiarity with those in authority would be allowed.

The foundlings were treated as chattel, the lower rung of a system designed to benefit the upper class. "It seems to be that the Governors," my mother went on, "the very people who had the power to make reforms, to liberate us from a repressive, long outdated system, were themselves the very people who most benefited from the system and consequently perpetuated it." Or perhaps, she mused, "the Governors were guilty of nothing more than the British tendency at the time to cling to the past, to carry on the way things had always been done."

Whatever the reason, as my mother saw it, she had been

allowed to go home with her mother not because it was in her best interest but simply because she had become too difficult to be of value to the Foundling Hospital as a future servant. Her attempt to escape was the final straw that led to her release, the letter granting Lena custody having been written just one day after Dorothy had been returned to Berkhamsted.

And so, in a roundabout way, it *was* her courage that brought about her freedom.

Once the decision had been made, Dorothy was given only an hour or so to bathe and share that final meal with her classmates. She hardly knew what to expect when she followed Miss Wright into Mr. Nichols's office. As Dorothy entered the room, she saw Mr. Nichols sitting at his desk. To his right stood a slender woman of medium height, wearing a tailored navy suit, a white silk blouse with a brooch at the neck, and a navy cloche, gray wisps of hair visible beneath. Her face was pale, her large blue eyes her most arresting feature. Dorothy froze as the woman stepped toward her.

"How's my little girl?" she asked, placing a hand on Dorothy's shoulder and kissing her cheek.

Dorothy blushed, never having been kissed before.

That first sight of my mother disappointed me, but it made no difference to my extreme excitement and desire to go home with her. It was simply that I had expected to see someone more like Margaret's foster mother, more "rounded," less tall and stiff, more "motherly" as I remembered her when Margaret and I ran away to her house.

There was little conversation. Mr. Nichols indicated that the taxi was waiting and that they should be on their way, but

Dorothy was not told where they were going. Lena took her hand and led her through the entry hall and down the few steps, out into the fresh air, toward their new life together.

I LONGED TO turn the page of my mother's manuscript to find out what happened next, to read the details of her time with her mother—the love they felt for each other, the healing I could imagine taking place after so many years of separation. I saw the two of them by the hearth in an old farmhouse, the crackling fire providing warmth as they chatted, my mother sitting beside Lena, leaning gently against her knee, home at last.

But the chapter I yearned for wasn't there. The pages had been removed, with a brief note in my mother's unmistakable handwriting under the heading "Shropshire": "Not included."

The Foundling Hospital's files provided little in the way of additional information about the next ten years of my mother's life. But I did find a letter written by Lena not long after Dorothy had been returned to her home.

May 16th, 1944

Dear Sir,

I am most grateful to you for your letter and enclosure of last Thursdays date which came duly to hand. I am sure you were pleased to hear how contented and happy Dorothy is in her new surroundings and not the least she is already of some considerable help to us. If I may I would again like to express my deep sense of gratitude to the Governors of the Foundling Hospital for the great benefit they have so freely given to me, and to yourself for your most courteous letters and consideration.

I am greatly indebted to the Staff, Teachers and Matron. I would like you to convey sincere thanks for all they have so well done and kindly done for this child.

Yours truly,
Miss L. S. Weston

That was the last letter from Lena on file. But three years later Dorothy's foster mother, Louise Vanns, wrote informing school administrators that Dorothy would be spending a month with her. She also indicated that Dorothy wished to visit the school in Berkhamsted. Attached to the letter was a handwritten note, written by the secretary to provide some background on Mrs. Vann's request:

This child was a worry to Miss Wright when in the Schools; and I believe she was the girl who once ran away. After restoration, she wrote several times to Miss Wright, who was doubtful if the girl was attending school.

I never learned what might have been said in those letters to Miss Wright. They were not contained in the file. Nor would I ever discover what transpired during Dorothy's visits with Miss Vanns, or the years she spent on the farm with her mother and her uncle.

The last piece of correspondence I was able to find was written on June 4, 1947, and did not identify the recipient, beginning simply with "Dear Sir":

In reply to your request to write to you, I am pleased to say that I am very well and very happy back with my own mother and uncle. I am at present staying with my foster mother for a holiday and I am enjoying it very much.

I am very grateful for the interest you have taken and I have heard from Mr. White to say that I might visit the school any time. I wish, which I think is very nice of him. Mrs. Vanns and I will be going to Berkhamsted sometime during the next two weeks. I hope I may be fortunate enough to meet you too. Thanking you.

I remain
Yours faithfully
D. Soames

The letter had been written by my mother as a young teen. Her penmanship was usually instantly recognizable to me, but not this time—the characters lacked their usual grace, the neatly crafted bends and curves. The writing in this decades-old letter was more practical and indelicate.

I was surprised to learn that Dorothy had stayed in contact with Mrs. Vanns and Miss Wright, two women who had caused her so much pain. In the recollections she set down years later, she had no kind words for either of the women, describing them only as cruel and uncaring. Perhaps it is simply a quality of being human that draws us back to those who shaped us during our formative years—like a moth to a flame.

In search of more clues, I rummaged through a stack of old files I had kept in the attic and happened upon a page filled with names and addresses, all of them in either England or other parts of Europe. There were Westons on the list, along with some surnames I had never heard before. Hoping that I could find someone to fill in the missing pieces of my mother's story, I wrote to each of the addresses, brief letters asking for any information relating to my recently deceased mother. I received two replies.

One was a short, typewritten note from a woman in England who believed she might be a distant cousin of my mother. Those who would know more had passed away, she told me. I thought about reaching out to her, but while polite, the tone of her letter did not indicate a willingness to engage more. Perhaps my inquiry had served as a reminder of a dark chapter in the Weston family history. I had read in the Foundling Hospital files that, other than her brother, no member of the Weston family had known that Lena had given birth to a child. What a surprise it must have been when a twelve-year-old girl unexpectedly appeared on the family farm. Did Lena fabricate a story to explain Dorothy's sudden arrival (and did she even call her Dorothy)? I remembered the letter I found in my father's files staking claim to the Weston farm following Lena's death. It had included a reference to me—that I looked like a Weston. Perhaps the Weston family had refused to acknowledge my mother as a member of their clan, challenging her right to inherit from her own mother. My mind churned with possible scenarios, but I was left with only more questions than answers.

The second reply to my entreaties came as an early-morning phone call from an unknown number in Switzerland. An unwanted marketing call, I assumed as I sent it to voice mail. But the caller, a woman identifying herself as Patricia, left a message. She started to say something else but began to cry, and the voice mail ended abruptly. I returned her call to learn that she and my mother had been friends many years before. Presumably this was the "Pat" that I had heard my mother speak of when I was a child. They had spent their twenties together in San Francisco and had stayed in touch through Christmas cards over the years. My letter had been her first knowledge of my mother's death.

She spoke fondly of my mother and was deeply saddened to hear that she had died. Over the next few weeks, she answered some of my questions about my mother's past—but I soon learned that my mother had been as secretive with others as she had been with me. Patricia had never heard the name Dorothy Soames, nor had she heard of the Foundling Hospital. She knew nothing of the Weston family, but had always assumed that they were well-to-do—my mother had talked of going on "hunts" in her youth, and her friend had assumed she'd been well educated at an elite private school. Well into her eighties, Patricia's health was failing, and she was unable to offer much more.

I could only assume that my mother's tales of fox hunting were just another sliver of the narrative she had meticulously constructed detailing her aristocratic past. There were no horses at the Foundling Hospital, and while she may have learned to ride on the Weston family farm, it's unlikely that Lena would have had the means to introduce her daughter to a sport that was generally reserved for only the wealthiest members of society. It wasn't a fib shared within my family. I had been riding horses since the age of six, practicing dressage and show jumping on countless childhood afternoons. One summer my mother even sent me to a camp so that I could spend two weeks learning the art of steeplechase with four other children. But in all that time, I'd never seen my mother so much as touch a horse.

I had all but given up hope of finding anyone who could fill in the missing pieces of my mother's story when I received another unexpected call, this time from England.

"My name is Bernice, and I knew your mother."

She had gotten my telephone number from the secretary of the Old Coram Association, an organization comprised of former foundlings and their family members. I had written to them early on in my search, hoping to find someone who knew my mother as a child, but nothing had come of it, the inquiries that I had sent over a two-year period remaining largely unanswered.

I was at the gym when I answered Bernice's call. Not wanting to put off the precious chance of a conversation with someone who'd known my mother back then, I huddled on a ramp outside. It was unseasonably cold in Florida, where I was living at the time, and there was a light drizzle. I barely noticed the raindrops dripping over the eaves onto my bare legs as I listened to her steady voice, her memory surprisingly sharp as she recounted events that had happened eighty years ago.

Bernice wasn't a name I recognized—but of course it wasn't her name at the time.

"Back then, my name was Isabel," she told me. "Isabel Hockley."

She was the little girl who lived on Carpenter Lane when Dorothy was still with her foster mother. My mother's best friend—and possibly my namesake, I realized in that moment. My middle name is Isabelle, and my eyes welled up as I wondered whether, despite the spelling difference, I had been named after her.

I listened intently as she described the cast of characters that I had learned about through my research and from reading my mother's memoir. She remembered Miss Wright, flat hair parted down the middle with waves on each side. "We called her 'The Rook' because of her pointed face," she said. I envisioned Miss Wright, with a nose like the bird's long beak, her eyes round and beady.

"Now, Miss Douthie, we called her 'The Cat.'"

"Why 'The Cat?'"

"It was her hands, you see." She went on to describe the hospital's central staircase, which still stands today, its thick banister and slick veneer too tempting for a child to resist. "We would slide down the banister. It was such fun!" I heard the joy in her voice as she recounted what I assumed was one of the few happy moments in her childhood.

"One time I had climbed onto the top of the banister, and Miss Douthie caught me just as I was about to slide down. Her hands were like claws as they grabbed me. They just snatched me up! That's why we called her 'The Cat,' because of her claw-like hands.

"We were really quite naughty," she added. "Always getting into trouble, which meant the cane. But we couldn't help ourselves, I suppose."

Like my mother, Bernice had only kind words for Miss Douthie. "She was really wonderful, so different than the others." When I pressed her on why, her answer was simple. "I suppose it's because she cared."

I interspersed questions throughout our conversation, hoping to discover even the smallest sliver of new information: *What was my mother like?* Intelligent and clever. *What did you eat during your midnight feasts?* Anything we could find. *Did you go to Bovingdon Air Force Base for Christmas?* Yes, it was one of the best nights of my life!

But I grew silent as she described the abuses she suffered at the hands of Nurse Rance, who she described as cruel, beating the girls with a hairbrush or cane. And how during swim lessons, Miss Woodward wouldn't allow the girls to jump in the pool themselves. Instead, she would line them up and walk down the line, sadistically pushing them in, one after the next, taking pleasure in the fear she invoked.

She also told me of the day she was dropped off at the Foundling Hospital. Her foster mother left without a word. "She just disappeared, and that was that. I was never the same."

"How so? How were you different?"

"I'm not sure. But I loved my foster mum, and I know that she loved me, so when she left without so much as a word, it just finished me. It's why I became so foul-tempered, I suppose."

She described my mother as one of her closest friends, but with the caveat that they were only as close as they could be. After all, life at the Foundling Hospital was so regimented and uninteresting. For Bernice, life wasn't much "worth living" during those dark years. "There wasn't much to talk about. You just got through the days the best you could."

Bernice confirmed many of the details of my mother's early years, yet I longed to know more, whether she knew what happened after my mother left the Foundling Hospital. But she had little to offer, nothing that could help me put the pieces together, only that she remembered when my mother was reclaimed, how astonishing it was.

"And you, what happened next for you?"

Bernice was a retired nurse. She had never married or had any children. "I had bad luck with men, you see. One of 'em knocked me around and I swore 'em off after that."

We ended our call with a promise to see each other during my next visit to England. Disappointed at not finding the answers to my lingering questions, I reread my mother's unfinished manuscript, hoping to glean a missed detail. I learned nothing new, but grew increasingly curious about where she had learned to write so eloquently. The children at the Foundling Hospital were taught only rudimentary life skills, and after rejoining her mother, Dorothy likely never attended school again. How had she learned to express the details of her past with such skill, clarity, and grace? My mother's written reflections were so different in tone from the volatile outbursts of the secretive woman I had known my whole life.

Some of the missing pieces came together on their own.

Searching online genealogy sites, I found a record of my grandmother's death. Lena Weston died in 1973, unmarried and alone, her brother, Harry, preceding her by several years. At the time of her death, I was seven, and my mother was forty-one. My grandmother had been alive when I was a child, and it was her death my mother mourned when I came upon her crying in the hallway all those years ago.

The Shropshire farm that was the subject of the letter I'd found in my father's files—the property I'd naively assumed to be a grand estate, proof of my mother's aristocratic heritage—was described in Foundling Hospital reports as untidy, with no indoor plumbing or electricity. Her claims of noble lineage, which as a child I'd regarded as tantalizingly plausible, now seemed far-fetched. True, her unknown father might have been a duke or an earl who had an illicit affair with Lena and refused to acknowledge the child. But I found no evidence of that.

I now understood my mother's tales in a different light. They served to hide the shame of her illegitimacy while buttressing her sense of self-worth. But what I couldn't understand was why she had kept the knowledge of my grandmother completely hidden from my sister and me. Lena Weston died when I was seven years old. It would have meant something to me to know I had a grandparent, to have met her. I could only assume the two women had become estranged. There was no record of Lena having written to my mother after she'd left the farm and moved to the United States, a stark contrast to those stacks of letters, spanning twelve years of separation, she'd sent when Dorothy was at the Foundling Hospital. Despite the denied requests for visits and terse typewritten responses, the letters had kept on coming. What could have come between these two women, after Lena had fought so tirelessly for their reunification?

Other questions I pondered revolved around me. Had my

grandmother known that she had a granddaughter? Had she written to ask about me?

Hoping to understand the missing pieces of my mother's story, I did a bit of research on the reunification of parents and children who have been in government custody. I was unable to uncover anything from my mother's time, but there was no shortage of materials from the last few decades. The volume of information was overwhelming, both in the United Kingdom and the United States. There were scholarly articles, sociological studies, even fact sheets for parents on what to expect when bringing their child home from foster care, and tip sheets for foster parents on how to make the process go more smoothly for the biological family. While I found little to shed light on reunifications during my mother's childhood, I did glean a few key points from my research. Family reunifications should not be abrupt; instead they should be the result of a gradual process in which the child is refamiliarized with his or her family of origin through a series of parental visits. Following reunification, there should also be competent case management and a care plan developed with input from the parents, along with after-care support for parents from one or more governmental agencies. Even with all of these resources, studies found that many reunifications—anywhere from a third to a half, or even more—fail. The reasons are many, and include parental instability and drug use. Comparisons between children in modern foster care and the systematized abuse my mother experienced certainly wouldn't stand up to academic scrutiny, but one thing my reading made clear was that once the bond between a parent and child has been broken, it is difficult to mend.

When Lena and Dorothy were reunited, the statistics were already against them, their reunification all the more likely to fail due to the absence of any kind of support. There was no gradual reintroduction of a mother and daughter who were strangers to each other, no advice given on what to expect once the pair returned home. Lena's only instructions consisted of when and where to fetch her daughter.

Again, scouring my mother's would-be book, I found one small clue embedded in a sentence she had written. The line wasn't about her own experience of reunification, but about other foundlings who had been reunited in the 1950s, just after long-needed reforms had finally been instituted at the Foundling Hospital. When policies were liberalized in the wake of a scandal following the death of a child—abused not at the Foundling Hospital but under the care of an ill-chosen foster family—birth mothers were given the option of contacting their foundling children. Many did. But, as my mother noted, "most of these meetings were not successful in that bonding and lasting relationships between mother and child failed to take place."

Maybe that was my mother's way of telling me what went wrong. Lena and Dorothy had tried to repair their bond, but the wounds from Dorothy's early separation and mistreatment had been too ragged to heal. It was a possibility that filled me with a compassion I'd never felt for my mother while she was alive. I thought of Lena—how she had longed to be with her daughter, and how heartbreaking it must have been to lose her, not once but twice. And I thought of my own mother, not the woman who continually criticized me, but the lonely girl yearning for a family to heal the trauma of her past. In that moment, sitting with Dorothy's heartbreak, I entertained the thought that perhaps she could have been a good mother, had her fate not been sealed centuries before.

As for me, I never became a mother. Given the resentment I'd long harbored toward my own, I had an intractable fear that any child of mine would reject me. In my thirties, my doubts were briefly eclipsed by a longing for a family of my own, and I explored the concept of adoption. I remember feeling hopeful after attending a workshop for prospective adoptive parents. Anticipating the feeling of motherhood, the chance of the rewards that my friends with children had described to me, I began to imagine that maybe I could be a good mother.

I'll be careful, I thought. I won't repeat the mistakes of the past.

I reached out to my parents to ask for financial support, the costs of adoption being too great for me to carry on my public interest salary. My father had always been generous, paying for my private school education and the down payment on my house. There was good reason for me to believe that he would help.

A week later, I received my answer. The white starched paper contained only one paragraph, typed on my father's law-firm letterhead, explaining that they could provide me with a small sum, a token, for my "project." But the letter came with a warning, a plea to reconsider. At the time, the news was filled with horror stories about conditions in orphanages in Romania and elsewhere, children abused and neglected and then pawned off on unwitting Americans eager to adopt. The child might be "defective," the letter said. *What then?*

I never filled out the paperwork. By the time I met my husband, I was well into my forties. Even if we could have conceived, running around after a toddler seemed like a stretch, and my desire to adopt had long since passed.

It had also been too late for Dorothy and Lena, who would never find happiness as mother and daughter. I don't know if Lena died bitterly regretting the decision she had made all those years ago. But for Dorothy, there was still a bright light of hope—the same hope that had fueled her during the bleak days and nights at Berkhamsted, when she sneaked into the library to read about a distant land called America or called out for gum from smiling soldiers in passing convoys. That hope eventually took her on a journey across an ocean, where she would finally find what she had been searching for.

16

BELONGING

I refused to go, too embarrassed to be seen with her. The bar-beque, a Fourth of July celebration, was just up the street, and all the neighbors would be there. There would be hot dogs and hamburgers, sparklers, roman candles, and my favorite, the small pellets that turn into magic snakes as they wriggle around on the pavement. But a few minutes before the party started, my mother had come down the hall to show off her outfit—a floppy hat and a wool overcoat adorned with tattered patches she had apparently sewn on. Underneath the coat she wore a vintage dress from the 1930s or '40s, the outfit completed with lace-up boots. She was carrying a mini American flag in one hand, and in the other a small leather suitcase with a sign pasted to one side:

> Give me your tired, your poor,
> Your huddled masses yearning to breathe free,
> The wretched refuse of your teeming shore.

Send these, the homeless, tempest-tost to me,
I lift my lamp beside the golden door!

"I'm an immigrant landing on Ellis Island!" she exclaimed, her face beaming with pride at her cleverness and creativity. The only problem with her getup was that the barbeque wasn't a costume party. I rolled my eyes as any teenager might, but my mother was undeterred.

"I owe my life to this country, and I am not ashamed to let everyone know that!"

Though she rarely shared anything personal with me, I had always known how she felt about being an American. When it came time to take her citizenship test, she studied for weeks, boasting afterward of her perfect score. She wore her citizenship with pride, speaking often of how lucky she was.

Her ardent patriotism took on a different hue as I learned more about the secrets she'd kept so hidden. For her, America was a land of kind people, like the soldiers she had met at that long-ago party. It was also a place that would allow her to forget her past.

FOUNDLINGS DIDN'T MINGLE with the opposite sex, not on the playground, the classroom, or in the hallways. Born out of wedlock, they were thought to be prone to sin by the circumstance of their births. A bastard would only beget more bastards, or so the thinking went, and in any case, foundlings were being trained for a solitary life. The girls could expect long hours as domestic servants and masters who frequently prohibited staff from having boyfriends, or "followers," as they were called at the time. The boys might spend long months in military service or at sea. There was no room in their futures for dreams of marriage and children.

From the day that the Foundling Hospital opened its doors, boys and girls had been kept in different wings, each a mirror image of the other. The construction of the separate dormitories had been funded by one of the hospital's governors, Thomas Emerson, a wealthy merchant who was particularly sympathetic to the plight of women ruined by "unscrupulous" men. He viewed himself as a protector of women, and left annuities for his sister and a servant that were off-limits to their husbands. (It's likely that his progressive views were limited to white women, however, given that he earned his massive fortune from sugar plantations in the Americas that operated on African slave labor.)

Even foundlings who passed away under the hospital's care were segregated by gender, buried in different sections of the cemetery. In the early years the children dined in different wings of the hospital, but at Berkhamsted, perhaps for the convenience of the kitchen staff, the children were seated in a single large dining hall, divided down the middle by a pair of folding oak doors. The top half of the doors was outfitted with panels of opaque glass, turning the figures on the other side into shadows. In the everyday world of the Foundling Hospital, the opposite sex was visible only as a blurred outline glimpsed through a pane of frosted glass.

The separation between boys and girls was strictly enforced. Many children had spent their first five years in the countryside forging sibling bonds with foster children of the opposite sex. Those early bonds were severed without warning or explanation when they entered the Foundling Hospital. Dorothy had spent her first five years being raised with two foster brothers, both of whom ended up at the Foundling Hospital. During their years at the institution, they never spoke. Only a few exceptions to the separation of the sexes popped up in the accounts I read. Boys in their first year at the hospital ate at a boys-only "infant table" on the girls' side of the dining hall, although no talking was allowed. I also read of an instance in which fraternal twins, a boy and a girl who'd been raised by different foster families, were allowed to meet for the first time since their births over a birthday cake—a rare moment of kindness on the part of the staff, who typically did not acknowledge birthdays. The movable oak doors in the dining hall were folded back for the occasion, and the two were allowed to peek at each other at close range for the first time, their heads cocked at identical but opposite angles, with identical grins.

The boys and girls were effectively raised in two separate schools and supervised by two separate sets of staff members. By many accounts, the abuse suffered by the boys may have been worse. The boys' headmaster was considered particularly cruel, and was given to beating the boys with a cricket stump—a thick stick that could easily break a bone. During one of my trips to England, I met a former foundling who recounted an incident when she had peered into the gym, where she saw a boy hanging upside down, being brutally beaten by the gym teacher.

Despite the hospital's efforts to completely separate the sexes, hormones led to natural curiosity on the rare occasions when male and female foundlings did cross paths, an event that usually took place in the chapel. Centrally and prominently located, the building was the crown jewel of the Foundling Hospital campus. With wide and lofty interiors and high arched ceilings, it comfortably accommodated all of the students and staff. Dorothy would spend much of her time during daily chapel services gazing at the colors that cascaded through the magnificent stained-glass windows along the side walls. A central aisle separated the boys and girls, and when Dorothy was about eleven or twelve, she began to make furtive eye contact with a boy across the aisle.

A few months before her departure, the staff allowed for a rare exception to the otherwise rigid segregation of the sexes during a Christmas event held in the assembly hall.

> The seating was moved and the entire school, including boys, gathered around a tall decorated Christmas tree. . . . We sang all the well-known, well-loved carols, received candies and were free to socialize. Possibly we were at liberty to mingle with the boys, but I recall we mostly stayed apart, out of shyness. . . . I remember looking for the boy I exchanged smiles with in church. I daringly dashed over to him and gave him one of my candies then swiftly raced back. When I turned around he was still standing there, smiling at me.

Naturally Dorothy and her fellow foundlings were kept in the dark about sex. There was no instruction on the differences between boys and girls or about menstruation and reproduction, and discussion of such matters was strictly forbidden. Sharing information about menstruation, a major transgression, would result in a caning. Girls who had started their periods were separated, branded as "infirmary girls," as they were required to wash in the infirmary during their menstrual cycles, rather than with the other girls in the dormitory.

My mother had a dim view of these practices:

> What might the answer be to the puzzling question of why we girls were kept ignorant about the workings of our bodies and, most crucially, of reproduction? Was this appalling policy a matter of prudence rather than prudishness as I had

at first thought? Could the withholding of such vital information from the girls, as well as the obsessive segregation of the boys and girls, have been because the Governors wanted to prevent future alliances with the opposite sex, not to have them even think about sex? Could the Hospital's thinking have been that such alliances among Foundlings might on leaving the school lead to marriages and offspring and a desire for independent living, thus likely causing the loss of valuable domestic servants they had placed, and for the boys, drop-outs from the military?

As my mother recognized, the institution was willing to go to great lengths to safeguard its investment in future servants, an investment that would be greatly devalued by an imprudent pregnancy.

There were unintended consequences to the hospital's policies, however. As my mother remarked in her recollections, the refusal to discuss the differences between the sexes left female foundlings "vulnerable to every kind of mistreatment and exploitation." Interviews with former foundlings supported my mother's view, revealing that many were uncomfortable speaking and interacting with the opposite sex. Some felt profound shame, their illegitimacy a secret that had to be hidden. Others fell victim to their own ignorance. There were reports of foundlings who didn't know that they were pregnant until it was pointed out by a friend or colleague. One thought that a condom was a receptacle for a man's menstrual blood, as she had no understanding that only women menstruated and certainly no concept of what a condom was. Yet another was raped, but didn't understand that until many years later.

As for my mother, who hinted at "further difficulties in dealing with the opposite sex," the hospital's rigid segregation led to what she termed an "acute awkwardness and discomfort" around men. In her early years, there was only one occasion during which she experienced joy and comfort in the company of the opposite sex. It's no wonder where her dreams would lead her.

I DON'T KNOW when or how my mother traveled to the United States, but I do know why.

> It all began with those kind American servicemen at Boving-don Acrodrome. Because of them it eventually culminated in my emigration to America. America offered hope, opportunity, acceptance and liberation from the rigid British system.

My mother emigrated in the 1950s, but I was not able to find her name on any government records. Whether she traveled by ship and how she found the money to pay for her passage are equally unknown to me. These subjects were never discussed in my family, and her manuscript skips over that entire period. Somehow, at some point, my mother made her way to San Francisco.

She found a job at a bank in the financial district and shared a small apartment with a few other young women. She was independent and free, with a fresh start that would allow her to leave her painful past behind. But the transition was not without difficulties. "Despite my inexpressible joy at being in America," she wrote, "I remember there was at the same time an intense emptiness in my life. More than anything I wanted a home of my own and an American husband of the kind that touched my heart as a child in England."

She didn't have long to wait. In the spring of 1960 after dinner at a little Italian restaurant in the lively North Beach area of

San Francisco, my mother and a coworker decided to hop on a cable car to visit the Buena Vista, a popular pub-like bistro famous for its trendy Irish coffee. Inside, there was a long bar and a row of round tables with views of Alcatraz and the San Francisco Bay. The two women found seats and had begun to chat when a well-dressed man with dark hair and large blue eyes approached my mother.

"Excuse me, may I sit in this chair?" he asked above the din. My mother nodded, and he extended his hand and introduced himself—though she was so nervous she missed his name. She told him hers. Eager to shed her identity as a foundling, when she came to the United States she'd let go of the name Dorothy Soames and adopted the name I assume she had been given at birth—Eileen Mary Weston.

The young man had served in World War II, he revealed, and the two talked until he asked if he could take her to dinner some night.

It wasn't the story I'd been told as a child. The version enshrined in family lore had them meeting at a party on Nob Hill, an affluent neighborhood of San Francisco first settled by railroad barons in the 1870s. Perched above the city, the location seemed like the perfect place for my parents to have met. But it was just another fib designed to hide my mother's shame, though this particular fabrication was run-of-the-mill, a harmless cover for my mother's embarrassment over having met her husband in a bar. I discovered the lie when I was thirty-nine years old, over dinner at a seafood restaurant in Ghirardelli Square. I had brought a friend along who innocently asked how my parents had met. I jumped in, ready to share the well-worn story of their courtship, until I noticed my parents smiling oddly. Only then did the truth come out.

As the day of their first date arrived, Eileen was excited, filled with hope for a future with a dashing young American GI. She was also fearful that she'd make a mistake and ruin everything. She didn't even know his name! Would he be offended by that? She had so little experience with men, she didn't know what to expect.

The night of their date, the handsome GI walked her to his car and opened her door. At the time, a person was required to have a copy of his license affixed to the steering wheel. While he walked around to the driver's side of the car, Eileen quickly leaned over and got a glimpse of his name—John Alderson Thompson. It was a nice name, she thought. John got into the car, none the wiser.

Several months later, my mother would take her third name in her lifetime, becoming Eileen Weston Thompson.

"WHY DID YOU marry her?" I asked my father when I was about fifteen. The question could have been interpreted benignly, a simple request for a story about how my mother and father had met, why he loved her so much. But my father knew what I meant.

"She can be quite charming, you know."

His explanation sounded hollow, too simple. I assumed he meant that my mother had tricked him.

The truth was more complex, but a facile gloss over the dynamic governing my parents' marriage suited me back then. A deeper understanding wouldn't emerge until I'd sifted through both of their backgrounds for clues. My father spoke often of his past, and the stories of his childhood and the years before he moved to California remained fresh in my mind. But as I revisited those memories through a new lens, my views of my parents' marriage slowly began to change.

Like my mother, my father had been separated from his mother not long after he was born, in the town of Rogersville, Tennessee. Originally settled in the 1780s, Rogersville is one Tennessee's oldest towns, and home to the state's first newspaper. Due to its remote location near the Great Smoky Mountains, the town was still sparsely populated, with only about fourteen hundred residents, in 1921, the year my father was born.

With no hospitals in the vicinity, John Alderson Thompson came into this world in the downstairs bedroom of his parents' home. Six days after his birth, his mother died of a postpartum hemorrhage, an event that cloaked my father's life in guilt, as if he had caused the blood to spill from her womb in the days following his birth. Some sixty years later, he shared with me his belief about what had happened in those last days of his mother's life. She must have known that she was dying, he told me, and he liked to believe she spent those six days holding him, loving him, and that as she took her last breath, she prayed for him.

John would soon be without a father as well. A man wasn't expected to raise a child on his own, so within months "Baby John" was moved to his aunt Azalea's house to be raised by Azalea and her husband, Hubert. The couple already had three sons of their own: Griff (born just six weeks after my father), Joe, and another John. To avoid confusion, my father would be called Johnnie and his cousin John T., and Griff and my father would be raised as twins. John thrived under Aunt Azalea's kindness and care, in the company of cousins whom he knew as brothers.

But his happiness was cut short at the age of six, when he was taken from the only mother he had known. His father had remarried, and John was summoned back to his birthplace, where he would be raised by a stern and mercurial woman named Jessie who had little love for her stepson. When John's father died a little over a decade later, she packed up and left, never to be heard from again. John would have to make his own way in life. He volunteered for the war against the Nazis and Japanese along with Griff, John T., and Joe. Griff was shot down over Czechoslovakia, perishing along with the rest of the crew of a B-24 bomber on a mission to Odertal, Germany. Joe came home from the war, but the horrors he had witnessed in the Pacific caused him to take his own life. Only Johnnie and John T. would make it back alive.

My paternal grandfather had been a prominent figure in East Tennessee before he died, a successful attorney and a member of the Tennessee legislature. When John returned from the war, he had no money; his stepmother had taken everything except a small plot of land that had been left specifically to him. But he was driven, taking advantage of the GI Bill that sent more than eight million World War II veterans to school. Before long he was a respected attorney who, like his father, was elected to serve in the Tennessee legislature. He also became a delegate of the 1953 Tennessee Constitutional Convention, which amended the state's constitution to eliminate the poll tax.

John was restless, however. During the war, he was stationed in the China-Burma-India theater, supporting China in its battle against the Japanese. He had traveled to Egypt, Iran, and Pakistan, eventually ending up in India. One of his first impressions of India, as he peered out of a transport plane flying at low altitude, was the sight of the Taj Mahal in full moonlight. For most of the war John was stationed in Assam, in the northeastern region of India. The American camp was surrounded by a jungle filled with venomous snakes—krait and cobra—and rumored to be crawling with tribal headhunters. There were always monkeys, hundreds of them, their incessant chatter providing a backdrop to the daily lives of the soldiers. Occasionally John would see a tiger or an elephant. Once he watched Tibetans walk single file near the camp, learning later that they had traveled hundreds of miles across the Himalayas to shop in the small town of Tezpur.

John had seen the world, and the small town of Rogersville would not contain him for long, and so he packed up his bags and made his way to California.

MY MOTHER HAD dreamed of meeting an American GI from the time that first convoy passed by the Foundling Hospital. Americans were kind and gentle, she decided, and John was no exception. He spoke softly to her, rarely raising his voice in anger, instead praising her cooking and her choices in design, always supporting her thoughts and opinions. And with a successful law practice, he became wealthy, allowing my mother to hire servants to meet her every need and never take a job of her own, something I viewed in a new light, given what I now knew about her past.

In addition to security and love, John gave my mother something she had always yearned for—respectability. She was the wife of a distinguished lawyer who came from a line of respectable men, prominent attorneys and politicians, a man whose great-great-great-grandfather Archibald Thompson had fought in the American Revolution. What a relief it must have been to marry into a family with a history, and a name that no one would ever question.

Seen from the outside, my parents' lives were ideal. My sister was born about a year after my parents married; I followed four years later. My mother took on the traditional role of a housewife, caring for us as my father made his way to work each day. His success allowed our family to live luxuriously, with expensive cars and homes, and vacations to exotic places where we would stay in the finest hotels—a far cry from the life Miss Wright had envisioned for Dorothy.

From my vantage point, their marriage was unhappy, but in the years closer to his death, my father told me often how much he loved my mother. Perhaps they shared a bond that I could never understand, both having lost their mothers at an early age, their formative years filled with heartbreak. At her funeral, he called out to her as they lowered the casket, his lonesome wails powerful, an animal cry coming from somewhere deep within his soul.

Love can take many forms, and though for much of my life I viewed my parents' marriage as a failed enterprise, I see things differently now. Both figures are more complex than I ever imagined, the bond between them formed by time and habit, but also through a shared journey of tragedy and loss. It's only in the shadow of their absence that I can reinterpret their union as an imperfect fairy tale. My mother's childhood dream had come true. She had married her American GI, and she was cared for and loved.

17

Reunions and Reckonings

My mother and I were about the same age when we each felt an irresistible pull to understand the past, and how it had shaped who we had become.

I can't claim to fully understand what finally compelled me to uncover my mother's secrets, an obsession that spanned the course of two years. I do know that the anger I'd shouldered for much of my life had taken its toll. The sheer intensity of my feelings for my mother, the loathing that was always simmering just under the surface, were burdens with a palpable weight. Perhaps I hoped that understanding my mother's past might provide me with a sense of peace.

But my mother's journey was not about anger—it was about shame.

Because I had spent most of my life not wanting to remember and didn't want anyone to know about this period in my history I had always tried to keep the Foundling Hospital years out of my thoughts. This was not only because of the shame I felt by being illegitimate, but also because of the fact that I was "allowed" to leave school two years early on account of what I believed was my bad conduct. I thought these reasons both degraded me and would cause me to lose esteem in the eyes of others. As a result, I have lived a life of lies.

That shame, she wrote, was also the reason she went to such great lengths to conceal the truth about her background. "However," she concluded, "in recent years and much to my surprise, I have been drawn back to those days and have tried to make sense of them."

And so, when I was eleven, my mother traveled across the Atlantic Ocean to Brunswick Square in an attempt to understand her past—just as I would forty years later.

MY MOTHER'S EFFORTS to isolate herself from the painful memories of her childhood had been so successful that she made a startling discovery—the Foundling Hospital as she knew it had shuttered its doors just a decade after her departure. Its closure had become inevitable as the chasm between society's increasingly progressive views on child development and the callous practices of the Foundling Hospital widened. In 1918 Parliament passed the Education Act, heralding a new commitment to quality education for children. The measure abolished fees in state elementary schools and raised the age at which children could quit school from twelve to fourteen. Further improvements were sidelined by the Great Depression of the 1930s, but World War II refocused England's attention on its children.

A further impetus for change arose from Operation Pied Piper—the government-led mass evacuation that Lena had attempted to use as leverage to reclaim Dorothy. The nation concluded from the experience that separating children from their mothers could wreak significant and lasting psychological damage. Of course the British government had been taking illegitimate children from their mothers for centuries, but with Operation Pied Piper, children of all classes and backgrounds experienced the trauma of parental separation, and the nation finally took notice of its effects.

It was also a ripe time for the field of child psychology, which flourished in the postwar era as researchers began disseminating ideas that would fundamentally change society's views on how children should be raised. Anna Freud, through her work with children separated from their parents during World War II, recognized the role that the family structure plays in helping individuals endure extended periods of stress. Donald Winnicott, one of Britain's first medically trained child psychoanalysts, put forth the idea that a mother instinctively knows how to care for her child without the need for expert advice. And John Bowlby (the same John Bowlby who, unfortunately, also believed unmarried mothers to be mentally ill) revolutionized the field of child development with his attachment theory.

These cultural shifts laid the foundation for what was to come, but a tragic event would be the tipping point in the demise of the Foundling Hospital. On January 9, 1945, less than a year after my mother had left, a twelve-year-old Welsh boy was murdered by his foster parents in Shropshire. While the boy had not been a ward of the Foundling Hospital, the institution's future was swept up in the onrush of public scrutiny of the treatment of unparented children in England.

Despite the ongoing war, the boy's death garnered a significant amount of attention—so much so that the crime led the minister of education, the home secretary, and the minister of health to create a commission to protect children who weren't being raised by their parents.

For a change, this commission would be headed by a woman— Dame Myra Curtis, an educator and civil servant. Instead of being appointed by virtue of their social connections, members of the commission would be medical professionals, educators, civil servants, and clergy, more than half of them female. In other words, for the first time in two centuries, the practices of the Foundling Hospital would be scrutinized by women.

Since King George II signed the royal charter for the Foundling Hospital, the opinions of women on how to care for children had virtually been ignored. The Ladies of Quality and Distinction without whom the Foundling Hospital might never have existed, who signed the first petition pleading with the king to care for foundlings, were ultimately sidelined in favor of male governors. These men would go on to opine as to the proper methods of child-rearing without soliciting female input, and would reject countless pleas for reunification, believing their care to be superior to that which could be provided by a child's mother. And in the end it was a commission comprised primarily of women that would finally bring this dark chapter of England's history to a close.

The scope of the commission's inquiry was broad, not limited to the Foundling Hospital but extending to foster care, group homes, and institutional care in general. It also considered the care provided to children who were homeless, disabled, or mired in the criminal justice system.

The Curtis Report, as the commission's findings were dubbed, was particularly critical of institutional care, rife with observations that were hauntingly similar to my mother's descriptions of life at the Foundling Hospital. The report criticized admission procedures that often caused children to experience "misery, bewilderment and fear," such as requiring newcomers to discard their clothes, take mandatory baths, and don identical uniforms.[62] Dressing the children alike perpetuated the stigma of poverty and suppressed individuality, the report found. The commission also noted that little attention was paid to recreation, and that children were allowed few personal possessions or toys. Lacking access to newspapers, pocket money, or rudimentary information about life outside of the institutions in which they were placed, the children frequently emerged without knowledge of the basics of sex and reproductive health, or even how to use money. As a result, they had difficulties developing an ability to look after themselves or fit into society at large.

Staff, the report found, was inadequately trained, or had no training at all, and paid little attention to the children. While many of the children were well cared for in terms of food, clothing, and accommodation, they frequently showed a "longing for caresses from strangers" that was "in striking and painful contrast to the behaviour of the normal child of the same age in his parents' home."[63] Highly critical of the assumption that girls should be trained as domestic servants, the report remarked that "nothing could justify the lack of care which seemed often to be shown in choosing employment best suited to the abilities of children deprived of normal home life, since the right kind of employment must be one means of compensating them for their loss."[64]

Its hundred and ninety-five pages chronicled countless other problems: too much isolation, lack of intellectual stimulation, failure to even consider allowing children to see relatives who "with encouragement might take an interest in them,"[65] and the enforcement of the stigma of poverty and shame. In short, it was everything my mother had described, chronicled in detail. For the first time, what she experienced at the Foundling Hospital was categorically and unequivocally condemned.

The report's conclusions were stark. Institutional care should be phased out, replaced with a system in which children would be put out for adoption, raised in private homes, or placed in smaller group settings with other children of various ages "under the care of a trained and sympathetic house mother or house mother and father."[66] Whatever the setting, the report recommended that "every orphan or deserted child coming within the range of public care should have a legal guardian to take the major decisions in his life and to feel full responsibility for his welfare."[67]

Most striking to me was that the report was commissioned in March 1945. Just eleven months after Dorothy Soames left the Foundling Hospital, practices that had been in place for two centuries began to unravel. For the first time, foundlings were allowed to go to their foster parents' homes for holidays, visits that would last as long as three weeks. Newcomers retained their given names, a sign that they would no longer be hidden in shame. Efforts were made to reunite mothers and children; appeals appeared in the *Daily Telegraph*, and a staff member was appointed to contact mothers to ask if they wanted to see their children.

Soon daily life at the hospital would bear little resemblance to the world in which my mother had been raised. Trained teachers were hired, kind-hearted and affectionate professionals who provided attention and tenderness to their charges. Children who had never been touched except in punishment received hugs, words of encouragement, and good-night kisses as they were tucked into bed each night. The dormitories were no longer so stark, as children were allowed to have toys and other belongings. In 1949 the strict segregation of the sexes was abandoned, and girls and boys began to receive mixed education.

My mother was overjoyed when she learned of the changes that came to the Foundling Hospital shortly after her departure:

> I can well imagine how exciting it was for my contemporaries when they were finally allowed to walk freely to town on weekends, unsupervised with pocket money to shop and visit the cinema; taught to ride bicycles and allowed to breeze around the countryside free as the wind; to be freed from the antiquated brown uniforms they had worn day after day, year after year, to be provided with modern clothing; to have a voice, to receive respect and affection.

"Gifts taken for granted by most parented children were at last bestowed on the children of the Foundling Hospital," she observed.

Still, the changes did not go far enough to satisfy what experts now recognize as the essential needs of children, and in 1954, two hundred and fifteen years after it had been granted a royal charter, the Hospital for the Maintenance and Education of Exposed and Deserted Young Children closed its doors. To mark the end of an era, its name was changed and a new policy was adopted: "to lay great emphasis on the home atmosphere for the children—primarily, of course, by restoration to the mother, and secondly by adoption and thirdly (and principally) by the choice of suitable foster parents."[68]

Today Coram no longer houses any charges, instead providing a range of direct services to vulnerable children and their families. One of the largest independent adoption agencies in the United Kingdom, the charity assists with approximately one in ten adoptions. But the institution views its role as much broader than placing children with permanent families, and its programs focus on nurturing children from their earliest days. As I read descriptions of Coram's offerings—early intervention practices to help children overcome trauma, the emphasis on keeping siblings together, the inclusion of sex education in its outreach programs—I wondered whether they had been developed as a response to lessons learned from the institution's history. Whether Coram simply evolved with the times or did the difficult work of institutional accounting, the arcane treatment that my mother endured had been firmly left in the past.

ALTHOUGH MY MOTHER was never allowed to see all of the files chronicling her life at the Foundling Hospital, her inquiries nevertheless brought unexpected and satisfying results. When she arrived at 40 Brunswick Square, she was met by J. G. B. Swinley, the director and secretary of the Thomas Coram Foundation for Children, as the institution was called before its name was shortened a second time. My mother was greatly touched by the visit, deeming it "the first time a Foundling official had acted with regard toward me."

Mr. Swinley was patient, taking the time to listen to my mother and hear about her life at the Foundling Hospital. They entered into a true dialogue, and she asked him why he thought the Foundling Hospital had closed, describing his response in an uncharacteristically breathless tone: "because it was realized that children needed LOVE!"

It was "an extraordinary statement for a former Foundling to hear," she concluded.

The conversation left such an impression that my mother was moved to send Mr. Swinley a donation. I found a copy of the letter she received in response tucked within the pages of her manuscript, the amount of the donation hidden.

20th June, 1977

Dear Mr. and Mrs. Thompson,

How very kind of you to send us a cheque for ███. We are extremely grateful.

I am so glad your visits here and to Berkhamsted were worthwhile. The more I hear about the Berkhamsted days, the more admiration I feel for those who like you not only survived them, but have made a success of their lives. That time seems to have been the nadir of the Foundling Hospital's history.

Yours Sincerely,
J. G. B. Swinley
Director and Secretary

Encouraged by the kindness she received and the news of the reforms, my mother continued her dive into the hospital's history and soon learned of another development to which she hadn't been privy—the creation of an association of former foundlings called the Old Coram Association. Founded in 1947, the organization had been bringing foundlings together to meet and share their stories for decades by the time my mother discovered its existence.

And so, in 1998, when I was thirty-two, and unbeknownst to me, my mother made yet another journey to England:

It was with a mixture of excitement and nervousness that I walked across the leaf scattered grass of Brunswick Square Gardens on October 18, 1998 to attend the Charter Day luncheon at 40 Brunswick Square in expectation of meeting at least a few of the girls from school. . . . The sky was overcast and I was glad of the slight drizzle on my face—I have always felt more alive in the cold moisture of the English climate. I was mindful that it was probably through that very door at number 40 that my mother parted with me when I was two months and one day old.

I expected that on entering the front door I would be politely ushered to the staircase going down below where undoubtedly the luncheon would be held in a basement room. After all, I thought without rancor, hadn't we Foundlings been shut away out of sight for most of our childhood? I had no reason to believe that our standing had been elevated.

Instead, after exciting recognitions and joyful hugs in the hallway with a couple of "girls" from school, I found myself propelled on the UP staircase. The handsome wooden staircase I was told was salvaged from the boys' wing of the old London Foundling Hospital. We passed historic paintings on the walls on our way up to the next floor where I was warmly welcomed by several other contemporaries, including my partner in crime, Margaret! All the while we animatedly caught up with each other's lives and commiserated in good humor about our travails at school, the leather straps and canes, the traumas with Miss Woodward and the swimming pool, and what we got away with. I was dizzily transported back to my Foundling days and my Dorothy Soames persona.

The former foundlings were ushered into a room rich with antique furnishings, paintings, and a beautiful, ornate plaster case ceiling. The crowd of some one hundred men and women mingled before taking their seats at long tables with white tablecloths.

What solace it must have been to reconnect with those who

had been lost to her and could truly understand her past. But further surprises were to come. As my mother took her seat that night, she gazed toward the head table and found that seated among the executives of Coram administrators and other honored guests were several former foundlings. She hadn't expected to see them sitting in positions of honor, and was even more surprised when they stood up and delivered eloquent speeches.

As my mother listened, she felt unimaginable joy. Finally, she reflected in recounting the enchantment of the evening, "my fellow Foundlings had a place and a voice!"

It was in reading these words that I realized the full import of this second trip to London—the impetus for my mother to put pen to paper for the first time and attempt to tell her story, finally baring the secrets that had haunted her for a lifetime.

It wasn't only her fellow foundlings who had found their voices at last.

MORE THAN THIRTY years had passed since the day I'd found my mother in a dimly lit room, filling a notebook page with a name that was now familiar to me, like that of an old friend. I had promised Bernice—or Isabel, as I thought of her—that we would visit, and so, for the third time, my husband and I made our way back to England. But this time, as the plane approached London's Gatwick Airport, I felt calm, with a sense of belonging, as if I were going home.

After a quick stop at Coram and the Foundling Museum, where we were met with generous smiles and warm hugs from the staff members we had met on our previous trip, we boarded a train to Berkhamsted to spend the afternoon with Lydia Carmichael, the head of the Old Coram Association and my mother's former classmate.

As we walked outside the train station, a woman in her eighties bounded toward me, her eyes lively and her cheeks crimson from the cold air. "You must be Justine!" she exclaimed as she threw her arms around me. "You look just like your mother!" I smiled, no longer bothered by the comparison, feeling even a hint of pride.

We spent the afternoon walking around the old hospital grounds, just a few minutes from Lydia's home. She hadn't always lived in Berkhamsted, Lydia explained, but an opportunity arose and she had decided to move back.

She didn't mind being so close to the source of so many painful memories. "I used to be ashamed of my past," she shared. "We all were. But now, I shout it from the rooftops! I'm proud to be a foundling." Indeed, she had become a celebrity of sorts, speaking to school groups and civic organizations, sharing stories of the Foundling Hospital's past with anyone who would listen. She has appeared on television and met several members of the royal family, including the Queen, the Duke of Edinburgh, Prince Charles, and the Duchess of Cambridge.

As we wandered around the grounds, Lydia, who had kept the name given to her by the Foundling Hospital rather than revert back to her birth name, shared stories all too familiar to me—how the children had stolen carrots from the Victory Garden, and marched when Miss Woodward died. Lydia showed me the room where they held their midnight feasts, their dormitory (now a classroom), and Miss Wright's office. But we decided not to venture down the steep flight of stairs that led to what had once been the bomb shelter, thwarted by a sign warning of asbestos contamination.

"Those nights were terrifying," she recounted as we peered down the ominous stairwell. "It was mad, you know. Mad! We had such a long way to go to get to the shelter. The sirens would go off, telling us the Germans were coming, but we had to queue up first, all thirty of us in our dormitory, to use the loo! What were they thinking?! Not about us, that's for certain."

I asked whether she knew where my mother had been locked up by Miss Wright. She couldn't remember, but did recall a girl who had been told to stay in a classroom as punishment. The staff had forgotten about her, and although the door was unlocked, she stayed there until the following morning, fearful that she would be punished if she left. The next day, she was instead punished for remaining in the classroom all night.

As Lydia and I wandered the halls, from time to time we would come upon framed photos of foundlings affixed to the walls, reminding the current occupants of the building's history. Most featured groups of identically clad girls and boys, lined up to meet distinguished visitors in the chapel or perched behind desks in their classrooms. One featured a few girls playing with toys.

"There I am," Lydia interjected as we leaned forward to get a closer look. "It was all staged, you know."

Most of the photographs of the foundlings were publicity shots, she explained, taken to accompany cheerful newspaper accounts extoling the virtues of the Foundling Hospital.

"They took the toys away from us after they took the pictures," she added. "They couldn't even let us keep the toys, that's how bad it was."

Our conversation meandered as we wandered through the halls where my mother had once lived, and occasionally Lydia would ask for details about my project. By now she knew all about the pile of dog-eared books, the countless files I had reviewed, the emotional journey that had brought me to these very halls.

As we walked down the staircase, my hands gently skimming

the banister where foundlings had once risked a caning just to feel the elation of gliding down the slick wood, Lydia paused, looking up at me. "Your mother would have been so pleased that you came all this way," she finally said. "It would have meant so much to her."

My stomach tightened in response. *She thinks this is a journey of love.* How could I possibly tell her the truth? But silence would have been a lie, a betrayal of the trust Lydia had offered me, and so I confessed. "Our relationship was difficult," I said, searching for the right words. "It was . . . troubled."

I tensed as she turned toward me, preparing myself for the reprobation I had come to expect. Instead, she smiled and rested her hand gently on my arm.

"Of course it was," she said. "How would she have known how to be a mother?"

It was so simple and matter-of-fact, no platitudes about motherhood or stories about the intrinsic difficulties of mother-daughter relationships. I uttered no response, but on the inside, I experienced a sea change. Instead of the usual voices filling my head, damning and defending myself all at once, there was only a stunned silence.

When I'd gathered myself, I asked Lydia whether she re-membered the day my mother had gone home to live with her biological mother.

"We called it being 'reclaimed' back then, not that it hap-pened often. Your mother was the first that I remember during my time there. It happened again, after your mother left, but that time they didn't tell us anything. It was another girl, about our age. One day she was there, the next day she was gone. She just disappeared! It was years later before we found out what happened to her, at a reunion or something of that sort, that she had been reclaimed by her mother. It hadn't gone well, I heard.

Her mother was a terrible person, treated her badly. It rarely went well. Too much time had passed, I suppose."

"Do you know what happened to my mother when she left? What her life was like with her mother?"

"I'm not quite sure, but you know, she sent me her book. It's probably in there."

The same book that my mother had sent me all those years ago—maybe Lydia's version would be complete.

"Why don't you and Patrick come over for a cup of tea, and I'll have a look for it."

Patrick and I sank into the soft couch in Lydia's cozy living room as her husband, Don, served us tea and cakes. As we waited for Lydia, Don shared that he too had grown up parentless, an orphan raised at a children's home in India. Lydia and Don had been married for sixty years, and I wondered whether their shared losses in childhood had created an uncommon bond, as had been the case for my own parents.

I listened as Don told us stories of his life in India as a child, but it was difficult to concentrate. *Would my mother have censored Lydia's manuscript in the same way she had mine? And if she hadn't, would I finally learn the truth about those missing years?*

"Here it is!" Lydia exclaimed as she bounded into the room, a broad smile on her face. I immediately recognized the sheath of papers in her hands as the same pages my mother had given to me. But as I thumbed through the pages, I saw the same handwritten note that had been in my copy where the chapters of her time in Shropshire should have been: "Not included."

Lydia was puzzled that my mother had kept the details of the reunification hidden.

"It's odd. We went through so much together. I wonder why she wouldn't want us to know?"

My mother had shared stories of beatings and brutality, of

shame and disgrace. What secrets were contained in those pages that were worse than she had already admitted? If she couldn't share her secrets with the girls who had suffered alongside her all those years ago, who could she tell?

We left Lydia's house with promises to stay in touch, and I tossed and turned that night as I reckoned with the awareness that my journey was coming to an end.

Before it could, there would be one more stop.

The following morning, Patrick and I arrived at London's Euston Station to catch the train to Polegate, a small town a couple of hours south of the city, to meet my namesake, Isabel, now called Bernice. I scanned a gigantic timetable in the station's atrium for our platform. Unable to find it, I approached a man dressed in a conductor's uniform.

"You're at the wrong station," he explained. "Your train leaves from Victoria."

Instantly, anxiety-fueled adrenaline filled my veins with such speed that I became light-headed. How could I have made such a stupid mistake? What was wrong with me? But before my mind could leap into the darkness, I felt Patrick's arm around my shoulder.

"It's going to be all right."

"I should have double-checked last night," I countered. "It's my fault. What if we don't make the train? What if we miss Bernice, and we came all this way and we never see her?"

As my mind raced with endless scenarios flowing from my carelessness, Patrick pulled me closer, resting his forehead against mine so that I could hear him above the din of one of London's busiest train stations. My heart rate calmed as I listened to his voice. People rushed past us, but their forms became shapeless blurs.

"It's not your fault. You're human, that's all. And it's going to be okay."

There are people out there who doubt whether their husbands or wives love them. I am not one of those people. Patrick loves me even more than the day we walked down the aisle, and I am sure of that. I see it in the way he looks at me—not when I am dressed up for a night out, or laughing at one of his silly jokes, but when I am huddled in the dark abyss of self-doubt.

In the early years of our relationship I would resist his tender words, allowing my mind instead to wander through well-trodden grooves that instinctively assessed guilt or innocence to the smallest of missteps. But Patrick has shown me another way, a paradigm that isn't based on culpability. "Love isn't about blame," he says often. I have an uneasy truce with the voices from my past, and it takes vigilance to keep them at bay. I rarely experience the destructive emotions that afflicted me in the early years of my adulthood—an achievement I attribute largely to a skilled therapist. But I credit Patrick's love with my ability to view myself with compassion. I can now look into the mirror with an unfamiliar confidence and admire my smooth brown hair and blue-green eyes, or take pride in my accomplishments— and more often than not, allow myself to make a few mistakes.

We made our connection at Victoria Station with seconds to spare, and an hour and a half later we pulled into Polegate. Isabel, or Bernice, as she now preferred to be called, met us at the station and hurried toward me as if we were lifelong friends. She was small and delicate, standing less than five feet tall. Her voice was soft, but, I soon learned, her wit was sharp.

We had lunch in a modest country manor that had been converted into a restaurant, where Patrick and I listened intently as Bernice recounted stories of her childhood and the cruel indifference of the Foundling Hospital staff. After lunch, we headed back to her small but comfortable apartment. Bernice showed us a collection of figurines she had carefully arranged on a sideboard in the living room. She picked up two small five-inch-tall dolls depicting a boy and a girl, each clad in the unmistakable brown clothing with white caps that the foundlings had once worn. As she cradled them in her hands, Bernice started whispering to them, calling each by name—Isabel, her own childhood name, along with the name of the boy who was her schoolgirl crush. I imagined them stealing glances across the aisle in the chapel, risking punishment for a tiny sliver of joy in an otherwise dreary existence. Bernice never married, but her eyes lit up as she murmured to the figurines.

The remainder of the afternoon was spent over tea, learning more about Bernice and her life after the Foundling Hospital. At the age of fourteen, she had been placed as a domestic in a house with many servants, where she scrubbed floors and changed linens for a wealthy family.

"It was just awful, and after about six months, I'd had enough," she said. "So one day I told 'em that they damn well needed to do their own cleaning." She giggled as she recounted her tale, holding her hand in front of her mouth. "And I told the Foundling Hospital that they could forget about putting me in another house, that I was done with them, too!"

Bernice was not alone in rebelling against the path that the governors of the Foundling Hospital had set for her. Lydia, whom we had met earlier that week, proudly embraced her status as illegitimate, refusing to accept the arcane narrative that her background was a shameful secret. And of course there was my mother, who had beaten all the odds, marrying her American GI and becoming wealthy beyond her dreams. I had come across other stories as well, of foundlings who became nurses, teachers, and engineers, and who were happily married with children. While none escaped the painful wounds of the past, I was struck by the number of foundlings who did more than just survive.

As the afternoon progressed, Bernice and I spoke comfortably, like we were old friends chatting about the past. From time to time, I would slip up and call her Isabel, instead of Bernice. But she didn't mind.

"I was never keen on Isabel, but now I have changed my mind. It brings back memories of your mother, my dear friend, and brought into being a lovely meeting with you."

Bernice insisted on walking us to the train station. It was a cold and blustery day, and the wind was picking up as storm clouds formed above us, but I was filled with a sense of warmth as we walked side by side. We said our goodbyes, and as I was about to make my way through the turnstile, Bernice pulled me toward her and whispered in my ear, "I knew it was you when I saw you at the station. I said to myself, there she is. There's Dorothy."

Tears streamed down my face as Patrick and I stood on the platform, the cold wind stinging my cheeks. But I hardly noticed as I stepped onto the train and headed back to London.

18

LOVE

I dreamt of my mother.

I was sitting in my favorite room of my childhood home, the breakfast room, small and cozy, with none of the grandeur of the rest of the house. Instead, it was furnished with a plain oval oak table surrounded by four wooden chairs, the only decor a simple vase with a rose from my mother's garden. Along one side of the room stood a row of windows with sheer white curtains that allowed the morning light to spill in, and in the glow was my mother, sitting across from me. Her face was at ease, with no sign of her usual frown or pursed lips. There was a pewter teapot next to her, and we both sipped hot tea as I listened to her tell me stories of her childhood. I interrupted her only to ask the questions that had been replayed so many times in my mind. *Did my grandmother know about me? Why didn't you tell me about her? How did you get to San Francisco? Who taught you to paint, and to play the piano?*

In the dream, she patiently answered my questions until finally, drained but with a sense of peace I had rarely experienced in my waking life, I realized that I now knew everything she had gone through. I looked at her and smiled. She smiled back.

In real life, my mother and I never spoke about her past as Dorothy Soames. Not when I first saw the name that portentous day when I was nineteen, not when she reached out to me with her story a decade later, nor when Alzheimer's began to chip away at her memory.

I often think about what our relationship would have been like had I dared to ask those questions, and had she dared to answer. But by the time my interest in her past was finally stirred, it was simply too late.

It was a Tuesday afternoon when I got the call—there wasn't much time left. My mother, who was now in a nursing home for the memory-impaired, had taken a turn for the worse and wasn't expected to hang on for longer than a few days.

My father was staying nearby at my sister's house in New Orleans, where we had relocated my parents when they were no longer able to care for themselves. In those last years, I visited often, every few weeks. With my mother in a facility, I was free to see my father alone for the first time in more than a decade. But our time together was bittersweet, at times filled with palpable regret, his ninety-year-old mind having lost its once characteristic sharpness.

Visits with my mother would last only an hour or so. The initial facility she lived in boasted a plentiful array of amenities, an attentive staff, and daily field trips. The rooms were bright and airy, the hallways thoughtfully decorated with articles of clothing and knickknacks from the 1930s and '40s, on the theory that being surrounded by familiar objects from the past is soothing for someone with Alzheimer's. But in the months before her death,

when her condition had declined, she was moved to another facility, drab and joyless, with hospital-green walls and a more
restrictive type of care, where the inhabitants rarely ventured
into the sunlight. I sometimes wonder if the place reminded my
mother of the Foundling Hospital, if the sense of being cloistered from the outside world in an institutional setting brought
her back to her unhappiest memories, even if she could no longer
quite grasp them. A few weeks before she died, I was told that
my mother had become resentful, feeling that she was trapped.
She had walked purposefully into the administrator's office and
with a look of defiance pulled down her pants and peed, right
there in the middle of the room. I was amused at the time. But
looking back, I believe this may have been my mother's last moment of defiance. Could she have been seeing Miss Wright's
stern face when she contemptuously emptied her bladder?

By the time I arrived at her bedside for the visit that would
be our last, she was no longer speaking. Her face was gaunt, her
breathing sporadic and raspy, her head tipped slightly to the side.
Occasionally, a nurse wandered in to wet her lips with a Q-tip
or adjust a pillow to make her more comfortable. The scene was
almost more than I could bear, but I knew what I had to do.
I approached the bed and looked down at my mother's hand,
wrinkled and peppered with large brown age spots. I took it in
mine, gently squeezing as I whispered, "I love you, Mom."

My words were a lie, a balm for a dying old woman.

After that, there was nothing left to do but sit and watch my
mother slowly die. Suddenly her head jerked to face me, and she
stared into my eyes. I felt as if she were trying to tell me something, but no words came as a tear rolled down her cheek.

Minutes later, she was gone.

I didn't know at the time what had happened to her as a child,
that her wounds were too deep for her to look beyond her own

anguish. I can only hope that my lie was convincing enough, that my mother died believing that she was loved by me.

Now I understand why I grieved her death so intently, why pain coursed through my body, leaving me exhausted and frail those weeks after she closed her eyes for the last time. I mourned not the loss of what I once had, but what had been taken from me before I drew my first breath or took my first steps.

It is lonely to have no love for one's mother. While I had hoped that my feelings would change, love cannot be forced or conjured up. Perhaps she was not the only one with wounds too deep to heal.

But in my quest to learn about my mother's past, I realized that I had come to know somebody special. Someone I wanted to hold, to comfort and protect. That person was a girl with a smattering of freckles and silky brown hair, feisty and courageous and, improbably, full of dreams. I had grown to love that little girl.

Her name was Dorothy Soames.

ACKNOWLEDGMENTS

First and foremost, I would like to thank my talented publishing team, Sara Nelson at Harper, Sarah Savitt and Rose Tomaszewska at Virago, and my agent, Mollie Glick, at Creative Artists Agency, for their attentive reading, astute observations, and unwavering support.

Special thanks to Coram, in particular Val Payman, for setting me on my path; to Lydia Carmichael and Bernice Cunningham, my mother's former classmates at the Foundling Hospital, for showing me the meaning of courage and resilience; to Alison Duke at the Foundling Museum, Katharine Hogg at the General Coke Handel Collection, and Janette Bright, who were so generous with their time, confirming details buried in the past; and to Ashlyns School, for allowing me to wander the hallways and classrooms where my mother once roamed.

My eternal gratitude to Arielle Eckstut and Savannah Ashour for their thoughtful insights and indispensable wit.

More thanks than can be made to all those who listened, read, advised, and encouraged, including Michael Alvear, Lisa Baudot, Rabbi Mark Bloom, Lisa Pujol Boe, John Coburn, the Cowan Clan (Cara, Dan, Ian, Jen, Kathleen, Meg, Paul, and Tesla), Laura Coyle, Paula Derrow, Alex Djordjevich, Samuela Eckstut, Izak Epstein, Angie Fallows, Zoe Lee Francis, the Fort family, Nancy Frehner, Sarah Gill, Hollis Gillespie, Mary Gresham,

ACKNOWLEDGMENTS

Denean Hanson, Katherine Hoogerwerf, Angela Hunnicutt, Sondra Jarvis, Lisa Kern, Laura Klein, Lisa Mackin, Julie Mayfield, Carolyn Murchison, Darcy and George Nichols, Emilie Rider, Amy Paradysz, Robin Steinberg-Epstein, Midge and John Sweet, T. Edward Smith, David Henry Sterry, Olive Sterry, Suzi Sublette, Valerie Suttee, Scott Sykes, Ashley Vann, and Cary Barbor Zahaby.

I can never adequately thank my husband, Patrick, for his encouragement, and for showing me that unconditional love really does exist.

NOTES

1. Foundling Hospital, *A Copy of the Royal Charter, Establishing an Hospital for the Maintenance and Education of Exposed and Deserted Young Children* (London: J. Osborn, 1739), 1.

2. Foundling Hospital, "Rules for the Admission of Children," as provided to Lena Weston, January 4, 1932.

3. Marie Stopes, *Sex and the Young* (London: Gill Publishing Co. Ltd., 1926), 134, quoted in Ross McKibbin, introduction to *Married Love*, by Marie Stopes (Oxford: Oxford University Press, 2004), xvi.

4. John Bowlby, *Maternal Care and Mental Health* (World Health Organization, Geneva H.M.S.O. 1952), 93, quoted in Virginia Wimperis, *The Unmarried Mother and Her Child* (London: Sir Halley Stewart Trust, 1960), 95.

5. John Brownlow, *The History and Objects of the Foundling Hospital: With a Memoir of the Founder* (London: C. Jacques, 1881), 3.

6. Ibid., 70.

7. Foundling Hospital, "Rules for the Admission of Children," (emphasis in original).

8. Foundling Hospital, *Regulations for Managing the Hospital for the Maintenance and Education of Exposed and Deserted Young Children: By Order of the Governors of the Said Hospital* (London: Foundling Hospital, 1757), 34.

9. "Report of the Gentlemen Appointed . . . to Consider of a General Plan," *Report of the General Committee*, p. 5, FHL 41, item 1,

quoted in Ruth McClure, *Coram's Children: The London Foundling Hospital in the Eighteenth Century* (New Haven, CT: Yale University Press, 1981), 46.

10. Jonas Hanway, *A Candid Historical Account of the Hospital for the Reception of Exposed and Deserted Young Children* [. . .] *with a Proposal for Carrying a New Design into Execution*, 2nd rev. ed. (London: G. Woodfall and J. Waugh, 1760), 16.

11. McClure, *Coram's Children*, 9–10.

12. Thomas Bernard, *An Account of the Foundling Hospital in London, for the Maintenance and Education of Exposed and Deserted Young Children*, 2nd ed. (London: Thomas Jones, 1799), 4–5.

13. Foundling Hospital, *Regulations*, 50.

14. Ibid.

15. Porcupinus Pelagius [pseud.], "The Scandalizade: A Panegyri-Satiri-Serio-Comi-Dramatic Poem" (London, 1950), quoted in McClure, *Coram's Children*, 105.

16. Foundling Hospital, *Regulations*, 49.

17. Ibid.

18. McClure, *Coram's Children*, 229–30.

19. *Psalms, Hymns and Anthems Used in the Chapel of the Hospital for the Maintenance & Education of Exposed & Deserted Young Children* (London, 1744), 66, quoted in McClure, *Coram's Children*, 232.

20. Charles Dickens, *Oliver Twist* (New York: Shine Classics, 2014), 7 (emphasis in original).

21. Ibid., 166.

22. Foundling Hospital, *Regulations*, 39.

23. Ibid., 17.

24. Jonas Hanway, *A Review of the Proposed Naturalization of the Jews; Being an Attempt at a Dispassionate Enquiry*, 2nd ed. (London: J. Waugh, 1753), 25 (emphasis in original).

25. Ibid., 40 (emphasis in original).

26. Jonas Hanway, *Solitude in Imprisonment: With Proper Profitable Labour and a Spare Diet, the Most Humane and Effectual Means of Bringing Malefactors, Who Have Forfeited Their Lives, or Are Subject to Transportation, to a Right Sense of Their Condition* (London: F. Bew, 1776), 109.

27. Ibid., 105 (emphasis in original).

28. Minutes of the General Committee, Foundling Hospital, 15:284, quoted in McClure, *Coram's Children*, 234.

29. Charles Dickens, *American Notes for General Circulation* (London: Chapman and Hall, 1842; rpt., London: Penguin Classics, 2004), 111–12.

30. Deborah Blum, *Love at Goon Park: Harry Harlow and the Science of Affection* (New York: Basic Books, 2011), 218.

31. Ibid., 219.

32. Minutes of the General Committee, Foundling Hospital, 3:30, quoted in McClure, *Coram's Children*, 233.

33. Christine Oliver and Peter Aggleton, *Coram's Children: Growing up in the Care of the Foundling Hospital, 1900–1955* (London: Coram Family, 2000), 35.

34. Ibid.

35. Blum, *Love at Goon Park*, 145.

36. William Cadogan, *An Essay upon Nursing and the Management of Children, From their Birth to Three Years of Age*, 2nd ed. (London: J. Roberts, 1748) 10.

37. Ibid., 3.

38. Ibid.

39. Ibid., 21.

40. McClure, *Coram's Children*, 124.

41. Charles Dickens, "Received, A Blank Child," *Household Words* 7, no. 156 (March 1853), 53.

42. Ibid., 50–51

43. Letter from Secretary to Mrs. Storer, Nov. 17, 1852, Letterbook A/FH/66/002/011/:1849-53, London Metropolitan Archives, quoted in Gillian Pugh, *London's Forgotten Children: Thomas Coram and the Foundling Hospital* (Stroud, England: History Press, 2007), 84.

44. Pugh, *London's Forgotten Children*, 106.

45. Ibid.

46. Ibid., 106–7.

47. James C. Humes, *Speak Like Churchill, Stand Like Lincoln: 21 Powerful Secrets of History's Greatest Speakers* (New York: Three Rivers Press, 2002) 116.

48. Juliet Gardiner, *The Blitz: The British under Attack* (London: HarperPress, 2011), 193.

49. Ibid.

50. Ibid., 197.

51. Cadogan, *An Essay upon Nursing*, 14.

52. Pugh, *London's Forgotten Children*, 58.

53. Cadogan, *An Essay upon Nursing*, 17–19.

54. Ibid., 5.

55. Ibid.

56. US War Department, *Instructions for American Servicemen in Britain* (Washington, DC: US War Department, 1942; reproduced from the original typescript, Oxford, England: Bodleian Library, 2004), 3.

57. Ibid., 5.

58. Ibid., 20.

59. Helen Berry, *Orphans of Empire: The Fate of London's Foundlings* (Oxford: Oxford University Press, 2019), 222.

60. Ibid., 223.

61. Minutes of the General Committee, Foundling Hospital, 13:162–63, 243, quoted in McClure, *Coram's Children*, 134–35.

62. Care of Children Committee (Myra Curtis, chair), *Report of the Care of Children Committee*, Cmd. 6922 (London: His Majesty's Stationery Office, 1946), 53.

63. Ibid., 160

64. Ibid., 70.

65. Ibid., 60.

66. Ibid., 160.

67. Ibid., 138.

68. Pugh, *London's Forgotten Children*, 117.

SOURCE MATERIALS AND
SELECTED BIBLIOGRAPHY

I would never have been able to piece together my mother's story if she had not taken the heroic step of writing down the details of her painful childhood. I was able to corroborate her account with various sources, including the archival files maintained by Coram and the London Metropolitan Archives, along with interviews of former foundlings and historians.

The Foundling Museum was indispensable in my efforts to reconstruct the daily lives of foundlings, particularly its Foundling Voices project, which is based on interviews with seventy-four men and women who grew up in the care of the hospital in the twentieth century, between 1912 and 1954.

I also read dozens of books, articles, pamphlets, and other materials most of which I have listed below, but a handful deserve special mention. They were my constant companions, always within reach, their pages dog-eared, their margins filled with my illegible scribbles: *Orphans of Empire: The Fate of London's Foundlings*, by Helen Berry; *Coram's Children: The London Foundling Hospital in the Eighteenth Century*, by Ruth McClure; and *London's Forgotten Children: Thomas Coram and the Foundling Hospital*, by Gillian Pugh.

Atwood, Margaret. *The Handmaid's Tale*. New York: Fawcett Crest, 1986.

Bernard, Sir Thomas. *An Account of the Foundling Hospital in London, for the Maintenance and Education of Exposed and Deserted Young Children*, 2nd ed. London: Thomas Jones, 1799.

Berry, Helen. *Orphans of Empire: The Fate of London's Foundlings*. Oxford: Oxford University Press, 2019.

Blum, Deborah. *Love at Goon Park: Harry Harlow and the Science of Affection*. New York: Basic Books, 2011.

Bowlby, John. *Attachment*. New York: Basic Books, 1969.

Boylston, Arthur. "William Watson's Use of Controlled Clinical Experiments in 1767." *Journal of the Royal Society of Medicine* 107, no. 6 (June 2014): 246–48.

Brownlow, John. *The History and Objects of the Foundling Hospital: With a Memoir of the Founder*. London: C. Jacques, 1881.

Cadogan, William. *An Essay upon Nursing and the Management of Children, From their Birth to Three Years of Age*, 2nd ed. London: J. Roberts, 1748.

Campanella, Richard. *Lincoln in New Orleans: The 1828–1831 Flatboat Voyages and Their Place in History*. Lafayette: University of Louisiana at Lafayette Press, 2010.

Carrington, Paul D. "Asbestos Lessons: The Unattended Consequences of Asbestos Litigation." *Review of Litigation* 26, no. 3 (Summer 2007): 583–611.

Curtis, Myra, et al. *Report of the Care of Children Committee*. London: His Majesty's Stationery Office, 1946.

Dear, I.C.B. and Foot, M.R.D. *The Oxford Companion to World War II*. Oxford: Oxford University Press, 1995.

Dickens, Charles. *American Notes for General Circulation*. London: Chapman and Hall, 1842. Reprint, London: Penguin Classics, 2004.

———. *Oliver Twist*. New York: Shine Classics, 2014.

————. "Received, A Blank Child." *Household Words* 7, no. 156 (March 1853): 49–53.

Dolan, Alice. "The Fabric of Life: Linen and Life Cycle in England, 1678–1810." PhD diss., University of Hertfordshire, 2015.

Foundling Hospital. *A Copy of the Royal Charter, Establishing an Hospital for the Maintenance and Education of Exposed and Deserted Young Children*. London: J. Osborn, 1739.

————. *Regulations for Managing the Hospital for the Maintenance and Education of Exposed and Deserted Young Children: By Order of the Governors of the Said Hospital*. London: Foundling Hospital, 1757.

————. "Rules for the Admission of Children." As provided to Lena Weston, January 4, 1932.

Foundling Museum. *Foundling Voices: An Oral History Project of the Foundling Museum*. London: Foundling Museum, 2011.

Gardiner, Juliet. *The Blitz: The British under Attack*. London: HarperPress, 2011.

Gärtner, Niko. *Operation Pied Piper: The Wartime Evacuation of Schoolchildren from London and Berlin, 1938–1946*. Charlotte, NC: Information Age, 2012.

Grassian, Stuart. "Psychopathological Effects of Solitary Confinement." *American Journal of Psychiatry* 140 (November 1983): 1450–54.

Das Gupta, Jyoti Bhusan, ed. *Science, Technology, Imperialism and War. History of Science, Philosophy, and Culture in Indian Civilization*, vol. 15, pt. 1. New Delhi: Pearson & Longman, 2007.

Hanway, Jonas. *A Candid Historical Account of the Hospital for the Reception of Exposed and Deserted Young Children; [. . .] with a Proposal for Carrying a New Design into Execution*, 2nd rev. ed. London: G. Woodfall and J. Waugh, 1760.

————. *An Essay on Tea: Considered as Pernicious to Health, Obstructing Industry, and Impoverishing the Nation*. London: H. Woodfall, 1756.

———. *A Review of the Proposed Naturalization of the Jews; Being an Attempt at a Dispassionate Enquiry*, 2nd ed. London: J. Waugh, 1753.

———. *Solitude in Imprisonment: With Proper Profitable Labour and a Spare Diet, the Most Humane and Effectual Means of Bringing Malefactors, Who Have Forfeited Their Lives, or Are Subject to Transportation, to a Right Sense of Their Condition*. London: F. Bew, 1776.

Holden, Katherine. *The Shadow of Marriage: Singleness in England, 1914–1960*. Manchester, England: Manchester University Press, 2007.

Johnson, David Alan. *The Battle of Britain and the American Factor, July–October 1940*. Conshohocken, PA: Combined Publishing, 1998.

Jungnickel, Christa, and Russell McCormmach. *Cavendish: The Experimental Life*. Bucknell, PA: Bucknell Press, 1999.

Kaplan, E. Ann. *Motherhood and Representation: The Mother in Popular Culture and Melodrama*. London: Routledge, 1992.

Kellermann, Natan. "Transmission of Holocaust Trauma—An Integrative View." *Psychiatry: Interpersonal and Biological Processes* 64, no. 3 (February 2001): 256–67.

Levene, Alysa. *Childcare, Health and Mortality at the London Foundling Hospital, 1741–1800*. Manchester, England: Manchester University Press, 2007.

McClure, Ruth. *Coram's Children: The London Foundling Hospital in the Eighteenth Century*. New Haven, CT: Yale University Press, 1981.

Mignot, Jean-Francois. "Child Adoption in Western Europe, 1900–2015." In *Cliometrics of the Family*, edited by Claude Diebolt, Auke Rijpma, Sara Carmichael, Selin Dilli, and Charlotte Störmer, 333–66. New York: Springer, 2019.

Mortimer, Gavin, "Cat's Eyes: John Cunningham's Wartime Nickname Concealed a Vital Military Secret—The Invention of

Airborne Radar." *Air & Space*, November 19, 2010. https://www
.airspacemag.com/history-of-flight/cats-eyes-72622832/.

Neal, Toby, "Happy Memories of a Shropshire Wartime Evacuee."
Shropshire Star, Shropshire February 2, 2014.

Oliver, Christine, and Peter Aggleton. *Coram's Children: Growing Up
in the Care of the Foundling Hospital, 1900–1955*. London: Coram
Family, 2000.

Peters, Ellis, and Roy Morgan. *Shropshire: A Memoir of the English
Countryside*. New York: Mysterious Press, 1992.

Pugh, Gillian. *London's Forgotten Children: Thomas Coram and the
Foundling Hospital*. Stroud, England: History Press, 2007.

Roberts, Andrew. *The Storm of War: A New History of the Second World
War*. New York: Harper, 2012.

Ross, Stewart. *Rationing at Home in World War Two*. London: Evans
Brothers, 2005.

Sheetz-Nguyen, Jessica A. "Calculus of Respectability: Defining the
World of Foundling Hospital Women and Children in Victorian
London." *Annales de demographie historique* 2, no. 14 (2007):
13–36.

———. *Victorian Women, Unwed Mothers and the London Foundling
Hospital*. New York: Continuum International, 2012.

Schmidt, William E. "Two 'Jovial Con Men' Demystify Those Crop
Circles in Britain." *New York Times*, September 10, 1991.

Silverman, Mark E. "The Tradition of the Gold-Headed Cane." *The
Pharos of Alpha Omega Alpha Honor Medical Society*, Winter 2007,
42–46.

Stopes, Marie. *Married Love*. Oxford: Oxford University Press,
2004.

Tarullo, Amanda, Jelena Obradović, and Megan R. Gunnar. "Self-
Control and the Developing Brain." *Zero to Three* 29, no. 3
(January 2009): 31–37.

Taylor, James Stephen. *Jonas Hanway, Founder of the Marine Society: Charity and Policy in Eighteenth-Century Britain.* London: Scholar Press, 1985.

US War Department. *Instructions for American Servicemen in Britain.* Washington, DC: US War Department, 1942. Reproduced from the original typescript, Oxford, England: Bodleian Library, 2004.

Wagner, Gillian. *Thomas Coram, Gent., 1668–1751.* Woodbridge, England: Boydell Press, 2015.

Williams, Edward Huntington, and Henry Smith Williams. *A History of Science.* Vol. 2. New York: Harper & Brothers, 1904.

Wimperis, Virginia. *The Unmarried Mother and Her Child.* London: Sir Halley Stewart Trust, 1960.

Zunshine, Lisa. *Bastards and Foundlings: Illegitimacy in Eighteenth-Century England.* Columbus: Ohio State University Press, 2005.

ABOUT THE AUTHOR

JUSTINE COWAN is an attorney and environmentalist who spent more than two decades exposing corporate corruption and holding polluters accountable. A graduate of UC Berkeley and Duke University School of Law, she lives with her husband in Atlanta, Georgia. *The Secret Life of Dorothy Soames* is her first book.